CLINICAL PSYCHOLOGY, 'RACE' AND CULTURE

ACKNOWLEDGEMENTS

We would like to acknowledge all those who have helped to sustain and bring this project to fruition. In particular, we would like to thank all those with whom we worked in clinical practice over the years: clients who have shaped our thinking; colleagues who have engaged in difficult though enriching discussions, our employing services which have enabled us to invest energy into this project and, of course, the Clinical Psychology, 'Race' and Culture SIG without which we could not have done this work. We would like to give very special thanks to Mary Bamber for her humour, her encouragement and her meticulous and efficient administration and typing.

CLINICAL PSYCHOLOGY, 'RACE' AND CULTURE:

A TRAINING MANUAL

Edited By

Nimisha Patel

Elizabeth Bennett

Maxine Dennis

Neelam Dosanjh

Aruna Mahtani

Ann Miller

Zenobia Nadirshaw

BPS BOOKS   THE BRITISH PSYCHOLOGICAL SOCIETY

First published in 2000 by BPS Books (The British Psychological Society), St Andrews House, 48 Princess Road East, Leicester LE1 7DR, UK.

A catalogue record for this book is available from the British Library.

Library of Congress Cataloging-in-Publication Data on file.

ISBN 1 85433 319 4

Typeset by Book Production Services, London.
Printed in Great Britain by MPG Books Limited.

Whilst every effort has been made to ensure the accuracy of the contents of this publication, the publishers and author expressly disclaim responsibility in law for negligence or any other cause of action whatsoever.

CONTENTS

PART 3: SPECIALITY MODULES

EDITORIAL GROUP

Elizabeth Bennett
Consultant Clinical Psychologist, Acting Head of the Newham Psychology and Counselling Service, East London and City Mental Health Trust and Newham Community Health Services Trust, London.

Elizabeth is a White British clinical psychologist who has worked in the NHS for 20 years and as Clinical Tutor for the University of East London (UEL) training course during five of these years. She came to psychology after studying Chinese language and history at the School of Oriental and African Studies, University of London and brought from this an interest in the psychology of difference and inequality which found little support in her undergraduate study of psychology. The support needed has come through her work in the multicultural borough of Newham, and through colleagues at UEL and the CPRC SIG.

Maxine Dennis
Clinical Psychologist in Psychotherapy working with adults at the Tavistock Clinic, Tavistock and Portman NHS Trust, London.

Maxine is of African-Caribbean descent with a longstanding interest in the teaching and integration of 'race' and culture issues within clinical psychology training. In addition, she is also concerned with the provision of culturally appropriate psychological and psychotherapy services. Currently Chair of the CPRC SIG, she has held various executive positions in the SIG and was a co-instigator of the manual.

Neelam Dosanjh
Consultant Clinical Psychologist and Head of the Primary Care Psychology Team in the Newham Psychology and Counselling Service, Newham Community Health Services Trust. London.

Neelam was born in India and identifies herself as an Indian Sikh. Her interest in the issues of 'race' and culture has arisen out of personal experiences as a minority person growing up in London, and continued professionally with published research on Asian women's ethnic identity. Neelam has contributed to the CPRC SIG Executive as a committee member and treasurer. She was also the regional officer for the London 'race' and culture meetings for four years. Neelam's particular interest is in using the psychoanalytic model to understand working with 'difference' at organizational, group and individual levels.

Aruna Mahtani
Principal Clinical Psychologist at the Medical Foundation for the Care of Victims of Torture and the Tower Hamlets Healthcare Trust in East London.

An Indian, Aruna has been committed to working with issues of 'race', racism and culture since she qualified as a clinical psychologist. She has been involved in developing accessible and appropriate mental health services for the Black and minority ethnic communities in East London, and in examining the relevance of Western psychological models. Currently working with refugees who have survived torture and organized violence, she has been involved in training and publishing work around these issues, and she was the first chairperson of the CPRC Special Interest Group.

Ann Miller

Consultant Clinical Psychologist at the Marlborough Family Service, Brent, Kensignton, Chelsea and Westminster Mental Health NHS Trust, and Honorary Teaching Fellow at Birkbeck College, University of London.

An Australian, Ann is of Celtic heritage, and has worked in Britain since 1973. Profoundly influenced by her experiences of London's multicultural society, and by what she has learned from the teaching she has done in South Asia and in Europe, she has been reflecting on the differences and the similarities between her own and other's cultures for many years. She is also a family therapy trainer and has developed both clinical services and training with the aim of making them inclusive of many different people and perspectives.

Zenobia Nadirshaw

Consultant Clinical Psychologist and Head of Learning Disability Services, Parkside NHS Trust, London.

Zenobia is a Parsee Zoroastrian from Bombay, India. In her 26 years of NHS work, she has acquired a wide range of experience of teaching, training and researching in mental health, learning disabilities and women's issues withinn the British Psychological Society and outside. Within local and national professional organizations, she has drawn attention at all levels to issues of 'race', difference and diversity. As a founder member of the Special Interest Group, former Chair of the Transcultural Psychiatry Society (UK) and BPS award winner for challenging inequality of opportunity, Zenobia remains concerned that a section of British society is not receiving authoritatively competent psychological care.

Nimisha Patel

Consultant Clinical Psychologist, working at the University of East London as Senior Lecturer and formerly as the Clinical Director of the Doctoral Degree Course in Clinical Psychology. She is also Head of Clinical Psychology at the Medical Foundation for the Care of Victims of Torture, London.

Born in Kenya, Nimisha is a Gujarati Indian who has lived in various parts of Africa and in Britain. She has served on the CPRC SIG Executive Committee as Treasurer and Chair. Her interests in inequalities and difference have been shaped by her own experiences of growing up and being educated in Britain and of working in the NHS as a Black woman. Her interests in training began within her own training in Hull, eventually leading her in 1991 to conduct the first survey of the teaching of 'race' and culture in clinical psychology courses. This, in turn, resulted in her instigating the working party on training and this manual for the CPRC SIG. Nimisha has also been the Chair of the editorial group since its formation in 1992.

OTHER CONTRIBUTORS

Gill Aitken — Clinical Psychologist, Adult Forensic Service, Mental Health Services of Salford, Manchester.

Nick Banks — Clinical Psychologist and Lecturer, Department of Social Policy and Social Work, University of Birmingham, Birmingham.

Sandra Baum — Consultant Clinical Psychologist and Head of Learning Disabilities Services, Newham Psychology and Counselling Service, Newham Community Health Services NHS Trust, London.

Oliver Davidson — Consultant Clinical Psychologist, Head of HIV/GUM Psychology and Psychotherapy Services, Camden and Islington Community NHS Trust, London.

Iyabo Fatimilehin — Consultant Clinical Psychologist, Royal Liverpool Children's Trust, Liverpool.

Sue Gibbons — Clinical Psychologist, Newham Psychology and Counselling Service, Newham Community Health Services NHS Trust, London.

Graham Gibson — Consultant Clinical Psychologist, Redford Lodge Hospital, General Healthcare Group, London.

Anne Goodwin — Consultant Clinical Psychologist, Central Nottinghamshire Health Care NHS Trust, Nottinghamshire.

Hermine Graham — Clinical Psychologist/Head of Compass Programme, Northern Birmingham Mental Health NHS Trust, Birmingham.

Richard Hallam — Consultant Clinical Psychologist, Reader in Psychology, University of East London, London.

Lih Mei Liao — Consultant Clinical Psychologist, Hunter Street Health Centre, Camden and Islington Community Health Services NHS Trust, London.

Vaman Lokare — Consultant Clinical Psychologist (retired).

Brigid MacCarthy — Consultant Clinical Psychologist, Tower Hamlets Healthcare Trust, London

Yasmin Mullick — Clinical Psychologist, Newham Psychology and Counselling Service, Newham Community Health Services NHS Trust, London.

Lesley Murphy — Consultant Clinical Psychologist, Queen Mary's Hospital, Kingston and District Community NHS Trust, London.

John Newland   Consultant Clinical Psychologist, Camden and Islington Community NHS Trust, London.

Hitesh Raval   Consultant Clinical Psychologist, Tavistock and Portman NHS Trust, London.

Mayuri Senapati   Clinical Psychologist, Newham Psychology and Counselling Service, Newham Community Health Services NHS Trust, London.

Kate Tress   Consultant Clinical Psychologist, Head of Clinical Psychology RFU, Royal Free Hampstead NHS Trust, London.

Shamil Wanigaratne   Consultant Clinical Psychologist/Honorary Senior Lecturer, National Addictions Centre, South London and Maudsley NHS Trust, London.

FOREWORD

It is an honour to be asked to write a foreword for this valuable addition to the growing range of Resource Packs for Trainers. As professional standards rise there is more pressure on trainers to cover everything to an appropriate depth. Similarly, trainees are having to pay attention to more and more issues as they develop their competence to practise Clinical Psychology. Some of the authors of this manual I have known for many years. It was also during my time as Chair of the Division of Clinical Psychology that we were able to support the SIG in their efforts to be heard. I feel, therefore, as though I have a personal as well as a professional interest in the success of the venture. Most of my clinical work has been with people who are different, although as a white British psychologist my knowledge of 'race' and 'culture' issues has grown through what my patients have taught me. The emphasis on individuality is crucial and the core of Clinical Psychology. But we can't understand another's individuality unless we have some constructs on which to base our judgements. This pack provides us with those constructs. It shows us the facts, and takes us gently but firmly through the things we need to know about ourselves and others who have a different background, culture and experience of living in Britain today.

It is very apparent that the authors speak with commitment and knowledge. Some of them have experienced discrimination and negative thinking from others who don't know any better. They have shown, in the manual, that the knowledge is there and can be shared; people can know better. They are to be congratulated on providing us with a way of sharing further.

This manual will be invaluable to Clinical Psychology trainers. I hope it will be well used and that we will see the benefits disseminated. Clinical Psychology is not the only profession that needs to address these issues and I sincerely hope that the manual will be bought and used by other professional groups.

Pat Frankish
BPS President, 1999

INTRODUCTION

THE HISTORY OF THE MANUAL

Clinical Psychologists provide a service to a population which is diverse ethnically and culturally. This has posed many challenges for the profession in the last few decades. When the Clinical Psychology, 'Race' and Culture group gained Special Interest Group status in 1991, one of the first tasks it undertook was a survey of Clinical Psychology Training Courses to discover how issues of 'race' and culture were being addressed in training. Trainers from 12 out of the then 26 courses responded to a questionnaire and most indicated that they were attempting to provide trainees with preparatory concepts and clinical skills. However, all respondents suggested that guidance from the CPRC SIG regarding training in the area of 'race', racism and culture would be welcomed.

A separate survey conducted by the SIG in the same year focused on the experience of trainees from all the Courses. They were asked whether issues of 'race' and culture had been addressed in their training and whether they felt adequately prepared to work within a multicultural and multiethnic society. Over a hundred trainees responded, with an overwhelming majority indicating that training in this area could be vastly improved.

The SIG therefore established a Training Working Party to look at how it could best respond to a clearly identified need. This Training Manual is one part of that response and we set about creating it with the following aims in mind:

- To draw together a range of clinical psychologists to share the richness, depth and variety of their thinking and experience to date in their areas of clinical specialism.
- To facilitate trainers in considering and integrating issues of 'race' and culture at every level of training, both academic and clinical, and in developing their own perspectives on these issues.
- To make current thinking accessible and enabling, rather than providing a 'cookbook' or a 'cultural handbook', with the implicit understanding that the contexts, processes and methods of teaching are constantly evolving.

Our guidelines to contributors were not prescriptive, but required that each module should outline relevant research findings and theoretical, conceptual and practice issues – and suggest texts which elaborate on each of these. Beyond this, contributors were free to develop their Module in the way which best suited their area of expertise. In some fields there has been little research or theoretical advances related to issues of culture and 'race', partly reflected in the varying lengths of the modules. The modules also vary in style and are not intended to give a full description of relevant issues in any particular area, but to provide a conceptual map which trainers can explore while developing their own perspective on the issues of difference and discrimination in their work. Each module also suggests some learning outcomes for trainees that trainers may find useful when preparing and providing their training.

The modules have been structured in this way to reflect our view that change is a continual process for both trainers and trainees, requiring not a fixed body of knowledge and politically correct perspectives, but a flexible scheme that allows trainers and trainees to create their own meaning, style and methods of clinical practice for working with a diverse population.

AN OVERVIEW OF THEMES

Some 'superordinate themes' emerged during the development of the manual, and these warrant some introductory discussion as they emerge in most of the modules.

Difference

In considering the question 'what is difference?' several ideas became clear in our thinking.

Difference is a **relational term**. Consider the following figures and ask yourself 'Which one is different?'

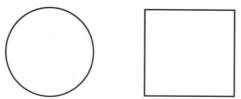

When asked in this abstract way, the question clearly makes no sense. However, from the standpoint of a Eurocentric clinical psychology, difference has come to be seen as an 'attribute of the other'. When clinical psychologists are exhorted to 'take account of culture' in their thinking and practice, the culture taken into account is generally that of Black and minority ethnic service users and very rarely that of the psychologists, or the psychology which informs their work. Thus, for example, aspects of the cultures of African-Caribbean people are seen as potentially contributing to the type of presentation which results in their over-representation among people diagnosed as schizophrenic. Aspects of European or White American cultures that might give rise to behaviours judged to be signs of madness are invisible in the literature. Similarly, an individual practitioner may strive admirably to understand the contribution of their client's culture to the conversation created between them in therapy, but will rarely give the same scrutiny to the role of their own culturally determined belief systems. Much of the literature on ethnic and cultural difference runs the risk of 'exoticizing' the experience of Black and minority ethnic people, further entrenching the 'normality' of the culture from which clinical psychology has risen. It must always be remembered that if 'you' seem different or 'unusual' from where 'I' stand, then 'I' am likely to seem different and strange from where 'you' stand. Thus, difference exists between people, not within individuals.

Defining differences in relation to ethnicity and culture is not a neutral activity. Hence, the gathering of 'cultural information' alone is not an adequate strategy for change and, as previously mentioned, developing some kind of a cultural handbook or directory is not the focus nor the intention of this Training Manual. White Western cultural groups, by virtue of their dominant position, have exercised their power to define the significance of differences ascribed to 'others' in relation to culture, ethnicity or 'race'. This process of ascribing a value to a particular difference is therefore a non-neutral activity. The values of dominant groups also become embedded in institutions, recreating power relations in organizational structures, procedures and processes. When such power relations and values are related to 'race' and culture, inequalities on the basis of ethnicity are established and maintained and institutional racism emerges as a discriminatory process with deleterious consequences for Black and minority ethnic people. Within the NHS, this translates into questions about the accessibility and acceptability of current services. To offer a simplified example, a middle-aged Indian woman may approach her GP for help, complaining of aches and pains and general malaise. The GP may assume that Asian patients tend to somatize their psychological distress. This may make it less likely that this woman is referred for psychological help and more likely that she will be prescribed medication, a medical approach which arguably serves to reify the original assumption. On the other hand, if a psychological approach is adopted, psychologists may see their task as the transformation of the way the client experiences and expresses her distress and her ideas on how healing is achieved to a position which is congruent with their learned beliefs. In both cases, the power imbalance in the relationship generally ensures that the world view of the health professional will prevail.

The task of this Training Manual is to focus thinking on *visible* ethnic and cultural difference, as this relates to the practice of clinical psychology. We do not intend, however, that this focus should help to obscure the importance of other forms of discrimination. Inequalities based on ethnicity are also experienced, for example, by Jewish and Irish people. In this regard, our aim has not been to be totally inclusive, nor indeed to be exclusive, for we recognize that many of the issues referred to in this Training Manual are relevant to all those who have been subjected to racial discrimination. In addition, the debate on how to make health services accessible and acceptable to Black and minority ethnic people often appears to rest on the assumption that our services are accessible and acceptable to all White users, regardless of age, class, gender, physical ability or sexual orientation. This is yet another assumption which requires scrutiny.

Difference in itself is not 'a problem'. As psychologists, we know the value of identifying and working with difference. Why else do we ask so many questions about it? For example: 'When are you more likely to feel panicky?' 'What kind of response from staff tends to make this behaviour more or less likely to occur?' 'How do you think you could manage the same situation differently?' Our formulations of psychological problems are based on information about the effects of different situations, different relationships, different ways of thinking. At the micro level of visual perception, for example, 'difference is information and no difference is no information'. The same is true at the macro level of interpersonal and intergroup relationships.

Alternative psychologies

In referring to psychologies practised by 'others', various writers in existing literature have used terms such as 'indigenous psychologies', 'alternative psychologies' or 'folk healing'. All these terms require deconstructing. For example, it is precisely our position as psychologists steeped in Eurocentric thinking that dictates what we view and term as 'alternative' or 'indigenous' and what we persist in calling 'psychologies'. The use of terms such as 'alternative' betrays what we assume to be the norm against which we evaluate different models. The use of the term 'psychologies' also reveals the roots of our psychological models, which have evolved in the West, based on the philosophy of Cartesian dualism. To assume that all models of human experience make the distinction between physical medicine and 'psychologies' is both to devalue different ways of construing and making sense of human experience, and to deny that different models of health and healthcare may even exist. The implications of this for what clients may or may not be offered, or what is imposed on them, and what the consequences are for them, are matters for clinical psychologists to consider in order to value the person in front of them, and to avoid colluding with the establishment and maintenance of social inequalities.

Adaptation versus paradigm shift

During the development of this Training Manual the following questions have arisen frequently: should the goal of clinical psychology be the adaptation of current therapeutic approaches, with greater attention given to where and how services are delivered to meet the needs of Black and minority ethnic clients? Or, is a complete paradigm shift required, to construct new ways of understanding human experience and new ways of addressing distress? Can new paradigms lead to a universal psychology, or will a series of equally valued ethnocentric 'psychologies' meet client needs more effectively?

Our view at this point is that change will come about, and has started to come about, through a series of small steps. For example, the 'cross-cultural' approach attempts to increase cultural sensitivity or competence through knowledge and understanding of non-Western cultures with the reference point, however, remaining that of the Western observer. Then there is the 'transcultural' approach, which implies a more two-way process but is still firmly grounded in Western models. The 'intercultural' approach involves a more explicitly collaborative therapeutic relationship but still employs existing Western models of therapy. Our starting point, and the starting point of this Training Manual, is that the context for any changes in practice needs to be a radical critique of existing psychologies to provide a coherent theoretical account of how inequalities are established and maintained, and thus point to how these inequalities can be addressed at every level of service provision.

Some of the arguments relating to these questions are presented in a number of modules. We have not seen our task as providing the answers, but providing at least some of the materials and concepts to help trainers and trainees consider the questions. The task as we see it is to help enable trainees to develop a conceptual framework and to question the theoretical and clinical basis of clinical psychology as we currently teach and learn it.

USING THE MANUAL

The contributors to this Training Manual are all clinical psychologists working in a range of specialisms. We do not consider ourselves 'experts' in the fields of 'race' and culture, but we are all practitioners who continue to think about the issues and who are committed to addressing them in our work. Much of the material we have provided presents trainers, service managers and individual practitioners with serious challenges to their practice, and this can seem both overwhelming and disheartening. The attempt to meet some of these challenges, as we have found in the process of developing the manual, can be frustrating, emotive and confusing, yet also enriching and enabling. Each time we met and recognized an idea or a way of viewing something which differed from our own, we were presented with an opportunity to learn and move our thinking on. As an all-female, mixed ethnicity editorial group, our discussions have inevitably been confined to the parameters of our own experiences as women, though enriched by our differing ethnicities and related histories.

One question we considered at some length was how the names of contributors would appear in the publication. Essentially this has been a Black-led project and we recognize that Black voices have been and are routinely subjugated in the psychological literature. On these grounds, we might have chosen to put Black authors' names first. However, most contributors chose to place their names in alphabetical order. Where this is the case, it should not be taken to reflect either the seniority or the level of expertise or contribution of those involved.

Over the years that we have been working and struggling together, our thinking has continually evolved and continues to evolve. The process of developing the manual has been one of intense debate, disagreement, discoveries and insights, and one which has injected a vitality into our own thinking and practice. It is this which has sustained us and inspired us to encourage others to engage in a similar process of discovery and learning.

In using this Training Manual, it is hoped that trainers will be able to draw from the different modules, follow up the relevant literature and develop their own thinking and ways of teaching. The materials are intended to be sufficiently flexible to allow trainers considerable autonomy in deciding how they can be meaningfully integrated into their existing teaching.

The Introductory Module in Part 2 outlines areas that enable trainers to set the context for training and skills development in relation to issues of 'race' and culture and it is intentionally more detailed and thorough than the subsequent modules. It is sufficiently broad-based and flexible for trainers to be able to adapt its contents and methods to the needs of their particular trainees. Course organizers are also advised that module leaders, lecturers and supervisors should be encouraged to refer to the Introductory Module as a supplemental resource.

The speciality modules which follow in Part 3 address some of the issues of 'race', racism and culture in a variety of clinical fields. These modules are designed to provide a conceptual map, with some suggested exercises and recommended annotated reading, rather than a thorough account of relevant issues. Trainers should develop their own thoughts, materials and style in a way which will enable trainees to examine theory and practice critically in a given speciality area in relation to issues of 'race', racism and culture. Many of the speciality modules also share similar issues, and trainers are therefore referred to other useful modules which could provide additional sources of materials.

Finally, we hope that trainers and trainees will enjoy and find useful the materials and resources provided.

RECOMMENDATIONS TO TRAINERS ON THE PROCESS OF TEACHING

The following are guidelines for trainers in using the Training Manual.

INTRODUCTION

Clinical Psychology is characterized by its ability to generate novel, individual solutions from a broad theoretical base rather than merely by its skilful application of techniques. Trainees need to be provided with a sound conceptual basis for their clinical practice, in *all* areas. Trainees and trainers alike will be looking for answers to the question: 'What do I do in clinical practice when working with difference?' While this is an entirely valid question, which needs to be addressed throughout training, we strongly believe that the beginning of this process, as set out in this manual, should focus on thinking rather than doing.

Reflecting on our theoretical base and our clinical practice from a new point of view is stimulating and exciting, and helps to refine and elaborate our approach to all our work. It can also create uncertainty, which is uncomfortable but, as psychologists, we should have a good capacity to tolerate ambiguity as there are few certainties in our profession! So, we recommend holding back from the rush into 'What do I do?' to concentrate initially on good, creative thinking.

TIMING AND SEQUENCE OF TEACHING

The Introductory Module should be started early in the process of training, to avoid a sense of being 'tagged on', but not too early. Some time should be allowed for the training group to become established and for trust to be built among trainees and between trainees and trainers.

1. Our experience has been, and feedback has confirmed, that academic, conceptual material should be presented first before moving on to more experiential work. This helps to reduce threat and also frames the work as part of academic psychology rather than as a personalized, feeling-based topic.
2. Subsequent modules can be utilized, as appropriate, for each individual training course.

THE TRAINERS

1.   The material is best presented by local staff, rather than by 'expert' outsiders, although sometimes the course may be structured to provide joint training by internal and external trainers.
2.   Personal awareness of the trainer's own position in, and response to, different hierarchies of power will be of great help in developing sensitive teaching practices. Trainers will need to look at their own personal assumptions about Black trainees' experiences. Self-reflection, active, open and ongoing discussions between Black and White trainers and attending relevant training events will all help in this process.
3.   Ideally, trainers should work in pairs. This will enable them to support one another, to develop their ideas and ways of working, and to deal with emotive aspects as they arise. It is desirable that the teaching team is made up of both Black and White trainers to combat potential marginalization.

THE TRAINEES

1.   Training groups will differ in their knowledge, experience and awareness of issues of 'race' and culture. Therefore, it is important to use the manual flexibly to avoid under- or over-reaching the level of the group.
2.   Trainers will need to be sensitive to the fact that material connected to prejudice or racism will impact in many different ways on their expectations about trainees, in the light of their own experience. Trainees should be given the opportunity to talk about their expectations and what their experience of being in a mixed group has been (see later sections).
3.   There is no homogenous Black trainee experience or White trainee experience. Both Black and White trainees should be asked about their experience of working with difference and racism.

TEACHING METHODS AND APPROACHES

1.   Trainers should aim to integrate teaching on 'race' and culture into the course curriculum and into the supervision of clinical practice, so that it becomes central rather than marginal.
2.   A facilitative, enabling approach, which acknowledges and respects different levels of awareness is preferable to an approach which is 'missionary'. The exploration of differences and diversity brought to the course by trainees should be treated as a basis for learning, rather than as a source of conflict and discomfort.
3.   In teaching sessions, small group or paired discussions, with time to consider feedback, have been found to be very useful. Trainees can try out their ideas with each other before risking 'exposure' to the whole group and to their trainers.
4.   The use of trainers' own case material is highly recommended. General, conceptual notions can be illustrated in this way, links can begin to be made

to clinical practice and trainees can be reassured that their trainers address these issues thoughtfully in their own practice – and that they may have some, but not all, of the 'answers'.

5. Leave plenty of space and time for reflection, feedback and the management of feelings. Each session might start with a brief discussion of how trainees have 'processed' material from the previous session.

6. Trainers should acknowledge that not all the expectations and needs of trainees will be met in the Introductory Module. There should be a continuing dialogue between trainers and trainees about their needs and how these can be met throughout their training.

Useful reading

Brummer, N. and Simmonds, J. (1992) Race and Culture: The Management of 'Difference' in the Learning Group, *Social Work Education*, *11*, 1. 54–64.

NOTES FOR WHITE TRAINERS

Whiteness, as a set of normative cultural practices is visible most clearly to those it definitively excludes and those to whom it does violence. Those who are securely housed within its borders usually do not examine it.

Frankenberg, 1993, p.228

In order to be able to use this Training Manual successfully in the development of the training curriculum, Course Directors will need to do some preparatory work with White trainers. This section is written mainly by the two White members of the editorial group and offers suggestions, based on our own experience, which we hope will be useful in this process. These suggestions include some initial thoughts and a number of exercises, which staff groups can undertake together. As the 'occupiers' of the centre ground/the normative space, White trainers have a particular role in relation to training about 'race' and culture: that of taking responsibility for thinking about how to create the space for the topic in ethnically mixed staff and training groups. In a very helpful article, Cooper (1997) also describes the necessity for White people to think for themselves about the matter of racism and not to rely solely on dialogue with Black people about it.

I should be capable of thinking for myself about these questions and not perpetuate in myself an anxious dependency on any racial "other" for answers. In turn this quite simply entails taking the risk of exposing the fact that one does not understand, that one is capable of failure in the effort to think and empathise.

Cooper, 1997, p.133).

To feel confident in doing this, we need first to reflect on our own 'race' and culture and on the implications of our membership of what is commonly assumed to be a dominant group. Many of us will have direct personal experience of discrimination on the basis of some kind of systematic difference – for example, age, gender, class, physical and intellectual ability – through our families, friends and work with clients, or in the course of our own lives. This kind of experience can be used to increase our understanding of discrimination which does not touch us directly. We need to increase our awareness of the impact of difference on Black colleagues and trainees. In our experience, the best starting point for this is a focus on 'Whiteness' rather than 'Blackness', recognizing 'being White' as one position among many, rather than the norm, and examining the privilege that is conferred by being White. We therefore suggest a number of exercises as starting points and we recommend that groups set aside one day or two half days for these.

Exercise 1: What was your first experience of discrimination?

(work in groups of three)

First, in a period of silent recollection, think of your first experience of feeling 'outside', 'other', set aside or discriminated against.

- When were you first aware of being discriminated against?
- What were the apparent grounds for it?
- Did you tell anyone about it? Who in the family would have understood?

Then two of the group discuss these thoughts while the third remains silent. After the initial discussion, think about the impact of the silent colleague on the conversation.

- What did you think they made of the conversation?
- Did you perceive them as being similar/different to you?
- What impact did their gender, 'race', class, age, religion, etc. have on this?
- What difference would it have made if a group of Black colleagues had been present?

The silent member of the threesome should then share her/his thoughts about being in the silent role.

Finally, all three discuss the effect of the exercise on them.

We also need to recognize the relative freedom from being hurt on the basis of visible differences that we enjoy as White people, and our relative freedom from injustice on the basis of ethnic origin. The aim of this type of recognition is not to engender guilt, but to enable us to be open, to give up 'being special' and to start to talk to each other about our part in redressing the imbalance of hurt and injustice.

Exercise 2: Being White and...

(small group discussion)

Explore the implications of being White and:

- being young/being old
- being middle-class or working-class or both
- being well-educated
- being male/female
- being able bodied/disabled

for your life-chances and choices, the cultural expectations that are placed on you, and your relationships with others.

Exercise 3: Unpacking White privilege (whole group)

White people can be the subject of racism on the grounds of their particular ethnicity, depending on the social/political context. However, White people cannot expect to have the same level of awareness of the racism which is based on colour as Black people who are subjected to it. In spite of goodwill, White people have to work at becoming aware of the many manifestations of racism, simply because they are not usually on the receiving end of it. This will apply to everyday interpersonal experience, which the next exercise addresses.

Exercise 3: Read McIntyre's list of statements on the daily effects of White privilege (see below). Each member of the group should have a copy of the list of statements and first read them individually. Then discuss in the group anything which surprised you or which introduced a new thought.

White privilege

- I can if I wish arrange to be in the company of people of my 'race' most of the time.
- If I should need to move, I can be pretty sure of renting or purchasing housing in an area which I can afford and in which I would want to live.
- I can be pretty sure that my neighbours in such an area will be neutral or pleasant to me.
- I can go shopping alone most of the time, fairly well assured that I will not be followed or harassed.
- I can turn on the television or open the front page of the newspaper and see people of my 'race' widely represented.
- When I am told about our national heritage or about 'civilization', I am shown that people of my colour made it what it is.
- I can be sure that my children will be given curricular materials that testify to the existence of their 'race'.
- If I want to, I can be fairly sure of finding a publisher for this piece on White privilege.
- I can go into a music shop and count on finding the music of my 'race' represented, into a supermarket and find the staple foods which fit with my cultural traditions, into a hairdresser's shop and find someone who can cut my hair.
- Whether I use cheques, credit cards or cash, I can count on my skin colour not to work against the appearance of financial reliability.
- I can arrange to protect my children most of the time from people who might not like them.
- I can swear, or dress in second-hand clothes, or not answer letters, without having people attribute these choices to the bad morals, the poverty, or the illiteracy of my 'race'.
- I can speak in public to a powerful male group without putting my 'race' on trial.
- I can do well in a challenging situation without being called a credit to my 'race'.
- I am never asked to speak for all the people of my 'racial' group.
- I can remain oblivious of the language and customs of persons of colour who constitute the world's majority without feeling in my culture any penalty for such oblivion.
- I can criticize our government and talk about how much I fear its policies and behaviour without being seen as a cultural outsider.
- I can be fairly sure that if I ask to talk to 'the person in charge' I will be facing a person of my 'race'.
- If the police stop me when driving or if there is an audit of my tax return, I can be sure I have not been singled out because of my 'race'.
- I can easily buy posters, postcards, picture books, greeting cards, dolls, toys and children's comics featuring people of my 'race'.
- I can go home from most meetings of organizations I belong to feeling somewhat tied in, rather than isolated, out of place, out-numbered, unheard, held at a distance, or feared.
- I can take a job with an equal opportunities employer without having co-workers on the job suspect that I got it because of 'race'.
- I can choose accommodation without fearing that people of my 'race' cannot get in or will be mistreated in the places I have chosen.
- I can be sure that if I need legal or medical help, my 'race' will not work against me.
- If my day, week or year is going badly, I need not ask of each negative episode or situation whether it has 'racial' overtones.
- I can choose blemish cover or plasters in 'flesh' colour and have them more or less match my skin.

Adapted with permission from chapter by P. McIntyre (1998) in Monica McGoldrick (Ed.) *Re-visioning Family Therapy: Race Culture and Gender in Clinical Practice*. New York: The Guilford Press, p.148.

Exercise 4: Designing a racist community / organization / course

This exercise addresses the manifestation of racism in its more invisible form of institutional racism.

The Task: to design a racist, sexist or ageist course. If you are part of a large staff group, you could split into smaller groups, each one working on one design. Otherwise, the group could choose to work on only one aspect, or work through each of them in turn.

Think about what structures and procedures you would need to have in place, the role of the media, of education and of the law.

Define the following aspects of your community/organization/course.

- The make up of the organization/course: Who's who? What are their positions and roles?
- How do people join the organization/course?
- How are decisions made? Who are the decision makers?
- How are informal and formal policies created?
- Where does the funding come from? Who controls the money/budget?
- What is the name given to your organization/course?
- What is the motto of your organization/course?

Work at making discriminatory practices subtle, so that they are not too easily discernible and could be seen as reasonable if challenged.

When the design is completed, discuss what light it might throw on the systems we are involved in.

EXPERIENCE OF BEING A BLACK OR MINORITY ETHNIC TRAINEE

The issues of 'race', culture and, specifically, racism are extremely complex and can arouse intense emotions for trainers and trainees alike. Since the main aim of this Training Manual is to enable trainers to facilitate learning on these issues in relation to clinical psychology, it is worth reiterating here that these issues cannot be addressed meaningfully without consideration of, and preparation for, how such training will be experienced by trainees. This section highlights some common dilemmas and difficulties which trainers need to be aware of, and to attend to, particularly in relation to Black and minority ethnic trainees. It is based on our experience of having been Black trainees ourselves and of training with mixed groups of trainees.

Black and minority ethnic trainees are invariably also a minority within clinical psychology training and in their year groups. Thus, being marginalized, excluded and oppressed on the basis of their ethnicities are experiences which can become very present in the arena of training and which also draw attention to the heterogeneity of a trainee group. Similarly, many trainees may have experienced exclusion and oppression on other dimensions of inequality: for example class, gender, age and disability. It is important that trainers acknowledge at the outset that each of us brings differing experiences of exclusion and oppression and that while the focus of your workshop or lecture may be to highlight and explore inequalities based on 'race' and cultural difference, this does not necessarily imply that only, or indeed all, Black and minority ethnic people are oppressed and that all White people are oppressors. Ultimately, trainers will need to work on setting a context for training to be facilitative, non-accusatory, non-oppressive, inclusive of all trainees and conducive to learning. Trainers must also be prepared to respond to situations where this has not been possible.

Focusing on 'race' and racism is often experienced as a duty and a demand, one which arises out of an explicit criticism, perhaps directed at the ideology underlying our profession and at our clinical practice. Such criticism points to a failure in the 'humanness' that informs practice, and to a failure of thinking (Lousada, 1994). Thus, training on issues of 'race' and racism necessitates an acknowledgement and agreement that these failures have impeded our professional practice and therefore that we all have an obligation to reflect on and manage our feelings in order to develop our practice. For some, these issues have a specific significance and meaning because of their experiences of having been excluded, marginalized or oppressed because of their colour or ethnicity.

For others, these issues resonate because of their membership of dominant groups in British society. Trainers will have to attend to Black and minority ethnic trainees as well as White trainees. The following highlights specific issues which we have found to be significant from the perspective of Black and minority ethnic trainees:

Terminology

Not all trainees from minority ethnic backgrounds will consider or refer to themselves as being Black or a minority ethnic person. Both descriptions mean different things to different people, and for an elaboration of these terms we would refer you to the Terminology section in the Introductory Module. However, in summary, the term 'Black' is a self-ascribed, political term for stating allegiance with all those who have experienced oppression because of their colour. It is important not to assume that trainees from Black and minority ethnic backgrounds will be familiar with, or agree with, or use, any of the commonly used terms referring to ethnic identity.

Homogeneity

Trainees from Black and minority ethnic backgrounds are not a homogeneous group and, by implication, their experiences are also not homogeneous. Their differing cultures, histories, class and gender are crucial in shaping their differing experiences in British society and within the training process itself. Assumptions should be avoided about their experiences or their ethnic backgrounds. Trainers should also ensure that Black and minority ethnic trainees are enabled and allowed to speak for 'themselves' as individuals and not be expected to speak as representatives of particular ethnic groups.

Disclosure

Not all trainees from Black or minority ethnic backgrounds will want to identify themselves as having experienced discrimination, as such, particularly in the context of training. There are many reasons for this, including the fact that some Black and minority ethnic trainees do not wish to use terms which focus on them as being 'different', particularly in relation to their peers. Sometimes, their own experiences of discrimination may never have been disclosed or discussed in a forum with their peers (particularly White peers), with colleagues, supervisors or tutors. This points to two key factors central to the training process: power relations and safety. These are elaborated below.

Power imbalance

The power imbalance inherent in the trainee–tutor and trainee–supervisor relationships can be further exacerbated when trainees from a Black or minority ethnic background are positioned overtly as being 'different' in relation to their peers. Often being 'different' is experienced as being 'special' in a derogatory way (as disadvantaged, less able, deficient) and is seen as being potentially problematic by tutors or supervisors. Thus, trainees may go to pains to avoid being singled out as 'different', particularly in a profession which constructs itself normatively as White. Trainees from Black and minority ethnic backgrounds often say that they felt unable and afraid to 'come out' about their ethnicities and related experiences during training because they had experienced subtle, covert and sometimes overt racism, perhaps unintentional, within their training, from tutors, lecturers or supervisors. It is such continued discrimination and oppression (in the context of training), however unintentional, that can further silence the very voices trainers might be trying to amplify.

Expert position

Trainees from Black and minority ethnic backgrounds often comment on being positioned as experts on 'Black issues', which include issues of racism, discrimination and cultural sensitivity. The inevitable costs attached to this expert position may far outweigh any benefits. Black and minority ethnic trainees often talk about ambivalent feelings towards the 'special' position of being an expert on certain issues. On the one hand, their often marginalized voices are given public respect, perhaps as token gestures, by trainers. But on the other hand, this is done without acknowledging that they are also involved in a process of learning in relation to issues of racism and culture in clinical psychology. Thus, the burden of the expert position can hinder training and the development of Black and minority ethnic trainees' sense of ethnic/professional identities. Trainers should allow Black and minority ethnic trainees to adopt both the expert position (with expertise in the experience of oppression based on ethnicity/colour) and the non-expert position (as a trainee clinical psychologist) while providing a forum to explore how such ambivalent feelings and paradoxical positions may create role conflict.

Furthermore, placing responsibility (explicitly or implicitly) on Black and minority ethnic trainees to be 'racial' or cultural experts, advocates or consultants can evoke feelings of discomfort, anxiety and resentment for them, while absolving White trainees of their responsibility for doing their own thinking about issues of 'race', racism and culture. It is worth reiterating that the history of racism is largely a White history (Pence, 1982) and that learning and thinking about, exploring and confronting the process of racism relevant to the theoretical bases and practice of clinical psychology need to be tasks for White trainees and professionals too, not just for those who have been at the receiving end of such racism.

Idealization

Black and minority ethnic trainees sometimes speak of feeling idealized or 'set up' by their White peers or by trainers. The exclusive and sustained focus on the resilience and immense capacity of Black and minority ethnic trainees and clients to endure oppression in their lives can be experienced as deliberate minimizing of the personal, social and economic costs of discrimination within the group itself. Trainers need to allow and enable a balanced exploration, but with great sensitivity to ensure that Black and minority ethnic trainees are not further marginalized or attacked, or that White trainees are not blamed and criticized in a way which halts their motivation to learn about issues of 'race', racism and culture and their relevance to their practice as a White trainee clinical psychologist.

Fear of being failed

Black and minority ethnic trainees sometimes comment on feeling that they are expected by their White peers and by trainers (Black and White) to voice the issues of discrimination and difference within their training group which their peers or their trainers themselves cannot name. Being silenced or choosing to stay silent can result in Black and minority ethnic trainees feeling increasingly frustrated, angry and resentful. But speaking out can incur the wrath and suspicion of their White peers. Sometimes there is a fear that White trainers are in a relative position of power to scapegoat, marginalize or even fail Black and minority ethnic trainees who speak out, if not immediately, later in their training. Clearly, trainers can offer no guarantees of absolute fairness in subsequent assessments or appraisals as often racism can be both unintentional and covert. However, awareness and acknowledgement that such fears and perceptions may exist can force tutors, lecturers and supervisors, as well as trainees, to consider ways in which oppressive and discriminatory processes may become inadvertently manifest within the training institution and its practices. Exploring the nature of institutional racism in workshops can be a constructive way in which dialogue can take place about the social and psychological processes that enable institutional inequalities to become manifest and that ensure their maintenance.

In conclusion, it is important for trainers to ensure:

1. **A safe environment,** conducive to learning.
2. **Explicit ground rules**, including rules addressing how a group will attempt to respond to racist comments which may be made during the session. How will trainees and trainers allow each other to 'make mistakes'? How should they be addressed?
3. **Support structures**, which Black and minority ethnic trainees may wish to use, confidentially, either within or outside of the course staff team.
4. **Trainers work in pairs**, wherever possible, ideally as one Black and one White trainer.
5. **Trainees are allowed to 'self-select'** when they divide into groups for exercises and role play.
6. **Trainers continue to explore their own feelings and experiences** as Black or White people, while continually developing their own skills and styles for managing the range of emotions and reactions which can result from training around issues of 'race', racism and culture. Working with other trainers who are different in relation to ourselves with regard to ethnicity, is

always a demanding but a very enriching and useful way to continually develop our skills in training with mixed ethnicity trainee groups.

7. **Enjoy the experience!** This is a process of immense discovery and learning for trainers too.

GUIDELINES FOR USERS OF THIS MODULE

This module aims to help courses reach the requirements of the British Psychological Society's criteria for the assessment of post-graduate training courses in Clinical Psychology, in relation to working in a multiracial and multicultural society.[2]

There has been a debate in the past as to whether this topic should be taught in its own specialist module. However, we recommend that issues of racism and culture should be integrated into every aspect of the Course, at both academic and clinical practice levels, and that the interrelations between racism and other forms of oppressive practices in society should also be examined. We are also of the opinion that because of the sensitive and complex nature of the material, this topic requires an Introductory Module of its own to set the groundwork for integration into the course as a whole.

We recommend that a minimum of 12 hours is required for this module and that it should be placed in the first year of the Course, preferably with a start towards the beginning of the course. We also recommend that trainers pay particular attention to the process of teaching, and that it is clear to all Course staff that this module does not replace the integration of a multiethnic perspective into all aspects of teaching.

AIMS OF THE INTRODUCTORY MODULE

1. To begin to develop a language which will facilitate discussion of the issues of 'race' and culture.
2. To introduce issues of ethnic and cultural diversity, power imbalance and racism as an important context for the practice of clinical psychology in a multicultural society.
3. To provide initial information about the partiality of our knowledge base: the history of psychological theory production; theories of culture; cross-cultural diversity in the construction of mind, self and emotion and 'alternative psychologies'.
4. To provide trainees with some basic tools required for a critique of psychological theory and practice.
5. To promote awareness that all people exist within and are shaped by culture, helping trainees to recognize the relationship and interaction between their own and other cultures.

---

1. This module was first published by the DCP in 1995. The following is a revised second edition.
2. See Criteria (1991) BPS Membership and Qualifications Board Committee on Training in Clinical Psychology with particular reference to Introduction, paragraphs vii and viii and Section 8.11.

Chapter 1

WHY LOOK AT RACISM AND CULTURAL DIVERSITY?

Social justice and professional integrity

Black and minority ethnic people are increasingly unwilling to accept the role of passive recipients of those services which others consider it appropriate to offer. They are taxpayers and they are entitled to expect relevant services, not as an afterthought or when additional resources are made available, but routinely. Decisions may have to be made about the degree of diversity which can be met specifically and how this can be done, but social justice requires that such decisions be made as far as possible within the context of mainstream policy and service planning.

We have the duty to recognize and challenge racism within the systems in which we work, including our own profession. In so far as 'competence' is an aspect of professional integrity, then competence in dealing with diversity and inequality should be emphasized. Humility, flexibility and willingness to ask questions thus become critical aspects of professional integrity. So too does the strength to take chances, to apply existing and increasing knowledge to new situations.

Statutory obligations

1. 1976 Race Relations Act, Section 20. Health Authorities have an obligation to ensure that the provision of services is not racially discriminatory in the types of services offered or the manner in which they are offered and, also, to provide services which are appropriate and easily acceptable to all ethnic groups in the population.
2. The Patient's Charter. The Government proposed a commitment to providing mental health services for minority ethnic groups. One of the nine national standards demands 'respect for privacy, dignity and religious and cultural beliefs'. This means that the Health Service must respond to individual needs of clients which arise from their religious and cultural beliefs.
3. The White Paper, *Health of the Nation*, indicated that 'local decisions about action to achieve targets will need to take into account particular needs of people from Black and minority ethnic groups'.
4. The White Paper, *People First*, stated that all services must be ethnically sensitive and meet the needs of different ethnic groups.

5. The National Services Framework for Mental Health (1999) advocates that 'mental health services need to develop and demonstrate cultural competence' (p.44).

Health Authority recommendations

The National Association of Health Authorities (NAHA) Working Party report on health care for Black and minority ethnic groups, *Action Not Words* (1988), first suggested that access to NHS provision should be equally available to all and be sensitive to the needs of all groups in society. The NHS therefore needs to adapt to a multicultural and a multiethnic British society.

The British Psychological Society's recommendations

1. The BPS Committee for Training in Clinical Psychology (CTCP, 1991) has reiterated the necessity of integrating a multicultural perspective into post-graduate training in Clinical Psychology.
2. The BPS Equal Opportunities Statement (1994) refers to ensuring 'the provision of relevant training materials in the area of Equal Opportunities and encouraging individual courses to ensure the adequacy of coverage of Equal Opportunity issues'.

    Thus, both government legislation and recommendations and BPS policy and training requirements, direct our profession towards the examination and the acquisition of an appropriate methodology which should equip us to provide accessible, adequate and appropriate psychological care for all our clients.

Chapter 2

BASIC INFORMATION ON DEMOGRAPHY AND INEQUALITY

The experience of individual and institutional racism is endemic in the sociopolitical context for many Black and minority ethnic people in Britain. The psychological consequences can be devastating and can lead to a sense of powerlessness, helplessness and an internalized negative conception of self. For the therapist, the task in hand is to explore this context and presenting issues, whilst also identifying the strengths and resources of the client/family, ultimately in an effort to empower them to live in a world which may be experienced as constantly seeking to disempower them (Patel and Fatimilehin, 1999).

Demographic data

According to the 1991 Census (OPCS, 1991), the total population of Great Britain was 54.9 million. Of this, the total minority ethnic population was just over 3 million (5.5 per cent). Nearly half of this 5.5 per cent was made up of people of South Asian ethnic origin, with Indian people comprising the largest individual minority ethnic group. The second largest group was of Black-Caribbean people. The third largest group was of Pakistani (CRE, 1992). Emerson and Hatton (1999), using statistical analysis, predict that by the year 2021, approximately one in ten young people aged 0–30 will belong to a minority ethnic group.The largest minority ethnic groups are less strongly represented in Wales and Scotland than in England. In Wales and Scotland, the Chinese and 'other' groups account for a larger share of the minority ethnic population (39.8 per cent in Wales and 38.5 per cent in Scotland, compared to 20.8 per cent in England). Details of regional patterns can be found in the Statistical Paper 1, CRE (1992).

Settlement patterns

The 1991 Census identified 81 separate national origins in addition to those of the United Kingdom (and other British islands). This information has been summarized by the CRE, as shown in Tables 2.1 and 2.2.

Table 2.1 *Ethic group composition of Great Britain. 1991 (thousands)*

Ethnic Group	Great Britain	England and Wales	England	Wales	Scotland
White	51,843.9	46,907.8	44,114.6	2,793.3	4,936.1
Ethnic minorities	**3,006.5**	**2,947.0**	**2,906.5**	**40.5**	**59.5**
Black	*885.4*	*880.9*	*872.4*	*8.5*	*4.4*
Black Caribbean	499.1	499.0	496.3	2.7	0.0
Black African	207.5	205.5	203.2	2.3	2.0
Other Black	178.8	176.4	172.9	3.5	2.4
South Asian	*1,476.9*	*1,444.6*	*1,428.8*	*15.9*	*32.2*
Indian	840.8	830.6	823.9	6.7	10.2
Pakistani	475.8	454.5	448.8	5.8	21.2
Bangladeshi	160.3	159.5	156.1	3.4	0.8
Chinese and others	*644.3*	*621.5*	*605.4*	*16.1*	*22.9*
Chinese	157.5	147.3	142.4	4.9	10.2
Other Asian	196.7	193.2	189.7	3.5	3.5
Other	290.1	281.0	273.3	7.7	9.2
Total population:	54,860.2	49,861.6	47,026.5	2,835.1	4,998.6

Table 2.2 *Ethic group composition of Great Britain, 1991 (percentages)*

Ethnic Group	Great Britain	England and Wales	England	Wales	Scotland
White	94.5	94.1	93.8	98.5	98.7
Ethnic minorities	**5.5**	**6.0**	**6.3**	**1.4**	**1.3**
Black	*1.6*	*1.8*	*1.9*	*0.3*	*0.1*
Black Caribbean	0.9	1.0	1.1	0.1	0.0
Black African	0.4	0.4	0.4	0.1	0.0
Black – other	0.3	0.4	0.4	0.1	0.0
South Asian	*2.7*	*2.9*	*3.0*	*0.6*	*0.6*
Indian	1.5	1.7	1.8	0.2	0.2
Pakistani	0.9	0.9	1.0	0.2	0.4
Bangladeshi	0.3	0.3	0.3	0.1	0.0
Chinese and others	*1.2*	*1.2*	*1.3*	*0.6*	*0.5*
Chinese	0.3	0.3	0.3	0.2	0.2
Other – Asian	0.4	0.4	0.4	0.1	0.1
Other – other	0.5	0.6	0.6	0.3	0.2
Total population:	54.860.2	49,861.6	47,026.5	2,835.1	4,998.6

Source: 1991 Census of Population, 1991, reproduced from Statistical Paper 5, CRE, 1993

The population comprising those whose country of origin was not the United Kingdom has often been referred to as 'migrant'. Migrants are not a homogenous group of people, but people who have migrated to Britain for different reasons with different expectations and different motives. There has been some distinction made between settlers, exiles and guest workers (Rack, 1982) and some of these terms are still relevant. Further explanations of these terms can be found in Chapter 3, 'Developing a language'.

The gender balance of the population differs significantly between the British population as a whole and persons born outside Great Britain. On the whole, females form a small majority of all persons resident in Great Britain, but females form a slightly larger majority of all persons born outside Britain.

Black and minority ethnic people using the Health Service

Until very recently there has been a noticeable lack of data on the use of the health service by Black and minority ethnic people. In order to deliver an effective, acceptable and appropriate service to all people from different minority ethnic backgrounds, it is essential that effective monitoring is undertaken. Currently, the Department of Health is taking some steps to improve the situation. Since 1994, data on the ethnicity of service users has been included as part of the Contract Minimum Data Set.

Of existing data, hospital records indicate that a disproportionate number of minority ethnic persons, both those born in Britain and in the Caribbean and West Africa, are detained under the Mental Health Act. (Ineichen *et al.*, 1984; McGovern and Cope, 1987). The degree of over-representation varies, but most studies suggest that it is between two and three times the rate for White people born in the UK (Littlewood and Lipsedge, 1989).

Almost all of the existing data on the use of psychological services by those from minority ethnic groups is anecdotal, although very relevant. In Britain, clients from minority ethnic backgrounds are rarely referred for psychotherapy or counselling services. (For further information please consult later modules and accompanying reading lists, particularly Smaje (1995), Teague (1993), Coleman and Salt (1996).)

Data on disadvantage and discrimination

Employment
- Studies by the Policy Studies Institute (PSI) carried out in London, Birmingham and Manchester show that at least one-third of private employers discriminated against Asian applicants, Afro-Caribbean applicants or both (Braham *et al.*, 1992).
- In 1995/96 the unemployment rate for people from ethnic minorities (18 per cent) was more than twice that of White people (8 per cent). Pakistani and Bangladeshi groups, at 27 per cent and 28 per cent respectively experienced particularly high unemployment levels (CRE, 1997).
- A higher incidence of unemployment over a 1–2 year period for Black men

and women (19 per cent and 23 per cent respectively) compared with 15 per cent and 13 per cent for White men and women. This was more prevalent among 16–24 year old Black women (39 per cent), Black men (36 per cent) and Pakistani/Bangladeshi women (36 per cent).

- It seems that if unemployment is high locally, the figures are even higher among minority ethnic groups.
- A formal investigation by the CRE of 168 large companies in Britain in 1993/94 found that although 88 per cent of companies had racial equality policies, fewer than half had programmes to put them into practice (CRE, 1997).
- Quoting surveys by Modood (1997), Patel and Fatimilehin (1999) conclude that 40 years following post-war migration, the majority of Black and minority ethnic people work primarily within the public sector in non-managerial positions or are self-employed, pointing to their likely social exclusion.

Housing

Institutional racism has increasingly been taken into account when analysing racism in housing processes in Britain. Studies in the last two decades looking at local authority housing departments across the country document institutional processes seen as racist whereby Black applicants for council housing waited longer than White people, and once rehoused received inferior accommodation to White people (Simpson, 1981; 1989). Furthermore, racial violence and harassment in and around the home are also very important factors in sustaining racial inequalities in housing. There appears to be a tendency among housing managers and politicians to avoid these issues because they may be seen as too intimidating, too difficult or as being matters for the police. None the less, racial violence and harassment around the home are frightening realities for many minority ethnic people. These can also impact on psychological health.

Education

For details of research and issues in the area of 'race' and education, please see the Child, Adolescent and Family Module.

Racial attacks and harassment

These are a reality for many Black and minority ethnic people, although the true extent to which they occur is difficult to gauge as it is dependent on the crimes concerned, their reportability and the production of evidence. It seems that Pakistanis are least likely to report even serious crimes to the police and these offences are usually not isolated one off incidents but involve repeated victimisation (Fitzgerald and Hale, 1996). It is therefore suspected that a fear of reprisal and dissatisfaction with police response is a deterrent for many.

- In 1996 the British Crime Survey (BCS) estimated that 382,000 offences (or just over 2 per cent of all offences reported to the BCS in 1995) were considered by the victims to be racially motivated. This accounted for 15 per cent of all crimes committed against minority ethnic people compared to 1per cent of offences against White people (CRE, 1999a).

- In 1997/8, the police recorded 13,878 racial incidents in England and Wales, an increase of 6 per cent over the previous year. In Scotland, the figure rose by 35 per cent from 811 to 1,097 incidents. An increase in reporting and in police recording may account for this rather than an increase in frequency (CRE,1999a, p.2).
- 21 per cent of all racial incidents involved assaults and 2 per cent were serious crimes against the person.

Of racial incidents recorded by the police in England and Wales between 1994/5 and 1996/7, serious offences made up 1,363 (3.7 per cent) of the 37,206 incidents: 866 were serious assaults, 482 were attacks involving explosives and arson, ten were homicides and five attempted homicides (House of Commons (1998) cited in CRE, 1999a).

Criminal justice system

The CRE (1999b) suggests that minority ethnic people, especially Pakistanis, Bangladeshis and Caribbeans who are young, poor, unemployed and living in high crime inner city areas are more likely to be victims of crime. Yet the picture is of Black and minority ethnic people making up a higher percentage of the prison population (Home Office, 1996).

Bucke (1997), looking at the 1996 BCS on vehicle and foot stops, found that Caribbeans are more likely than both Asians and Whites to be stopped by the police on more than one occasion: particularly, Caribbean males aged between 16 and 25 (53 per cent) compared to 47 per cent White and 36 per cent Asian males. Asian women were least likely to be stopped. Some studies suggest that Black juveniles are less likely to be cautioned and more likely to be prosecuted in comparison to White juveniles (Willis, 1993; Walker *et al.*, 1989).

Once stopped and searched, Caribbeans were more likely (12 per cent) to be arrested than Asians (6 per cent) or White people (6 per cent). Black people were five times more likely to be arrested than Whites in ten forces with large minority ethnic populations (Home Office, 1998). This seems to be the case even when there is weaker evidence against the Black or Asian suspect compared to the White suspect (Philips and Brown, 1998).

- Studies of Black people and sentencing have produced mixed findings: some have found no significant differences in the sentencing of offenders from different ethnic groups (Flood-Pape and Mackie, 1998), while other studies have produced disturbing indicators of discrimination (Smith,1994; Voakes and Fowler, 1989; Walker, 1988; Hood, 1992; Hudson, 1989; Fitzgerald, 1993).
- In 1997/8 13 per cent, i.e. 7 out of 53 deaths in custody, were of detainees from minority ethnic groups (CRE, 1999b).On 30 June 1997, 18 per cent of prisoners in England and Wales were from minority ethnic groups. They

accounted for some 18 per cent of all males and 25 per cent of the female prison population.

- In 1997/8, Black prisoners formed the largest minority ethnic group: of these 21 per cent were foreign nationals.
- In June 1997, per 100,000 population in England and Wales, 1,246 Black, 176 White, and 150 Asians were incarcerated (Home Office, 1997).
- The impact of institutional racism within the police force has been clearly stated within the Macpherson report on the inquiry into the murder of Stephen Lawrence (Macpherson, 1999).
- A disturbing aspect is the expectation of unfair treatment by the criminal justice system for minority ethnic people, a feature highlighted by available data and expressed in studies which focused specifically on their experience (Hood, 1992; Smith, 1994).

Chapter 3

DEVELOPING A LANGUAGE

Finding a common language between the therapist and the individual or family is an important aspect not only of joining or forming a therapeutic alliance, but of being able to work constructively together. Yet language is open to much misinterpretation, a factor necessitating the need for care in its usage.

This section aims to clarify the terms which will be relevant in the discussion of ethnic and cultural diversity and of inequalities based on ethnicity. The historical significance of words cannot be ignored in understanding their current usage. For example, in the area of what was termed 'learning disability', the advent of normalization led to a change in what were deemed appropriate terms in the field.

In the clinical setting we need to highlight the ways in which word usage is significant. Aspects of usage include the relevancy of terms to their context, pejorative dimensions of meaning, both conscious and unconscious, and whether language involves a self-classification or classification by others.

Commonly used terms within the discourse of 'race' and culture

'Race'/Racial categories

'Race' is a concept that has largely been discredited in biological science, but was particularly prevalent in the 19th and 20th centuries. For this reason it is usually placed in inverted commas in social science texts. The term assumes that humans can be clearly divided into distinct populations based on biological characteristics, usually coupled with the belief that these also determine behaviour and institutions (Littlewood, 1989). The concept of a hierarchy, with consequent notions of inferiority and superiority of different groups, was also built into the notion of 'race'. In everyday speech, 'race' almost always refers to differences in skin colour, and is often used in a derogatory manner. In anthropological circles 'race' has been related to a wide range of genetic characteristics: for example, skin colour, blood group and hair texture (d'Ardenne and Mahtani, 1999). The construct of 'race' may be used to understand culture and behaviour when these are, as Phillips and Rathwell (1986) note, more to do with social relationships, power and domination, than with biological differences.

Ethnicity

Fernando (1991) provides a useful framework for looking at the concepts of 'race', culture and ethnicity (Table 3.1).

Table 3.1: *'Race', culture and ethnicity*

	Characterized by	Determined by	Perceived as
RACE	Physical appearance	Genetic ancestry	Permanent: genetic/ biological
CULTURE	Behaviour Attitude	Upbringing choice	Changeable: acculturation/ assimilation
ETHNICITY	Sense of belonging	Group identity Social pressures Psychological need	Partially changeable

Source: Fernando, S. (1991) *Mental Health, Race and Culture* (reproduced by kind permission of Macmillan Press Ltd.)

Ethnicity, unlike 'race', is not fixed: it is situationally defined and concerns the maintenance of social boundaries. Ethnicity is a group identification, it defines an 'us' (the similarity axis being primary); its contents include culture or geography. 'Race' is a categorization, it defines a 'them' (the difference axis being primary). The us/them boundary is imposed from outside when 'race' is being talked about, and taken on from the inside when 'ethnicity' is the organizing theme (Dalal, 1993). Ethnicity is transactional, shifting and essentially impermanent. It signifies allegiance to the culture of origin and implies a degree of choice which 'race' precludes (Jenkins, 1986). Ethnicity is part of everyone's identity. The terms 'minority ethnic' or 'ethnics' imply that only minority groups are ethnic or have ethnicity. We need to keep in mind that both 'minority ethnic groups' and 'majority ethnic groups' have ethnicity. As Sashidharan (1986) and Fernando (1988) note, in psychiatry words like 'culture' and 'ethnicity' are not neutral but take on a politically loaded meaning. They may be used in an ethnocentric way, where non-Western cultures alien to psychiatry are seen as pathological. In this way culture becomes the 'problem' that accounts for the abnormal client.

Racism and institutional racism

These terms describe the systematic application of prejudice across personal and institutional contexts. Institutional racism refers to the reproduction within institutions of practices of power which discriminate against persons on the grounds of perceived 'race'. Individuals within these institutions may not necessarily hold overtly racist views. These practices maintain the status quo in institutions and can be practices both in the commission of racist acts or in the omission of acts which would redress the situation.

Racisms

Here one needs to take into account that discrimination is based not just on a Black–White binary. It is used to highlight the argument that racism takes different forms and is experienced in a variety of ways (Phoenix, 1999).

Racialization

Phoenix (1999) states that the term 'racialization' (Omi and Winant, 1986) is designed to convey the idea that the meanings associated with 'race' are not static but are dynamic social processes (see Phoenix, 1999, p.134 for details).

Immigrant

This term has a particular history in Great Britain. Clearly there is a difference between the dictionary meaning ('one who comes into a foreign country to settle there') and the common connotations associated with the term in Britain: namely, that immigrants are strangers by virtue of their colour and culture. It can be misused when loosely applied to those people born in Britain but who have parents who were immigrants. It often implies a sense of 'outsider' or 'intruder' into society, where the 'host society' is seen as stable and without fundamental conflicts within it – a stability which is disturbed by immigrants. Generally, it is used to refer to 'coloured immigrants' and therefore reinforces prejudice against a particular group. Its usage may be relevant in the cases where a person's legal immigration status is under discussion or a client's experience of migration is seen as clinically relevant.

Settler

Individuals may decide to settle in Great Britain and make it their home. Such individuals have full immigration rights. In contrast, refugees exiled from their country of origin and guest workers (Rack, 1982) migrated, as many did during the fifties and sixties, with the intention of returning to their country of origin. Clearly the clinical implication of differentiating between settlers, refugees and guest workers is considerable, particularly in understanding the factors possibly influencing or impacting on the psychological health of clients from different ethnic backgrounds.

Political correctness (PC)

The original term 'political correctness' referred to language which consciously tried to avoid racial, ethnic and gender stereotyping. In certain quarters rigid adherence to, and over exaggeration of, such politically correct stances became in itself a focus of derision. It is now seen by many as a euphemism for things having 'gone too far the other way': assumed over-compensation. It has gone through several stages demarcating the trivialization of people 'doing the right things' but with their 'hearts remaining unchanged'. The term has been misused and derided, essentially in a way that has suppressed alternative voices and viewpoints which attempt to challenge the status quo.

Western

In common parlance it is often assumed that Western implies a dominant White majority and is seen as the dominant culture. This is portrayed as the ideal by which other cultures are evaluated. Such ethnocentrism can be seen operating in South Africa, Australia, New Zealand, European countries and North America. It has a distinctive meaning when applied to European and Russian psychology. The Cold War added another level, where Western came to mean European and North American and not Eastern. However, it does depend on whose history is being looked at.

Dominant culture

The idea that some cultures are dominant and others not is part of the discourse of power that has been an important part of the deconstruction (at least intellectually) of such power. Dominance is not conferred by membership of a statistical majority, although it is associated with it in some circumstances, such as in European states. It refers to the validation of cultural practices, norms and values over and above the non-dominant cultures, and to its underpinning by economic, social and political structures.

Skin colour

While skin colour is not a term at issue in its own right, its inclusion relates to an important aspect of the clinical context. Skin colour and skin tone, along with facial features and hair quality, play a significant role in the lives of Black people. These immediately obvious and relatively stable characteristics have been used by both White and Black people to discriminate against, and make distinctions among, others and themselves. The visibility of difference created by skin colour has consistently attracted discriminatory behaviour. Thus, it is important, clinically, to think about the possible association of skin colour with perceived self-worth, intelligence, success and attractiveness, and about how skin colour is addressed in the therapeutic setting. It is the psychologist's responsibility to consider the timing and sensitivity of raising this issue. For a fuller discussion see the exercise 'Role play of inter-racial work' later in this module.

Coloured

This term has important historical links. It was originally used as a polite term to refer to 'foreigners' or 'immigrants'. This was quite vehemently rejected by the Black community, possibly because it was seen as a euphemism for the term 'foreigner' which had connotations of 'not belonging' or 'being unwanted' or 'Black'. It has links with the old South African apartheid system that classified some citizens as 'coloured' as a derogatory description of someone of dual ethnic background, perhaps also implying a sense of not belonging to either group.

Black

As Howitt and Owusu-Bempah (1994) note, the use of 'Black' as a generic, politicized description has had a rather chequered history in terms of its general approval. One of its particular problems is its varying acceptability in different communities, paradoxically because the term 'Black', adopted by some as a political act of self-labelling and self-unification, is experienced by others as yet another externally imposed description. The term 'Black' does create a major problem in some settings, in that it essentially strips the individual of any contextual referents. But of course this is exactly what some users intend the term to achieve – to identify and unite large groupings of people in terms of their shared experiences of socially disadvantaged status in White socio-politico-economic structures.

White

This is a term which some White people may not have thought about, its use often being implied rather than overt. Thus in conversation about 'race' issues the use of the term 'us' or 'we' often implies 'Whites' as opposed to those who are 'coloured'. When used in this fashion the term is very racist in its application (refer to Katz, 1978 and the earlier section, 'Notes for White Trainers' for further discussion of this term and related exercises).

Half-caste

This term is generally found to be offensive and patronizing in that it carries the negative connotations of deficiency and of being incomplete. More recently it has been superseded by the term 'mixed race'. Both terms are unsatisfactory since they imply acceptance of the notion of a distinct 'racial' group.

Mixed race

This expression is currently in transition. It refers to people whose parents are from two different ethnic backgrounds. It is inappropriate since it gives credence to the false notion of biological 'race' groupings and ignores the social identity of people. 'Dual ethnic background' or 'multi-ethnic background' are more recent terms. In therapy, it may be necessary to explore the importance of the individual's parentage to their self-concept/self-identify. When working with families, it may be important to explore issues from the parents' perspectives as well as those of the children.

Specific ethnic categories

Asian

This term is often misused to refer to 'South Asian' people, i.e. those originating in the Indian subcontinent. As Asia extends from Turkey through to China it is an unspecific and unhelpful term, particularly if it is being used clinically to stereotype or indiscriminately group people together. Where reference to a person's ethnic origin is made, we need to be more specific: Punjabi, Bangladeshi or Pakistani, for example, help to show respect for a person's ethnic identity and background.

West Indian

As with the word 'Asian', this term is not traditionally used in self-classification by the groups to whom it is usually applied as it has little true meaning. People who have migrated from the Caribbean have the roots of their identity in island differences – Jamaican, Barbadian, Trinidadian, etc. These, as well as the term 'West Indian', have little relevance for those born in Britain.

Afro-Caribbean

This is often used in preference to 'West Indian', but it can be ambiguous as it is normally used to mean Caribbean people of African rather than Asian origin, and there are many of the latter. The more straightforward 'Caribbean' is preferred by some, while 'African-Caribbean' is preferred by those who wish to emphasize their links with Africa.

British/English

These are also ambiguous. They can mean nationality/citizenship or ethnic identity. The ethnic majority group is not so clearly defined as we might think: consider the ethnic identity of the Welsh, the English, the Scottish and the Irish. Most of these groups take pride in their ethnic origins, even if they have moved away from their place of birth. The term has been adopted by some Black people to describe their identity.

Chapter 4
THE PARTIALITY OF ACADEMIC PSYCHOLOGY

Note to trainers: This section introduces some ideas and a basic structure for thinking about the Eurocentrism of academic psychology and its implications for the teaching and practice of clinical psychology. It does not provide all the materials that trainers will need for teaching on this topic. Core texts are recommended and described in the annotated reading list. Henriques et al. (1984), Howitt and Owusu-Bempah (1994), Littlewood and Lipsedge (1989) and Shweder and LeVine (1984) all provide useful discussions of the nature and history of theory production within psychology that will be helpful in elaborating this section.

In the teaching and learning of academic psychology there is generally an assumption that this body of knowledge is culture-free and has universal applicability. It is also assumed in the teaching and learning of clinical applications of psychological theory that these are sufficient to address people's problems irrespective of their culture. It is proposed here that we need to look at the possibility that the knowledge base of clinical psychology is *partial*, in both senses of the word:

(1)   'Pertaining to or involving a part only; incomplete'.*

Academic psychology is 'local knowledge', pertaining only to the culture which has produced it, i.e. usually White Western.

(2)   'Prejudiced or biased in someone's favour'.*

The dominant political and economic position of this White Western culture means that its world views, including psychological theories, hold the position of a privileged discourse. Thus, the psychological, behavioural and social processes it describes and attempts to explain have come to represent the norm against which other types can be measured and, often, be found to be deficient.

The first type of partiality, that our knowledge base may apply only to a subsection of human experience, can be seen as inevitable and, perhaps, unproblematic. The assumptions made when constructing a theory, the determination of what is worth studying and what is not and the inferences drawn from empirical findings, will all be shaped by the culture of the theory makers. It could perhaps be argued that the search for a universal psychology is fruitless, as theory makers can never remove their cultural lenses.

---

* Shorter Oxford English Dictionary, Third Edition, Clarendon Press, Oxford

The second type of partiality is more problematic. As long as one set of ideas or world views is privileged above others, those other ideas and world views will be devalued and other ways of giving meaning to human behaviour may be invalidated. It is this type of partiality which provides the notions of 'advanced versus primitive' and 'developed versus underdeveloped' in our discussions of human thought and behaviour.

Although there is evidence of purposefulness in the partiality of psychological theories (see Littlewood and Lipsedge for a history of theories of 'race'), bias need not be introduced into research methods or theory production intentionally or consciously. Bias routinely occurs because it represents the accumulated 'common experience' of being a member of a particular group. Scientific endeavour is characterized as objective but scientists, as human beings, cannot disengage from everyday shared assumptions about the nature of reality.

An illustration of this unconscious bias can be found in the frequently made 'observation' that Asian people tend to somatize psychological problems, and in the various attempts to explain this observation. Explanations tend to vary according to the orientation of the clinician. For example, a psychodynamically orientated psychologist might see evidence of denial, or even invoke 'conversion hysteria'. A systemically minded psychologist might look at the function of physical symptoms within the family, perhaps in relation to assumptions about gender roles within Asian families. A further stereotype is also sometimes invoked: that mental health problems carry a particular stigma for Asian people and are therefore disguised.

Some research has demonstrated that Asian people are no more likely to somatize than are their White British counterparts. Krause (1994) describes one such piece of research (the Bedford Study), showing that White British people are just as likely to somatize as are people from the Punjab, and that the nature of the physical symptoms reported is very similar among the two groups. Krause, however, goes beyond this finding to suggest that 'somatization' is itself a culture-specific notion, being given meaning only in the context of the 'mind–body split' which characterizes modern Western thinking. Thus, while two people from different cultural backgrounds may report the same physical symptom, the meanings given to it may be very different. The 'humoral paradigm', informed by traditional Ayurvedic ideas that underlies the thinking about health and illness of the Punjabis in the study, means that the terms they used to describe 'disease' all have not only physical but also psychological, social and existential referents. A checklist of symptoms may therefore yield very similar results for groups of people from diverse cultures, but if the results are then interpreted only by people from one of those cultures, this may still tend to obscure very real group differences – differences which may well be relevant to intervention processes.

As we all know, the questions asked in research will be important determinants of the answers found. The questions asked in psychological research are embedded within a particular social, cultural and historical context, so that the answers found are likely to relate most meaningfully to people who share that context. This factor clearly has implications for our practice of psychology. Currently we are taught, and we teach, psychological theory as if it had universal validity. If this is not the case, and at the moment the most we can say about this is 'not proven', then we run the risk, in a multicultural society, of at best misunderstanding and at worst devaluing and invalidating the experience of many users of our services.

THEORIES OF CULTURE

(See Shweder and Bourne, Chapter 6 in Shweder and LeVine, 1984)

Shweder and Bourne's (1984) categorization of the ways in which cognitive anthropologists have attempted to make sense of the 'diversity of human understandings' provides one useful framework for thinking about the nature of psychological theories. They identify three approaches:

- *Universalism*: This has as its cornerstone the idea that diversity is more apparent than real and that under 'surface difference' true universals can be found.
- *Evolutionism*: This is characterized by the assumption that White Western idea systems and world views represent the pinnacle, the most developed form of human understanding, while others' idea systems and world views represent incipient and less adequate stages in this development.
- *Relativism*: This holds that the idea systems of different cultures are fundamentally different and that each displays an internal coherency which can be understood but which cannot be judged. Others can be credited not with confusion, error or ignorance, but rather with an alternative vision of the possibilities of human life.

Each of these approaches has its strengths and limitations. Universalism allows the thrill of recognition that comes with the discovery of commonalities among people from different cultures – the possibility of a 'basic human connectedness'. True universals of human experience can perhaps be found. However, the pursuit of higher-order generality can result in impoverished descriptions, divested of the richness which makes up each individual's experience of the world. Unlike universalism, evolutionism does permit the existence of variety. It is a normative approach, however, which privileges a particular world view. Relativism is an egalitarian approach that denies privilege to any one particular idea system, but does not allow for the making of *any* value judgements between systems.

The Bedford Study involving somatization described above might be seen as an example of a universalist approach. On the whole, psychological theories assume universalism by failing to look at difference, but have a strong evolutionary bias. 'Stage theories' abound: for example, the works of Piaget, Luria, Kohlberg and Erikson are based on the notion that individuals move through an identifiable series of stages, with the end-point characterized by reason, logic, rationality and self-reliance – characteristics most highly valued within Western society. There are difficulties with such theories within the culture which produced them, but when they are used to define or describe people from a range of cultures, they tend to classify peoples along a 'primitive' to 'advanced' continuum, with White Westerners (particularly men) at the 'advanced' end.

ALTERNATIVE PSYCHOLOGIES

It was suggested above that the search for a 'universal psychology' might be fruitless. The term 'ethnocentric' tends to have a negative connotation, but can also be seen as a value-free description of what it is to be human: we are each shaped by our own culture, construct our view of reality within that culture and can reflect upon our own and others' cultures only from a particular world view. The current knowledge base of clinical psychology may relate most meaningfully to members of the culture which produced it. The search for universals, if conducted by people from diverse cultural backgrounds, might yield important findings, but might also leave us with 'an artichoke divested of its leaves'. An alternative could be the construction of a set of partial, culture-specific 'psychologies'that could stand alone but also inform and enrich each other.

Because of the dominance of the Western scientific paradigm, it is hard to find clearly articulated alternative psychologies. However, there is an important body of thought here, and it may be useful for trainers and trainees to look at some examples. Discussions of culture-specific views of self, personhood, child development and parenting, health and disease, for example, can be found in Fernando (1991), Kakar (1984) and Shweder and LeVine (1984). The 'Just Therapy' Centre in New Zealand has developed theoretical and therapeutic approaches specific to each of the cultural groups using its service (Waldegrave, 1990a). Culturally specific approaches to psychological healing and attempts at syntheses are described in Sheikh and Sheikh (1989). The issue of 'individualism versus collectivism', often seen as a crucial divide between Eastern and Western cultures, is usefully addressed in a collection of papers, edited by Kim and Berry (1993), which includes work by psychologists from Europe, Asia, Africa, Latin America and North America who argue that indigenous psychology requires each culture to be understood within its own frame of reference.

RELIGION

Western science is essentially secular and, consequently, academic psychology has very little to say about the religious or spiritual aspects of people's experience. It is probably true to say that psychologists tend to take a reductionist view of religious belief systems, while tending to ignore them in practice unless the client raises them for discussion. However, there is considerable anecdotal evidence that these belief systems are of great importance to many people seeking psychological services. Work done on the religious and spiritual dimensions of personhood and social life among people of African and Asian origin (Boyd-Franklin, 1989; Kakar,1984; Krause, 1994; Smith, 1981) and among Jewish people (Wieselberg, 1992) makes it clear that the ways in which many people's lives are structured by spiritual values is of great importance in both understanding and offering help to these clients. An appreciation of the part played by the socially supportive networks of some religious groups for their members can also provide useful resources for therapeutic work with clients. (See particularly Boyd-Franklin and Smith for the place of Black churches in the lives of their members and working with this therapeutically, and Wieselberg for an account of family work in the context of Orthodox Jewry.)

Chapter 5
THEORIES OF RACISM

Note to trainers: This section provides some 'pointers' for teaching as well as suggested reading. Trainers will need to read the texts in order to provide adequate teaching on this topic. Any experiential understanding of the processes and impact of racism which they have or can acquire will enrich their teaching.

Black and minority ethnic people who use psychological services will have been affected by racism in one form or another. Disadvantage and discrimination in employment, housing and education may have touched their lives, they may have received different treatment from mental health services on the basis of their ethnicities and they may have experienced 'everyday racism' in the community. These experiences may be directly relevant to the problems with which they present and may affect their readiness to use psychological services and trust individual White workers. Trainees need to be aware of the implications of racism for their clients and for their practice of psychology. Practice issues will be addressed throughout this Training Manual, some theoretical considerations are outlined here.

As discussed earlier in Chapter 4, the current construction of difference between cultures or ethnic groups is value laden. White Western culture views itself as the norm with which other cultures are compared, often unfavourably. One consequence is that 'difference' itself has come to be seen as an 'attribute of the other' rather than as a relational concept: i.e. Black and minority ethnic people are seen as different. Logically, of course, this makes no sense – if we are shown a circle and a square and asked to say which is different, we will probably answer that the question is meaningless and that they *differ from each other*. However, in everyday conversation, including that of psychologists, this illogicality tends to go unnoticed. For example, the problem of 'language barrier' in the therapeutic relationship is usually stated as 'the client does not speak English', rather than 'the client and therapist do not speak the same language'.

MODELS OF RACISM

Useful critiques of the ways in which racism has been modelled in the psychological literature and how these models are reflected in everday discourse can be found in Donald and Rattansi (1992), Henriques *et al.* (1984), Howitt (1991), Ridley (1995) and Wetherell and Potter (1992).

Cohen (1992, Chapter 3 in Donald and Rattansi), identifies five characterizations of racism in everday discourse:

- racism as institutionalized false consciousness
- racism as irrational prejudice
- racism as an expression of White power
- racism as a dimension of class rule
- racism as rational self-interest

He argues that all of these have 'propaganda value', but that none is necessarily adequate as a theoretical explanation of racism since all attempt to explain a complex phenomenon by citing a single, simple cause. He suggests that what is needed is respect for the 'relative autonomy' of different levels of explanation, each of which may contribute something useful to analysis and intervention in the different sites and forms of racism.

Wetherell and Potter (1992) examine models of racism which locate the problem within the individual, either in relation to particular individuals – the 'character structure' or 'pathological' model – or as a universal phenomenon, the 'errors of information-processing' model. The latter, resting as it does on the question of 'rational' versus 'irrational' judgements, is seen as highlighting the classical dilemma of positivism – 'facts versus values'. They argue that the question: 'When is prejudice "irrational"? and when is it "justified denigration"?', can never be answered empirically.

Henriques *et al.* (1984) trace the development of psychological theories of racism and argue that the emphasis placed on 'individual errors of information processing' results in racism being seen as an individual, exceptional phenomenon that exonerates society as a whole and obscures the existence of institutionalized racism.

Ridley (1995) defines racism as 'any behaviour or pattern of behaviour that tends to systematically deny access to opportunities or privileges to members of one racial group while perpetuating access to opportunities and privileges to members of another racial group.' (p.28). He also suggests a 'behavioural model' of the types or levels of racism:

I. Individual Racism	II. Institutional Racism
A. Overt (always intentional)	A. Overt (always intentional)
B. Covert	B. Covert
1. Intentional	1. Intentional
2. Unintentional	2. Unintentional

PSYCHOLOGICAL UNDERSTANDING OF THE EXPERIENCE OF RACISM

If trainees are to work well with Black and minority ethnic clients, they will need to recognize the potential significance of the experience of racism and gain some understanding of it at more than simply an intellectual level. This can be done in a number of ways: through experiential work in teaching sessions; through supervised 'learning from the client'; by reading some of the fictional, non-academic and clinical accounts included in the reading list (see under 'Further Reading') and by the use of relevant videos. There are many accounts of experiences of racism in literature, film and theatre. For some current accounts, we suggest Tizard and Phoenix (1993), Wilson (1993), Fenton and Saddiq (1993) and Essed (1991).

Chapter 6

IDENTIFYING AND PLACING ONESELF WITHIN A CULTURAL FRAMEWORK

DEFINITIONS OF CULTURE

There is a struggle to achieve a workable definition of the term 'culture', mainly because culture is continually evolving and changing. The term is construed in diverse ways, indicating that it is a complex, value-laden topic and, therefore, gives rise to a variety of definitions.

D'Ardenne and Mahtani (1999) have defined culture as 'the shared history, practices, beliefs and values of a racial, regional and religious group of people'. They viewed this term as referring to something dynamic and permeating the way people live their lives, although it is often used to explain any difference between one group of people and another.

In a similar vein, Sue and Sue (1990) have construed culture as 'consisting of all those things that people have learned to do, believe, value and enjoy in their history. It is the totality of ideals, beliefs, skills, tools, customs, and institutions into which each member of society is born.'

THE NEED TO UNDERSTAND ONE'S CULTURE

Every individual not only creates a culture but is produced by it. There is an assumption that is often held by White people that culture is possessed only by people who are different from themselves. It is important for every individual to recognize their own culture and how they are shaped by it as it provides individuals with a frame of reference and an identity both culturally and racially. This undoubtedly will, consciously or unconsciously, have an influence on the interactions and relationships between one's own and others' cultures.

CULTURE AS CONSTITUTIVE OF WORLD VIEW

The role or function of one's culture frames the process of one's world view and can act as a social standard by which individuals can judge, select and negotiate the respective value systems that each individual brings into an interaction or relationship. Values are the standards by which individuals direct their actions and define, interpret and judge all social phenomena.

One's values, beliefs, norms, morals and prejudices can be identified and explored by scrutinizing the development of one's world view. The most significant aspects in the makeup of an individual's world view include cultural upbringing and life experiences such as family, social, religious and spiritual beliefs, gender, age, sexuality, 'race', class, employment, environmental, philosophical, political and psychological dimensions. World views are not only composed of our attitudes, values, beliefs etc. but they affect how we think, make decisions, behave and define events.

It is important for clinicians to become aware of, and recognize, the development of their world view and how it may impact on others, in particular on those who are racially and culturally different from themselves. Insensitivity in this regard simply reinforces clinicians' opprtunity to respond according to their own conditioned values, assumptions and perspectives. But processing and understanding the make-up of one's world view enables clinicians to be more insightful, understanding and accepting of others' world views in a non-judgmental way.

One of the recognized difficulties in the examination of one's self- and world view is the emotional impact of beliefs and feelings associated with cultural differences and racism. It is not unusual for White individuals sometimes to become defensive or to flee from situations that require examining their attitudes towards ethnically different groups, since these situations create intense anxiety. It seems, however, that unless one explores this dimension, particular prejudicial attitudes may continue to persist and there may be difficulties in the recognition, respect and acceptance of racial and cultural differences. It must be remembered that differences are not the problem: the problem lies in the perception of what difference means.

Chapter 7

MODELS OF 'RACIAL' AND CULTURAL IDENTITY

There has been increased interest and work in the area of 'racial' and cultural identity and the development of adults. Each individual has a distinct world view and cultural heritage and the belief that all British White people are the same, or all Black and Asian people are the same, has led to numerous problems. For example, by responding stereotypically to the culturally different client or responding to a culturally similar client in an assumption-led manner, we fail to recognize within-group or individual differences.

An understanding of identity development can sensitize clinicians to the role of oppression and racism in individual development. Identity models are useful in recognizing differences among people who are the same or different 'racially' and culturally. The models can also allow clinicians to realize the potentially changing and developmental nature of 'race' and cultural identity among clients. Sue and Sue (1990) have written about the counselling implications when working with clients using identity models. It seems that the models, although they require extensive refinement, can be useful for clinicians in exploring their own identity development, and in identifying when it would be possible to raise the issue of difference with a client: for example, for a client who may be denying their own 'race', the models can help to determine when and how would it be suitable to address and work with this problem. This may have implications for the therapy relationship and whether the client continues to attend. Such issues highlight the complexities and difficulties in the area of identity development and the recognition of difference.

In Britain, there is a lack of research in the area of adult racial and cultural identity development, although ways of working with racial identity development in children have been proposed by Banks (1992) and Maximé (1986). Research has been conducted in the field of the clinician's cultural/'racial' identity and on client preference for a clinician of a similar 'race' and culture. Helms (1984) suggests that the high failure-to-return rate of many culturally different clients seems to be linked to mental health professionals' inability to assess and incorporate the cultural identity of the client and how this factor has an impact on their construction of the problems.

A FRAMEWORK FOR BLACK IDENTITY DEVELOPMENT

The early models of 'racial' identity development, conducted largely by Black American social scientists and educators, incorporated the effects of racism and oppression. Such models of Black identity are largely based on research on the psychology of 'nigrescence', which means 'the process of becoming Black'. They describe the developmental stages Black people traversed in moving from a self-hating to a self-healing and culturally affirming self-concept. Nigrescence is a resocializing experience, transforming a non-Afrocentric identity into one that is Afrocentric.

Cross's original model (1971) of a four-stage process has been viewed as deficient because it underestimated the role Black nationalism played in the lives of many who achieve internalization. What follows is a brief overview of Cross's revised model (1995), where he suggests that the development of a Black person's racial identity is often characterized by a movement through a five-stage process, the transformation from pre-encounter to internalization–commitment.

1. *Pre-encounter*
Persons in this stage hold attitudes towards 'race' that range from low salience, to 'race' neutrality, to anti-Black. A high value is placed on things other than their Blackness. 'Race' is attributed some significance not as a proactive force or cultural issue but as a social stigma. In anti-Black attitudes their vision of Blackness is dominated by negative, racist stereotypes; conversely, they may hold positive 'racial' stereotypes of White people, favouring a Eurocentric cultural perspective. They may oppose multicultural education as wasteful or 'inferior'.

2. *Encounter*
A series of eye-opening episodes cumulatively affect the person's ongoing world view. The person's Eurocentric thinking is disrupted by an encounter with racial prejudice and precipitates an intense search for Black identity. The encounter stage involves two steps: first, experiencing and personalizing the event – the person realizes that his or her old frame of reference is inappropriate, and he or she begins to explore aspects of a new identity; the second part is portrayed by a testing phase in which the individual tries to validate these new perceptions, and a desire to become more aligned with a Black identity. The encounter stage brings a range of emotions such as anger, guilt and shame. In this stage the 'Afrocentric' person is beginning to emerge.

3. *Immersion—Emersion*
This stage brings a transition period in which the person begins to demolish the 'old' perspective while constructing a new frame of reference. The person is familiar with the identity to be destroyed but lacks knowledge about the complexity of the new identity. This stage of being in-between arouses intense anxiety, and the person looks for clear guidance to enable a movement forward. White becomes inferior, inhuman and oppressive, and Blackness becomes supe-

rior. Group identity is significant for social support and the nurturing of the developing identity. For a total immersion into Blackness, the emergence aspect of this stage requires more control of emotions and intellect; the need to become more critical of what it means to be Black. This stage brings the most difficult process of nigrescence to an end.

4. Internalization

By working through the problems in the transition period, the new identity is internalized. The new identity gives high salience to Blackness. From a psycho-dynamic perspective, this identity serves three functions in the everyday life of a person: '(a) to defend and protect a person from psychological insults that stem from having to live in a racist society; (b) to provide a sense of belonging and social anchorage; and (c) to provide a foundation or point of departure for carrying out transactions with people, cultures and human situations beyond the world of Blackness' (Cross 1995: 113). The person's concept of Blackness becomes more expansive and sophisticated.

5. Internalization–Commitment

This stage is characterized by an openness about being Black, and a positive self-esteem emerges through a commitment to express the new identity. This commitment will enable the person to be involved in the resolution of problems and will be of lasting political significance.

Comments on the model

The limitation of Cross's model is that it fails to address gender, class and age (Robinson, 1998; Mama, 1995). Thus, 'the Black individual is still assumed to be a unitary subject (albeit a Black one) devoid of gender and class' (Mama, p.162). Through the five-stage process, Black people are a primary reference group, but the individuals seem to neglect their prejudices about sex, age, 'race' and class. Cross's (1995) response is that people who successfully resolve the conflicts in their racial identity can then shift their attention to other identity concerns such as gender, sexual preferences, religion and class. Parham (1989), cited in Robinson (1998: 16), proposes that identity development recycles throughout adulthood. Parham presents a life-cycle nigrescence model based on a modification of the Cross model. Parham views the Black person as a dynamic subject moving beyond the linear stage models of Black identity development. Helms (1994) views racial identity as ego statuses rather than developmental stages. His model is comprised of five ego statuses and information-processing strategies.

A FRAMEWORK FOR WHITE IDENTITY DEVELOPMENT

The majority of identity models have focused on the Black person. A number of authors have recognized the need for White people to deal with their concepts of Whiteness and to examine their own racist attitudes and world views (Helms 1984; Ponteretto, 1988). It is a common view that White people deny that they belong to a 'race' (Katz and Ivey, 1977). Since, as Robinson (1998) argues, the majority of social and health care workers are White individuals, this is an important area of study.

Hardiman (1982) proposed a model describing a developmental sequence of beliefs, values, feelings and behaviours that White people pass through in developing a new, non-racist White identity. Helms (1990:49) argues that the development of White identity in the US and the UK is closely intertwined with the development and progress of racism and that 'the greater the extent that racism exists and is denied, the less possible it is to develop a positive White identity'. Thus, in Helms's view, a positive White identity involves the process of abandoning racism and the development of a non-racist White identity. Helms's (1990) revised White identity model evolves through a six-stage process of:

1. *Contact* This stage is defined by a lack of racist awareness and participation in it. Black people are evaluated according to White criteria. There is minimal cross-racial interaction and an adherence to stereotypes.
2. *Disintegration* This stage is characterized by the individual's acknowledgement of their Whiteness in a racist society. There may be a belief that all individuals should be treated equally.
3. *Reintegration* The reintegration identity is a racist identity accompanied by a belief that White privilege should be protected. A significant event is required for the person to question and abandon his or her racist identity. Individuals can hold negative attitudes about inter-ethnic situations at work and there is general hostility towards Black people. Hostility and anger are likely to diminish if the person can understand the socio-political implications of being White.
4. *Pseudo-independence* There is a growing responsibility for racism at an intellectual level but cultural difference may still be interpreted from a White perspective.
5. *Immersion-emersion* Profound questions of an existential nature are faced: such as, 'Who am I racially?' This phase requires an emotional catharsis to re-experience previous emotions that were denied or distorted.
6. *Autonomy* There is an abandonment of personal, cultural and institutional racist practices and a development of a more flexible world view. There is a greater acceptance of oneself and others.

THE RELATIONSHIP BETWEEN RACIAL IDENTITY AND COMMUNICATION

Robinson (1998: 24) presents a useful summary of the issues pertaining to this relationship, proposing that 'the manner in which people express their racial identity resolutions influences the quality of their interactions with one another, especially in situations in which "race" is salient'. In relation to mental health, for example, recognizing the within-group variability among Black clients may help the clinician in understanding how the racial identity attitudes of a client may influence the establishment of a workable relationship with that client

(Parham, 1989). In addition, knowledge of a client's racial identity attitudes should not replace a clinician's sensitivity towards the client's experience of discrimination. 'To replace a simplistic psychological labeling would be a perverse misuse of racial identity theory' (Robinson, 1998: 24).

Robinson details Cross's racial identity model, emphasizing the relationship between Black clients receiving mental health care and the issues pertinent to each stage. For example, in the pre-encounter stage, the Black client may believe that White workers are more competent than Black workers; in the immersion–emersion stage, Black clients may be more suspicious and hostile towards White professionals; in the internalization stage, the Black client may become more comfortable with his or her racial identity and the 'race' of the professional is likely to become less important.

In summary, although they require more research in Britain and with different minority and White groups, racial identity development models provide a useful framework for both White and Black service providers. They enable them to gain more knowledge and understanding of themselves in their identity development as well as their clients in the same process.

Chapter 8

WORKING WITH INTERPRETERS

All clients have the right to be understood in their own language (Shackman, 1984). This is a premise that must be considered throughout training. The 1976 Race Relations Act makes it illegal to discriminate in the provision of services on the grounds of 'race'. However, the reality is that clients whose first language is not English are frequently denied psychological services. When challenged, the usual response given is that there is a lack of resources. Clinical psychologists must be clear that by not providing a service to non-English speaking clients, they are discriminating against a group of people. When a psychologist and a client do not share a common language, it is the responsibility of the psychologist to ensure that a trained interpreter facilitates their communication.

Working with interpreters is an essential clinical skill that clinical psychologists need to develop, and not something that is added on as an afterthought. Professionals have often taken the shortcut approach of using children or other family members as interpreters. This can be viewed as both unethical and unprofessional, but it is up to the individual psychologist to consider the effect of using family members versus trained interpreters; there may be exceptions where a family member has a beneficial impact. It is essential that interpreters and staff working with them are both given adequate training, and that they develop a good working relationship.

Throughout this Training Manual, the authors refer to the importance of working with interpreters. Different skills will be needed when working with specific client groups – for example, working with children and families requires different skills from working with adults. Trainers can develop exercises to fit the particular needs of working with interpreters in their specialist modules.

This section highlights the general areas to be considered before, during and after the interview.

BEFORE THE INTERVIEW

- Check that there is compatibility and fluency in the spoken language or dialect.
- Discuss with the interpreter both the content of the interview and the way in which you will be working.
- Explain your psychological model and the need for translation of psychological terminology that may not exist in the client's language: for example, depression, anxiety.

- Arrange the seating in the room in such a way that there is good eye contact between the psychologist, interpreter and client(s).

DURING THE INTERVIEW

- Ensure that the client understands that all information will be confidential, particularly when the interpreter and client are from the same community.
- Use clear and straightforward language and avoid jargon.
- Observe the non-verbal behaviour of the client and maintain eye contact with both the client and the interpreter.
- Encourage the interpreter to intervene when necessary. Interpreters can be extremely useful as 'cultural consultants'. When properly facilitated, their knowledge of the history, politics and culture of the client can add to the interview.
- Allow enough time.

AFTER THE INTERVIEW

- Ensure that there is enough time for debriefing with the interpreter.
- Discuss any difficulties that may have arisen.
- Check whether the interview has stirred up any feelings for the interpreter.

ANNOTATED READING LIST

Suggested initial reading for all trainers and trainees. We strongly recommend this article to all trainers using this manual:

Brummer, N. and Simmonds, J. (1992) 'Race' and culture: The management of 'difference' in the learning group'. *Social Work Education*, 11, 1.
Although this article is written for use by social work trainers, it is highly relevant to the process of training Clinical Psychology and other trainees. It is one of the best articles of its kind in its consideration of the dynamics of the learning group process.

Essential reading: Books

Boyd, Franklin N. (1989) *Black Families in Therapy.* New York: Guildford Press
This American book takes a clear look at a wide range of issues including: spirituality and working with religious leaders, different family forms and kin networks, skin colour, addressing racism and addressing difference, and the position of White and Black therapists working with Black clients.

d'Ardenne, P. and Mahtani, A. (1999) *Transcultural Counselling in Action.* 2nd ed. London: Sage Publications
This is the second edition of a book written by two clinical psychologists who use a transcultural model for their own work with a multiracial client group in London's East End. Cultural issues are highlighted throughout at individual, community and global levels. It offers a guide to counsellors and professional helpers, to providing an effective, sensitive and appropriate service to clients from outside their own culture. The authors also examine the current literature on counselling across cultures and consider the impact of racism on counselling practice.

Donald, J. and Rattansi, A. (Eds) (1992) *'Race', Culture and Difference.* London: Sage Publications/OU
A difficult text but one which illuminates the area in new ways, taking a critical look at accepted 'theories of difference'. It has an excellent chapter which considers the psychological effects of centuries of institutionalized racism on White identity.

Fernando, S. (1991) *Mental Health, Race and Culture.* London: Macmillan Education, in conjunction with MIND
A major contribution to the area of 'race' and culture in mental health, widely regarded as a classic text. Highly recommended for trainers and trainees.

Henriques, J., Hollway, W., Urwin, C., Venn, C. and Walkerdine, V. (1984) *Changing the Subject: Psychology, Social Regulation and Subjectivity*.: London: Methuen

A useful text in general, whose most fundamental argument advances a new theorization of subjectivity central to a politics of social transformation. Henriques' chapter on 'Social Psychology and the Politics of Racism' traces the development of theories of racism.

This book is currently out of print but can be obtained through libraries.

Hopkins, A. and Bahl, V. (Eds) (1993) *Access to Health Care.* London: Royal College of Physicians

This publication places the health of Black and minority ethnic people firmly on the NHS agenda. It acknowledges the fact that minority groups with distinct disease patterns and different cultural backgrounds experience many forms of discrimination. This book contains commissioned articles that will help health professionals to respond to the full range of health needs in multiracial Britain.

Littlewood, R. and Lipsedge, M. (1997) *Aliens and Alienists: Ethnic Minorities and Psychiatry*. 3rd ed. London: Unwin Hyman

The authors, both psychiatrists, assess the psychological consequences of migration and the experience of racism (individual and institutionalized) for members of minority ethnic groups. They give a useful potted history of medicine and racism, drawing on anthropological as well as medical sources. They present a number of case histories and conclude that mental illness can be an intelligible response to disadvantage and racism. A thoughtful, scholarly and humane account, very well worth reading.

Rawaf, S. and Bahl, V. (Eds) (1998) *Assessing Health Needs of People from Minority Ethnic Groups*. London: Royal College of Physicians and Faculty of Public Health Medicine, in collaboration with the Department of Health

This book is a good source of reference and guidance for public health physicians, primary care teams and those with a special interest in improving the health of minority ethnic groups. The 25 chapters provide a sound theoretical and practical framework on how to carry out health needs assessment in multicultural Britain. They provide a knowledge base for the understanding of various aspects of health service delivery and approaches to dealing with minority ethnic health. This book also highlights the fact that minority ethnic health is not the business of the NHS alone but also of the communities it serves. Healthy alliances have developed with the community and voluntary organizations and the academic institutions. The book includes experiences of the main minority ethnic groups (Asians, Africans and Chinese) but also those of refugees and asylum seekers.

Shweder, R. and LeVine, R. (Eds) (1984*) Culture Theory: Essays on Mind, Self and Emotion*. Cambridge: Cambridge University Press

A collection of papers by social scientists, mostly cognitive anthropologists. The focus is on the role of symbols and meaning in the development of mind, self and emotion. An invaluable contribution to the consideration of theory-production and assumptions underlying White Western psychological theory. Mostly very accessible, and compelling reading. Particularly useful chapters: 1, 6, 12.

Sue, D. and Sue, D. (1990) *Counselling the Culturally Different.* New York: Wiley

This is an American text. It provides a conceptual framework for multicultural counselling with proven therapeutic methods for specific groups. It highlights key issues of ethnic and racial identity formation, including White identity development, and culturally specific concepts of the family and their relationship to counselling. There is an emphasis on the damaging effects of political and racial biases inherent in the mental health field and on the need to develop culture-specific communication/helping styles for culturally different clients. The text moves from the theoretical to the practical in three sections covering: Issues and concepts: viewing the complex interplay of values and social and political forces in the counselling relationship. Counselling specific populations: guidelines and detailed methods. Critical incidents: case vignettes portraying issues and dilemmas.

Essential Reading: Articles

American Psychological Association Office of Minority Ethnic Affairs (1993) Guidelines for providers of psychological services to ethnic, linguistic and culturally diverse populations. *American Psychologist, 48,* 1, 45–48

An interesting paper which summarizes the American Psychological Association's Board of Minority Ethnic Affairs' (BEMA) work on service delivery. It provides a useful outline of key points for psychologists working with ethnic, linguistic and culturally diverse populations. Well worth a perusal. As yet, there is no British equivalent of this paper.

British Journal of Guidance and Counselling (1993) Symposium on Transcultural Counselling, 2, 1 Jan

Lokare, V. (Ed.) (1992) *Counselling Psychology Quarterly* Special Issue on Transcultural Counselling, 5, 3

These two special issues contain many very useful and interesting papers.

Holland, S. (1990) Psychotherapy, oppression and social action: Gender, race and class in black women's depression. Chapter 14 in R. Perelberg and A. Miller (Eds) *Gender and Power in Families*. London: Routledge

This chapter is based on thinking developed in the innovative community psychology project the author ran in White City for many years. She examines in it a model of therapy which firmly acknowledges and works with the personal and political context of women's lives.

Montalvo B. and Guttierrez M. (1988) The emphasis on cultural identity: A developmental-ecological constraint in C.Falicov. (Ed.) *Family Transitions: Continuity and Change Over the Life Cycle* London: Guildford

This chapter offers a sophisticated analysis of issues to do with cultural identity including various uses and misuses of the concept.

National Association of Health Authorities (1988) *Actions not words: a strategy to improve health services for Black and minority ethnic groups.* NAHAT, Birmingham (0121–414 1536)

This is one of many articles which concedes the pervasiveness of racism in health services. The report mentions many areas of concern and makes many recommendations. Sadly, since its publication, very few of its recommendations have been implemented.

Patel, N. and Fatimilehin, I. (1999) Racism and mental health. In C. Newnes, G. Holmes and C. Dunn (Eds) *This is Madness: A Critical Look at Psychiatry and the Future of Mental Health Services*. Ross-on-Wye: PCCS

'Race' and Culture in Clinical Psychology Training (1993) A report of a training day at the University of East London
Copies available from Nimisha Patel or Mary Boyle, Department of Clinical Psychology, UEL, The Green, Romford Road, Stratford, E15 4LZ.

Further reading: Academic Books

Essed, P. (1991) *Understanding Everyday Racism: An Interdisciplinary Theory*. London: Sage Publications
This book compares contemporary racism in the US and the Netherlands through in-depth interviews with 55 Black women. Essed reinterprets many of the definitions and everyday practices that the majority of society has come to take for granted. She address-es crucial dimensions of racism: how it is experienced; how Black women recognize its covert manifestations; how they acquire this knowledge and how they challenge racism in everyday life.

Hiro, D. (1992) *Black British, White British: A History of Race Relations in Britain*. London: Paladin
Dilip Hiro charts the fortunes of Britain's African, Asian and Caribbean communities over the last four decades. He describes their cultures, their reasons for migration and the overt and covert racism they have encountered. He considers questions such as: Is assim-ilation or social pluralism the way forward? What does it mean to be 'British'? Why do people believe that Blackness precludes Britishness? A very useful factual text, which also stimulates thought.

Kakar, S. (1981) *The Inner World: A Psychoanalytic Study of Childhood and Society in India*. Oxford: Oxford University Press
The book provides a very thought provoking account of what the author calls the 'social psychology' of Hindu society, defining the work as 'a study of the psychic representation in individuals of their society's culture and social institutions'. The account diverges from the a-cultural and a-historical accounts of the dominant academic tradition, providing a model of psychological thinking which is not Eurocentric. Kakar's work was both influ-enced by and influenced that of Erik Erikson.

Kareem, J. and Littlewood, R. (Eds) (1992) *Intercultural Therapy*. Oxford: Blackwell
The lack of psychotherapy provision for Black and other minority ethnic groups resulted in the setting up of Nafsiyat, the Intercultural Therapy Centre in London. Poverty, depri-vation and social powerlessness have affected the mental health of minority ethnic groups. There is no single model for intercultural therapy and a range of views is pre-sented.

Smaje, C. (1995) *Health 'Race' and Ethnicity: Making Sense of the Evidence.* London: Kings Fund Institute

Provides one of the most comprehensive accounts to date concerning the health of people from minority ethnic populations in Britain, their use and experience of health service and the history of attempts to address their needs in the formulation of health policy.

Personal Accounts

Adams, C. (1987) *Across Seven Seas and Thirteen Rivers: Life Stories of Pioneer Sylheti Settlers in Britain.* London: THAP Books

Oral history collection of Bangladeshi pioneers who migrated to Britain in the 1920s, 1930s and 1940s with families now living in the East End of London.

Fenton, S. and Sadiq A. (1993) *The Sorrows of My Heart: Sixteen Asian Women Speak about Depression.* London: Commission for Racial Equality

Gifford, Z. (1990) *The Golden Thread: Asian Experiences of Post-Raj Britain.* London: Grafton Books

Based on conversations with over a hundred Asian women and men, the book gives an opportunity to perceive Britain and the British through Asian eyes. The contributors discuss their experiences of migration and integration, describe what they value in their private and public lives and talk of politics, racism, marriage, relationships, spirituality and religion. Unfortunately currently out of print, but worth getting hold of. Easy to read, providing useful insights for non-Asian trainers and trainees.

Shan, S. (1985) *In My Own Name.* London: The Women's Press

The story of a Sikh woman living in Britain and battling both against the conventional restrictions of her family and the hostility of a strange country. Not 'representative', but a very personal account.

Wilson, M. (1993) *Crossing the Boundary: Black Women Survive Incest.* London: Virago Press

A particularly good account of the intertwining of racism and women's experience.

Fiction

All fictional works have been chosen for their intrinsic merit, quite apart from what may be learned from them.

Morrison, T. (1998) *Sula.* London, Vintage

Morrison, T. (1999) *The Bluest Eye.* London, Vintage

Morrison, T. (1997) *Tar Baby.* London, Vintage

Toni Morrison won the Nobel Prize for Literature in 1993 – deservedly so, as her books are stunning works of art. They have been described as 'black America singing its past'. They are written from the point of view of girls and women of different ages, who, though experiencing the double oppression of racism and sexism, 'refuse to be victims'. Her characters are real, vital and full of hope.

Washington, M. H. (ed.) (1981) *Any Woman's Blues. Stories by Contemporary Black Women Writers*. London: Virago Press

A collection of short stories by nine contemporary Black women writers which constructs a picture of Black American women's lives as seen by themselves. The editor provides an erudite introduction that maps the history of writing by Black women, relating this to political changes. She describes this history as a process of 'reclaiming the past and a central place in that past'. Many themes are explored, including the hostility between Black women and White women.

Chen, Y. (1980) *The Dragon's Village*. London: The Women's Press

This is an autobiographical account (forerunner of *Wild Swans*) of the life of a young woman revolutionary who became involved in the land reform movement in rural China in the early years of the revolution.

Marshall, P. (1959) *Brown Girl, Brownstones*. London: Virago Press

The book is written from the point of view of the daughter of Barbadian settlers, living in New York during the Depression and World War II. It is an account of the efforts of Black settlers to overcome poverty and racism, and a story of what it is to grow up Black and female in the US.

Sidhwa, B. (1978) *The Crow Eaters*. London: Fontana

The book explores the life of a Parsi community in Lahore over several generations. Bhapsi Sidhwa herself describes it as a satire. It is a very funny book, full of larger than life characters, giving a rich portrait of daily life and family relationships.

Thurman, W. (1970) *The Blacker the Berry*. New York: Collier Brooks Macmillan Publishing Co

First published in 1929. The book deals with the issue of prejudice within (as well as outside) the Black community. It focuses on Emma Lou's process of self-discovery.

Larsen, N. (1989) *Quicksand* and *Passing*. (First published 1928/29.) Republished by Serpent's Tail: London

Nella Larsen was born in Chicago in 1893 of a Danish mother and a Black American father. She was a celebrity in the 1920s and 1930s, but died in obscurity in 1963. These two books (published together in one volume) represent a very early, and ground-breaking, exploration of sexuality and racism from the point of view of a woman of multi-ethnic background.

Upex-Higgins, I. (1991) *Aloes and Brown Sugar*. London: Cube Publishing

Upex-Higgins, I. (1993) *Charcoal Woman*. London: Cube Publishing

A collection of powerful poems written by a Black, female social worker addressing issues of inequality using her experiences as a mother, partner, sister and a professional.

Ahmad R. and Gupta R. (Eds) (1994) *Flaming Spirit*. London: Virago Press

A stimulating collection of short stories written by Asian women writers in Britain. Topics addressed include adolescence, identity, religion, migration and sexuality.

USEFUL RESOURCES

GAMES, EXERCISES, ROLE PLAYS AND HANDOUTS

The following section offers suggestions of various exercises, games and role plays which could be used in the Introductory Module or to complement other modules.

Small and large group exercises. These address:
- the individual and his/her origin and its meaning
- individual experiences/events that have been important in the acknowledgement of different cultures and ethnicities
- assumptions that lie behind stereotypes
- the significance of power in the understanding of difference.

Games. These address:
- assumptions that can be made on the basis of names, physical appearances and identities
- assumptions that can be made about behaviour
- issues and feelings to do with inclusion and exclusion.

Role plays. These address:
- assumptions, issues and dilemmas that are pertinent to the therapist and client when considering 'race' and difference.

Exercise 1: Introductory warm-up

Description
Warm-up for first session.
Go-round of introductions: each person says their first name, why they were named this and what the name means to them.

Duration
2 minutes per person
10 minutes discussion

Aims
- To help people remember names.
- To establish how people want to be addressed.

- To raise awareness of cultural traditions in naming practices.

Notes for trainers
- Useful as a gentle start to training sessions.
- In discussion, draw out: implicit naming practices (e.g. patriarchal vs matriarchical family names) and explicit commonalities and differences; individual vs familial usage of first name.

Exercise 2: Terminology

Description
Three large pieces of paper are put up on the walls, headed 'ACCEPT-ABLE', 'UNACCEPTABLE' and 'NOT SURE'.

Group members are asked to write on the three sheets, writing words relating to racism and cultural diversity under the heading they think most appropriate.

They are told not to discuss their choices.

The whole group then discusses each list.

Duration
15 minutes for list writing
30–45 minutes for discussion

Aims
- Begin to develop a shared understanding of terms.
- Reduce threat by having suggestions made anonymously.
- Promote awareness of the functions and the fluidity of naming.

Notes for trainers
- Trainers can refer to the section in the manual on terminology for ideas on the usage of various common terms.
- In discussion, introduce an examination of why certain terms are acceptable or not, and who decides what is acceptable.
- Try to avoid dogmatism; the exercise should allow trainees to explore and extend their understanding of relevant terminology.

Exercise 3: Important events that have informed ideas about different cultures

Instructions
Divide group into small groups of three or four. Take five minutes each to talk about an experience or event that has informed participants about a culture other than their own.

Return to large group. Small groups to report on how they found the exercise and then individual members can choose to describe the experiences and events they discussed.

Duration
15 to 20 minutes per small group
30 minutes group discussion

Aims
• To raise awareness of individuals' formation and upholding of ideas, biases and beliefs about other cultures from their own experiences.

Notes for trainers
• Participants should be familiar with each other as individuals may disclose personal details.
• Trainers to attend to affective component if participants talk about the experience of or observation of racism.
• Trainers to attend to the useful and positive events that increased participants' knowledge of other cultures.

Exercise 4: Articulation of own culture

Instructions
Divide into pairs. Take five minutes each to describe the main features of your culture to your partner. Your partner will feed back to the group on your behalf – negotiate what is acceptable feedback.

Give 'warning' at four minutes and signal 'changeover' time.

Duration
10 minutes for paired discussion
2 minutes per person for feedback
15 minutes for discussion

Aims
• To raise awareness of own cultural context, specifically that all trainees are shaped by their own culture.

Notes for trainers
- Can be threatening if used too early in the life of a group. Participants should be feeling relatively safe if they are to use this exercise well.
- White trainees are sometimes unsure what 'culture' means, in relation to themselves. You can offer definitions supplied elsewhere in the manual: for example, shared history, practices, beliefs and values, if such questions arise. Further prompting can be given: for example, 'What are your attitudes to family life in relation to roles, duties or obligations ?' 'What part does religion play in your life?' 'What is your view of inequities in society?' 'What counts as "success" for you?' However, trainees' own attempts to define and articulate their culture can be illuminating.

Exercise 5: Labelling

Instructions
Each person writes down (in capital letters on an A4 piece of paper) an adjective describing an aspect of themselves which they really dislike, or which they would hate if anyone else saw it in them. The papers are to be folded once then placed in the middle of the room. The trainees are then given one of the folded papers and a pin and told to pin it on their fronts so that it can be read by others. If by chance they receive their own paper they should put it back (folded) and be given another one. Everyone then walks around the room in silence until they have seen every other person's label. Part way through the walk the trainer gives the following instruction: 'You may decide that you don't like your label and that you want to get rid of it, but in fact you have to keep it on. It's very important you keep it on.'

The trainer finally asks everyone to return to their seats. Once this is done they should discuss the exercise in pairs or small groups (self-selected) and/or, if there is consensus, the large group. The timing and method of removing the label can also be observed and discussed.

Duration
20 minutes minimum depending on the size of the group, but the walk or the discussion can be extended.

Aims
- The exercise is designed to help trainees focus on the experience of being judged by a negative label not of their own making and which they cannot remove. The metaphor is most closely related to racism on the grounds of a characteristic which cannot be 'hidden' (like skin colour). It can also be used to explore the process of projection.

Notes for trainers
- This exercise can be used fairly early in the life of the group but requires adequate containment and debriefing.
- The emotional intensity can be maintained in this exercise by discouraging talking during the walk, and by inhibiting too much laughter. The discussion should aim to cover how people felt and include how closely people identified with their label and whether and why they wanted to get rid of it. Comparisons can be drawn between feeling able/unable to 'remove' pejorative labelling.

Exercise 6: 'Stereotyping'

Instructions
Provide each trainee with a copy of the 'Statements Questionnaire' (included at end of exercise). Tell them that this is a forced choice exercise. Each trainee completes the questionnaire individually, followed by a group 'throw-in' and discussion.

Duration
10 minutes for completion of questionnaire
30 minutes for group discussion

Aim
- To raise awareness of, and question, the origins of stereotypical thinking/racist thinking.

Notes for trainers
- This exercise requires sensitive handling and should not to be used too early in the life of the group. Remind participants about not being judgemental towards one another as this is not a test of 'political correctness' but an opportunity to look at common psychological processes and the creation of stereotypes. Because the exercise involves statements which illustrate racist assumptions, some of which are more subtle than others, it is important that the trainers feel very confident that they are aware of the implications of the statements and are able to handle constructively the range of likely responses, *including those that are racist*. It is also important to be aware of the impact of this exercise on trainees from Black and minority ethnic groups.

Questionnaire to be used with Exercise 6: 'Stereotyping'

Under each statement please circle one of the responses

1. Black people are just as racist towards White people as White people are towards Black people.

    Strongly agree / agree / disagree / strongly disagree

2. People coming to live in this country should adopt the customs that exist here.

    Strongly agree / agree / disagree / strongly disagree

3. Children should only be fostered by families who replicate their ethnicity.

    Strongly agree / agree / disagree / strongly disagree

4. Children are not racist.

    Strongly agree / agree / disagree / strongly disagree

5. The effects of racism impair a child's development.

    Strongly agree / agree / disagree / strongly disagree

6. It is vitally important for ethnic minorities to hold on to their cultural differences and traditional family norms.

    Strongly agree / agree / disagree / strongly disagree

7. Women are oppressed in Asian families.

    Strongly agree / agree / disagree / strongly disagree

8. Asian families do not allow their children enough freedom.

    Strongly agree / agree / disagree / strongly disagree

9. It is inevitable and proper that the values of the host nation will be adopted by the children of immigrants.

    Strongly agree / agree / disagree / strongly disagree

Exercise 7: Assumptions made about identities

Instructions

Participants to form a line with one end of the continuum stating 'most English' and the other end 'not English'. Once individuals have lined themselves up, each one has to explain their choice of position. This can be done by saying 'I feel more English than you because ...'

Duration
Variable time depending on size of group: allow 30–40 minutes.

Aims
• To raise awareness of assumptions participants have of one another.
• The game enables the individual to focus on identifying themselves.

Notes for trainers
• Small group discussions can be useful for individual participants to share how this game felt, to share any surprises to themselves or about one another.

Exercise 8: Inclusion and exclusion

Exclusion

Instructions

Whole group or small groups (minimum six in group).

All group members, **except two**, hold hands tightly to form a circle. The excluded two are outside the circle and attempt to 'break in'. The aim of the 'circle' is to keep the two out. Reassemble, and feedback by whole group.

Duration
5 minutes to attempt to enter the circle
15 minutes for feedback and discussion

Aims
• To raise awareness about how it feels to be in a minority and excluded.
• Opportunity to talk about being part of a dominant group which excludes others.

Inclusion

Instructions
Same groups are re-formed, with the same pair outside the main group. The main group has to 'welcome in' the two people outside.

Duration
5 minutes for welcoming
15 minutes for feedback and discussion

Aims
- To raise awareness of how it feels to be welcomed by those who have excluded you in the past.
- To provide insight into 'outsiders'' caution, when welcomed by those who have excluded them.

Notes for trainers
- A group discussion can be useful, linking the exercise to the experience of members of minority ethnic groups. White trainees may gain awareness not only of the experience of exclusion but also of some mistrust and reluctance to accept an apparent 'welcome' at face value, from those who have previously excluded them. This is relevant to therapeutic contacts between White professionals and Black clients, when the professional will need to understand, and not be hurt by, an apparent lack of trust on the part of the client. The idea that 'trust must be earned' applies to *all* therapeutic encounters but may be particularly relevant to encounters between White professionals and Black clients.

Exercise 9: Assumptions and stereotypes in clinical practice

Instructions
General group brainstorm of common stereotypes and assumptions held regarding people from minority ethnic backgrounds.

Role play
Ask for two volunteers who will not have to speak during the role play. Assign ethnicities and roles. For example:
Client   Black, African-Caribbean, female
Therapist   White, English, male

Ask the rest of the group to brainstorm possible assumptions held by the client regarding the therapist, then by the therapist regarding the client, writing them on a board for the group to see.

In role, ask how each person (client and therapist) felt about the exercise and about comments by the rest of their group. Ask them to de-role.

Discussion with entire group.

Other variations can be used, time permitting. It is advisable that at least two variations are used so the group is able to explore issues around therapists and clients of different ethnic backgrounds working together. For example:

Client	White, Scottish, male
Therapist	Black, Indian, female
	or
Client	Black, Pakistani, male
Therapist	White, English, female

Group discussion
Discuss with the group the implications in clinical practice of possible strategies to deal with assumptions. For example:

* Making the assumptions of the therapist explicit by listing them as possible hypotheses to be tested in clinical sessions.
* Making assumptions and hypotheses explicit to the client/family with the aim of dispelling assumptions and stereotypes by collaborating actively with the client/family in enhancing understanding and facilitating change. For example, saying to a client/family: 'I'm assuming that ..., but perhaps you could tell me if I'm assuming incorrectly, or perhaps you could explain this further to me.'

Duration
10 minutes for the general brainstorm
10 minutes for each role play, with group ideas
20–25 minutes for group discussion

Aims
* To make explicit that all of us (clients and therapists) hold stereotypes and assumptions about people who are different from us.
* To make such assumptions and stereotypes accessible in clinical practice, enabling us to directly combat racist assumptions and to explore other assumptions which can facilitate reflection on the experience of difference.
* To initiate some thinking and discussion of the issues of White and Black therapists and clients working together.

Notes for trainers
- Useful to have two trainers.
- Trainers need to be very sensitive to the difficulties trainees may have making explicit some of their assumptions. It is helpful in the beginning to state that the exercise is based on the premise that all people hold assumptions.
- Trainers need initially to spend some time with each other discussing the possible implications of this exercise for a specific group, particularly considering the composition of the group.
- Trainers need to ensure that Black trainees are not marginalized or made invisible in this exercise, since Black trainees may feel very uncomfortable hearing potentially racist assumptions. They may also feel that their experience as a Black person working with Black or White clients raises many issues for them which are not acknowledged or addressed in their training by their trainers and their peers.

Exercise 10: Role play of interracial work

Instructions
Divide group into pairs and individuals to role play the various relationships; any configurations may be used.

1. Black female psychologist sees a Black female client.
2. Black female psychologist sees a White female client.
3. White male psychologist sees a Black male client.
4. White male psychologist sees a Black female client.
5. White female psychologist sees a Black male client.

Each pair to be given the following vignette:

The client has been referred by the GP to the psychologist because of low mood, low self-esteem and difficulties in forming relationships.

- The psychologist in the role play is to assess the difficulties by asking questions; the client is to inform the psychologist of his/her problem.
- Participants can say whatever feels comfortable.
- Psychologist to have some ideas about the client's difficulties. The client to attend to types of questions asked.
- Each pair to feed back to large group.
- Large group discussion. Trainer to draw out:
  - any similar issues that were apparent in all the configurations
  - which issues were different and why were they specific and assumed to be related to that configuration.

Each participant to de-role.

Duration
20 minutes for each role play
Feedback and discussion variable, maximum 60 minutes

Aims
• To raise awareness of the kinds of issues, assumptions and dilemmas that may become pertinent to the client and the therapist: for example, issues of gender, power, the psychologist as the 'expert'; 'over-identification' with the client, the ability to raise the issue of 'difference' within the relationship; the psychologist's biases and beliefs about the client's difficulties, etc.
• To enable trainees to develop an awareness, sensitivity and skill when working with difference, being able to think about the therapeutic encounter, and being able to examine oneself.

Notes for trainers
This exercise is a variation on the Assumptions and Stereotypes Exercises (numbers 6, 7, 8 and 9) and should be thought about in the light of these.

• Useful to have two trainers.
• Trainers to have thought about the issues and dilemmas that are likely to arise from the configuration before conducting the role play with trainees.
• This role play can be used at various stages of training to gather insight into trainees awareness and sensitivity about issues of difference.
• A useful role play to highlight problems that arise in the therapeutic relationship particularly when 'difference' exists between therapist and client.
• Trainers to acknowledge and inform trainees that there is no right or 'expert' way of working with difference, and that the aim of the role play is to increase sensitivity and awareness.
• May be useful to do role plays in threes by including an observer of the therapeutic relationship.
• It may be useful for trainers to have discussions with one another after the role play to attend to any specific issues or needs that may have arisen.

Handout for trainees[1]

Guidelines for evaluating your course in relation to issues of racism and culture

1. Examine teaching modules for their attention to issues of power and culture in the content of the module, both in relation to theory production and to examples of work chosen to illustrate clinical issues: for example, do clinical examples reflect a multicultural population?
2. Examine research findings for their implications about the nature of 'racial'/cultural differences and their privileging of a White, ethnocentric position.
3. Examine theories and models of psychological distress/psychological health for their implicit value systems and ethnic/cultural orientation.
4. Examine assessment instruments for their relevance to the client in terms of the nature of the measures and the samples on which they have been standardized.
5. Examine models of therapeutic intervention for their implicit value systems (e.g. self-disclosure, goal orientation, use of status and expertise), and for their negotiation of issues of power within the therapeutic relationship. How are religious or spiritual values accounted for or explored?
6. Examine models of intervention for their account of variables which constitute the relationship between therapist and client: e.g. 'race', gender, age, class, economic status, disability.
7. Examine the placement experiences for their range of clients from different ethnic/cultural backgrounds and for the supervision you receive in acknowledging and working with differences, inequalities and power imbalances.
8. Examine the nature of the venue in which you see clients to determine whether this is an accessible and comfortable place for the client.

1. Photocopying permission granted

Handout for trainees[2]

Observing the organization where you are on placement

This assignment is to be carried out in the organization in which you are currently based.

Make systematic observations on the following:

1.   What are the ethnic origins of clients who use the service? Is the pattern representative of the pattern of population in the catchment area of the service?
2.   What are the staffing ratios of ethnic majority/minorities?
3.   What is the status of positions filled by staff from minority and majority ethnic backgrounds?
4.   What in the physical setting shows the waiting area or workplace as a place where people from Black/minority ethnic backgrounds might feel comfortable? For example, pictures, books, papers, toys, etc.
5.   What agencies are there in the locality which are largely run or used by minority group clients either in the public or voluntary sector? For example, advice centres, centres for elderly, youth and religious groups. Do these agencies refer clients?
6.   Is there a policy in the organization on equal opportunities or on anti-racism? How are these disseminated, discussed or implemented?
7.   What ongoing staff discussion is there on racism and clinical practice?
8.   Are interpreters available? How are they trained in assisting the delivery of psychological or other services? How can they be accessed?

2. Photocopying permission granted

Handouts: notes for trainers

The following notes are for trainers and they are related to the previous suggested handouts for trainees.

Guidelines for evaluating the course

Trainers can use trainees' responses to the handouts as an audit tool when evaluating teaching modules.

This should be discussed with the trainees in the Introductory Module, but it would be very useful to make arrangements to follow it up with them at different stages of the Course. Trainees' responses could be included in Course Reviews and as such it would be useful to treat this not just as a trainee handout but as a guideline for all Course trainers and supervisors.

Observing the organization where you are on placement

The results of this assignment should be presented and discussed within the Course and in supervision. It should be discussed within the Introductory Module but should also be followed up in subsequent modules. Because of the relatively powerless position of trainees within their placement organization, they may or may not wish to discuss it in their placement context. The more their supervisors are involved in the process of the Course sensitizing itself to issues of racism and culture, the readier they will be to support the trainees in this exercise.

RECOMMENDED TRAINING VIDEOTAPES

The following videos are recommended for use with different trainee groups.

Being White (1987)
30 minutes. Videotape and teaching notes.

Aimed at a White audience, *Being White*, with accompanying teaching booklet, is an excellent resource for stimulating discussion of both individual and institutional racism.

Out of the Shadows (1988)
50 minutes.

This film traces the history of the Black contribution to British society from 1500 to 1950. It is packed with information probably unfamiliar to a British audience, a point which is significant in itself. It is accompanied with useful notes. A good introduction.

A Corner of a Foreign Field (1985)
52 minutes.

This film examines the contrasting attitudes towards marriage, culture, religion and a sense of 'homeland' that exist between two generations of families from Pakistan. Provides valuable insights into Pakistani culture and also demonstrates the dynamism of culture through the differences between the generations.

I See From Here (1988)
14 minutes.

A group of young Asian women from different cultures, and with different views, talk about what it is like to be a young Asian person living in Britain, straddling two cultures. It is a concise film, leaving many areas open to discussion: How can White people avoid tokenism? Whose job is it to educate White people about Asian cultures? What relevance do movements like feminism have for Black women?

Counselling Black Clients: Pre-counselling and Initial Interviews (three linked videos)

1.	Personal and Relationship Issues	28 minutes
2.	Issues of Identity	24 minutes
3.	Dealing with Prejudice and Discrimination	12 minutes

Each video contains initial interview trigger scenes lasting approximately 4–8 minutes where a range of South Asian and African-Caribbean client difficulties are explored by a black psychologist. A booklet of teaching notes is provided. Useful for examining cultural and racial issues as they arise in the therapeutic setting.

These videos can be obtained from:
Television Service
The University of Birmingham
Edgbaston
Birmingham B15 2TT
Tel: 0121 414 6492

Organizations with useful resources

King's Fund Institute
The King's Fund Institute aims to improve the quality of health policy-making in the United Kingdom through independent analysis, monitoring and evaluation of health and health services. It sponsors research in this area and also runs conferences to disseminate findings, often through SHARE.

SHARE
This is the national health and 'race' project funded by the Department of Health, at the King's Fund Centre. The aim of the project is to encourage changes in service provision, to disseminate information to support change, to increase awareness of services for Black users and to enable good practice to be shared.
They publish regular reference lists and lists of resources of individuals and organizations who are committed to development in this area. They have also produced *Asian Mental Health*, a bibliography (Department of Health, 1995).

King's Fund Centre
126 Albert Street
London NW1 7NF
Tel: 020 7307 2400
Fax: 020 7307 2801

MIND (National Association for Mental Health)
The Black and Minority ethnic Team at MIND has produced very useful bibliographies of articles, books and directories of organizations in the Voluntary Sector. They can be contacted at:

MIND Mail Order Department
Granta House
15–19 Broadway
London E15 4BQ
Tel: 020 8522 1728

AIMS OF THE SPECIALITY MODULES

- To introduce the main issues of 'race', racism and culture in the various speciality modules which include clinical specialist modules and others which concern psychological practice.
- To provide an overview of the relevant literature, where it exists, for each speciality area.
- To provide an outline of the usefulness or limitations of some of the concepts, theories and practice relevant to each speciality area.
- To introduce relevant issues in relation to service delivery in some of the speciality areas.
- To suggest some learning outcomes for trainees, related to each speciality area.
- To provide exercises which trainers can use or adapt as part of their teaching in each speciality area.
- To provide key annotated references for each clinical area which trainers and trainees may find useful.
- To enable trainers to build on teaching suggestions in the Introductory Module, encouraging continuity in the development of ideas and skills related to working with a diverse, multi-ethnic population.
- To enable trainers and trainees to develop their own conceptual frameworks for critically examining issues of power, discrimination and difference in psychological theory and practice.
- To enable trainers and trainees to develop appropriate competencies in working with issues of culture and 'race' and in combating discrimination in clinical practice and in related organizational structures.

Chapter 9

CHILD, ADOLESCENT AND FAMILY

Iyabo Fatimilehin, Hitesh Raval and Nick Banks

Introduction

When Bernard Coard, in a stirring and now famous publication, drew attention to 'How the West Indian child is made educationally subnormal in the British School System', he focused much of his exposition on the practices of psychological assessment at the time (Coard, 1971). Since then, the debate in the field about psychology's contribution to the problematizing of Black and minority ethnic children has continued.

Although children and young people have a natural capacity to question the received wisdom of adult beliefs and practices, they are also highly vulnerable recipients of ideas from the adult world which attempts to shape and form them. Issues of power are inevitably at stake when working with all children, and specifically so when working with children from minority ethnic groups. The historical and social construction of childhood and so-called adolescence is informed very centrally by cultural beliefs and practices. A consideration of the ways in which psychology contributes to our view of childhood needs to take into account the means by which culture, racism and the legacies of colonization shape the opinions which clinical psychologists form about children. The field of clinical psychology, in the setting of a multicultural society, needs to be enriched by the multiple perspectives from which childhood can be understood and these guidelines are intended to provide a framework for doing so.

THEORY

Important points to consider:

1. The effects of growing up in a minority versus majority cultural grouping and its relationship to the social context (i.e. issues of power, dominance of particular cultural values, oppression, racism, poverty and isolation) and sense of self (Ghuman, 1999). The generational aspects associated with acculturation, loss of history and loss of a wider social context for cultural values (e.g. Coard, 1971; Smith, 1991; Mirza, 1992; Tizard and Phoenix, 1993; Wilson, 1993; Kingsbury, 1994).

2. Normative views of child development to include studies from a range of cultures of, for example, the construction of childhood and adolescence, autonomy in adolescence, etc. (e.g. Kakar, 1981; Ho, 1981; Spencer *et al.*, 1985; Phinney and Rotheram, 1987; Jahoda and Lewis, 1988; Adler, 1989; Wilson, 1989; Lamb *et al.*, 1992; Harwood *et al.*, 1995; Nobles and Goddard, 1996; Holliday and Curbeam, 1996; LeVine *et al.*, 1996; Scheper-Hughes 1987). Child rearing practices in different cultures, and different parental expectations for social, physical and emotional development at different ages (e.g. O'Reilly *et al.*, 1986; Bernstein, 1991; Morelli *et al.*, 1991; Woollett and White, 1992; Bronfenbrenner, 1993; Reder and Lucey, 1995; Levine, 1995; Hillier and Rahman, 1996).

3. Formation of self-identity and racial/ethnic identity in children across different cultural groups and its influence on the child's emotional and psychological development (e.g. McRoy *et al.*, 1984; Wilson, 1987; Banks, 1992; Maximé, 1986; Tizard and Phoenix, 1993; Parker, 1995; Bernal and Knight, 1993; Kerwin and Ponterotto, 1995).

4. Family life-cycles and patterns of family organization across different cultural groupings. The evolving patterns of family functioning, organization, rites of passage and demands/conflicts, with their association to psychological functioning for families (McGoldrick *et al*, 1982; Wilson, 1992; Falicov, 1995; Delaney, 1995; Brookins, 1996; McAdoo, 1996).

5. Cultural explanations of childhood psychological problems and potential ethnocentric bias in psychological descriptions (e.g. Boyd-Franklin, 1989; Vargas and Koss-Chionio, 1992; Hillier *et al.*, 1994; Jackson, 1996). The consequences for children from different groups of family breakdown due to death or separation. The compounding effects of racism on children's experience of abuse (Mars, 1989; Wilson, 1993a; Maitra, 1995).

6. Effects of migration patterns and adjustment to new lifestyles for children and families (Maitra and Miller, 1996; Burnham and Harris, 1996; Lau, 2000).

7. Working with children and families of refugees (e.g. Athey and Ahearn, 1991; Dagnino, 1992; Jareg, 1992; Van der Veer, 1992; Richman, 1993; Gibbs, 1994; Woodcock, 1995; Richman 1998)).

8. Educational issues as they impact on young Black people. The importance of cultural appropriateness in the content and process of teaching, the issues of exclusions and inclusions and referral to psychiatric or psychological services. The aspirations of Black children encouraged by the educational system, implicitly and explicitly (e.g. Hare, 1985; Rattansi, 1992; Gillborn and Gipps, 1996; Bourne *et al.*, 1994; OFSTED Report, 1996).

9. Children in the care of the local authority. The impact of the Children's Act on placement issues for Black and minority ethnic children. The impact of family separation on children. The consequences of early separation and failed substitute family placements at different ages. The significance and importance of contact with birth family for emotional, psychological and identity needs. Black children's particular placement needs with regard to cultural identity and community connectedness. Issues related to transracial placements. The process and rationale for adoption and fostering.

Issues related to children of mixed parentage, their specific identity needs (e.g. Ahmed *et al.*, 1986; Williams, 1987; Banks, 1992; Jackson and West-moreland, 1992; Barn, 1993; Gaber and Aldridge, 1994; Banks, 1996).

10. Working with children and families with chronic physical health problems. The prevalence of specific health problems in Black and minority ethnic com-munities, e.g. sickle-cell and thalassaemia disease, diabetes, coronary heart dis-ease. Awareness of cultural issues in families coping with chronic illness; roles and responsibilities of various family members; community and religious beliefs about health and illness (Armstrong *et al.*, 1993; Bailey-Holgate, 1996; Belgrave and Lewis, 1994; Keese, 1995; Midence *et al.*, 1993; Watson, 1984).

11. For the children of parents with mental health problems, considering the effect on them of the services provided for their parents. (See the Adult Mental Health module, keeping in mind the fact that the recipients of these services also have children.)

PRACTICE

Of all the areas of clinical psychology training, working with children can often most directly revive personal issues and vulnerabilities for trainees. For this reason, the following issues related to good practice in working with Black and minority ethnic children and their families will frequently require work to be done at the personal level to help trainees to identify anxieties and blocks to learning. Under the next three headings of interviewing, assessment and inter-vention, the following are offered as goals for the trainees' learning in these areas.

Interviewing
1. Being able to understand and address difference during a therapeutic ses-sion (Ho, 1987; Faulkner and Kich, 1983; Boyd-Franklin, 1989; Ho, 1992; Ridley, 1995).

2. Dealing with difference in language and meaning during therapy (e.g. working with a family when not all the family members speak English, working with an interpreter, issues when the child becomes an interpreter and ethical reasons for not using children as interpreters). Useful literature can also be found in the section on interpreters in the Introductory Module.

3. Finding out from families about their belief systems surrounding the pre-sent problem (e.g. Ho, 1992; Dwivedi and Varma, 1996; Krause and Miller, 1995).

4. Developing an understanding of institutional inequalities (myths sur-rounding the reasons for a Black child or family being referred, expectations of the referrer, therapist and family, etc.). Useful literature includes: Boyd-Franklin, 1989; Fatimilehin and Coleman, 1998; Bourne *et al.*, 1994.

5. Interviewing using different approaches and styles (for example, assess-ment of directive versus non-directive approaches to work with the family, conjoint or sub-system work, cultural meanings involved in talking to a child in the presence of the parents) (Krause, 1998).

6. Becoming aware of the impact on therapy and the therapeutic relationship of the different cultural experiences that the trainee and the child and family bring to therapy (Lau, 1984; Dwivedi and Varma, 1996) and the methods of group work with children that are culturally relevant (Patel, 1997).
7. Becoming aware of the social and political implications of asking particular types of questions (for example, sexual functioning, questioning male/female roles, autonomy in adolescence, questions relating to immigration status, inappropriate use of interpreter to ask personal/sensitive questions).

Assessment

1. Ensuring that assessments are carried out with a wide perspective to take account of both client's and trainee's experience and understanding of racism (Thomas, 1992).
2. Becoming more skilled and sensitive in using psychometric assessment and being aware of the limitations of the given instruments when working with client groups on whom the instruments were not standardized. Developing qualitative assessments where necessary (e.g. Dasen, 1984; Lonner and Ibrahim, 1996; Whyche and Novick, 1992; Jackson, 1996; Cline and Frederickson, 1996). See also the Neuropsychology Module.
3. Using different methods of interviewing children and families, for example, with an interpreter. Developing an awareness of the different use of language in therapy (e.g. De Zulueta, 1990). Developing a knowledge of when it is appropriate and inappropriate to use interpreters in interviewing, therapy and assessment.
4. Gaining an understanding from families about their cultural norms and beliefs. Becoming aware of how this process impacts on the therapeutic relationship and therapeutic work.
5. Using the family and other available resources to find out about the family's culture (for example, from literature, community resources, consultants).
6. When there is a lack of shared understanding between the trainee clinical psychologist and the family about the nature of the presenting problem, the trainee needs to develop a way of constructing some common ground without alienating the family.

Intervention

1. Appreciating the necessity of examining existing interventions for their appropriateness for every client within a racial, cultural and religious context.
2. Learning the application of existing intervention approaches in culturally respectful ways (Boyd-Franklin, 1989; Bott and Hodes, 1989; Burnham and Harris, 1996).
3. Exploring with families in a respectful way the alternative types of intervention they may have already tried or know to be available (for example, spiritual, healing, ayurvedic).
4. Integration of psychological and social interventions (for example, use of community resources, voluntary sector family services).

5. Understanding varying levels at which the clinical psychologist can intervene in the contexts which affect children, young people and families (e.g.
organizational, social, political).
6. Thinking carefully about the implications for the child and family of different types of verbal and written reports and letters and where they are sent.
Becoming aware of what this could mean for clients from different cultural
groups (for example, being aware of the way routine communication with
a school or social services department may be interpreted by the family as
unhelpful if the family have taken pains to keep their business private from
institutions).
7. Assessing the usefulness of expert vs collaborative approaches for each
family in the light of cultural expectations and preferences.

SERVICE DELIVERY

The development of culturally competent and appropriate psychological services for children, young people and their families from Black and minority
ethnic groups requires considerable attention. This is particularly in the light of
the still relatively small numbers of Black clinical psychologists in the profession
(Fatimilehin and Coleman, 1998; 1999). The following are suggestions as to areas
that trainees can become familiar with in thinking about their potential contribution to service development.

1. An assessment of the best contexts from which to deliver services to children, young people and their families, taking into account accessibility or
lack of it, from the point of view of potential users. This can include looking for new bases from which to deliver culturally appropriate services (for
example, more community-based services), as well as examining ways in
which current methods of service delivery can be improved.
2. Exploring possibilities of collaboration with existing community resources
without exploitation (for example, co-working with youth workers, playgroup leaders, religious leaders or counsellors), or developing ways to support community workers and seeking support from them.
3. Liaising with other professionals and voluntary agencies about the range of
services available to support children and families from minority ethnic
groups. Collaborating with other agencies to learn about different
approaches to working with children and families.
4. Considering the resource implications for child services in becoming more
culturally appropriate: for example, toys, books, pictures, ways of employing interpreters, cultural consultants, etc.
5. Learning ways of understanding how institutional racism impacts on the
lives of children, young people and their families. Considering the effects of
their contact with the different institutions which impinge on them. Learning about the ways in which institutional racism can affect referral and service delivery. Examining ways in which it operates in institutions of which
the trainee is a part and considering ways of addressing it.

6.   Considering ways in which clinical psychology can be promoted to all communities, including the possibility that the terms both 'clinical' and 'psychology' may be problematic. Looking at ways in which clinical psychologists can make their services both user friendly and culturally acceptable to different communities. Looking for examples of good practice in different services.

7.   Consulting with, and being accountable to, the local community for meeting the needs of their children (Waldegrave, 1990; Tamasese and Waldegrave, 1993).

LEARNING OUTCOMES

Trainees will:

1.   Have an understanding of their own personal and professional issues when working with racial and cultural differences and with children's experiences of racism.

2.   Be able to develop and acknowledge an understanding of their own racism and/or ethnocentrism.

3.   Be able to use their understanding of the racism experienced by families to have a fuller appreciation of the other problems being experienced by the child and family.

4.   Have an understanding of the different ways of carrying out an assessment which are appropriate to their clients' cultures.

5.   Have an appreciation of child development and ways in which life cycle stages get constructed differently across different cultures. They will also have an appreciation of a wide variety of child rearing practices and some understanding of different transitional rituals which affect children.

6.   Have an awareness and respect for the way in which childhood is constructed differently in different cultures and some understanding of the implications of these constructions when working with children and families who are affected by multiple cultural contexts.

7.   Learn a range of interviewing skills which are sensitive to working with children and families from a different ethnicity to their own.

8.   Have experienced working with an interpreter, from an appropriate ethnic/cultural group.

9.   Have experienced working with a co-worker from a community, voluntary sector and/or religious group.

METHODS OF TEACHING

1.   Lectures on the theoretical topics.

2.   Videos (e.g. television programmes about children experiencing racism, growing up in the UK as a member of a minority ethnic group).

3.   Reading of recommended novels and autobiographies (e.g. Soyinka, 1981; Alibhai-Brown and Montague, 1992) See also the further reading section in the Introductory Module.

4. Role plays to include practice of talking with children about self-identifications and their relationships with others who are ethnically different from them. Developing skills in talking about discrimination and/or racism and using awareness of the child's perception of the trainee in doing so (Kitzinger and Kitzinger, 1999 for general approaches to talking with children; Ho, 1992 for working with children from minority ethnic groups; Vargas and Koss-Chioino, 1992).

5. Family of origin and family tree work with trainees looking at their own cultural heritage and differences. Discussing experiences of growing up in different cultural contexts. This needs to take into account the limitations of the genogram as an authentic representation of family structures which may include non-related kin and kinship networks which do not follow nuclear family forms.

6. Clinical presentation to consolidate theory using cultural genograms (Hardy and Laszloffy, 1995).

7. Visits to schools and day nurseries and talking to children and staff, looking at materials for teaching child development and for appreciating the sophistication that young people can show about their understanding of the world.

8. Trainer to present an interview of an adult/family/child from a minority ethnic cultural background (on audio tape or video) about living in Britain or their experiences of Child Services including Child Mental Health Services.

9. Trainees to interview two families who differ from them in terms of their colour, ethnic background and religion, with a view to helping the trainee learn about another culture. This is especially pertinent for White trainees.

10. Trainees to have worked with a minimum number of clients from different cultural/ethnic backgrounds than their own, as part of the clinical placement requirements. The minimum number must be representative of Black minority groups in the local population, and in any case must not be fewer than two families over the course of training.

Suggested exercises

Exercise 1: What do I 'see' in my first week at school?

Aim

To sensitize trainees to young children's experience when entering a new sphere outside the family which impinges on their degree of comfort in relation to their 'race' and ethnicity in the new situation.
(This exercise can be adapted to entering secondary schoo.l)

Instructions
Trainees to get into groups of three and select one person to be a child of

five, entering school for the first time and a second person to be the 'interviewer'. 'The child' should have a gender and an ethnicity selected by the person playing the role. 'The interviewer' should also have a stated gender and ethnicity. 'The interviewer' talks to the child for ten minutes about what she/he notices about being in school at the end of the first week. The 'talk' can be verbal or through play material. The observer (of a specific gender and ethnicity) then discusses their observations with the interviewer. 'The child' listens. The three then de-role and consider what impact the gender/ethnicity of the interviewer might have had on the interview.

Feed back to large group.

Timings
10 minutes for set up
10 minutes for the interview
5 minutes for the interviewer/observer discussion
10 minutes for the small group discussion
20 minutes for group feedback of findings.

Exercise 2: 'Telling it like it is' or 'Ways families manage discrimination'

Aim
To think about different ways that families have for dealing with children's experiences of discrimination.

Instructions
Form a family of four to five people of a particular 'race' and ethnicity, including a teenage child, an 'adult child' and a younger child. The teenage child has had an experience of discrimination which has been upsetting.

The experience may have been direct or observed. 'The family' then role play a meal time during which 'the teenager' chooses ways to express their upset. 'The family' then responds.

Debriefing: after the role play, the family de-role. Members then choose one or two other people with whom to think about the role play they were in. They are invited to reflect on the effect *on them* of the exercise, and on any parallels or insights they may have relating to their own and their family's way of dealing with discrimination.

Large group discussion.

Timings
10 minutes (about) for setting up 'the family'
15 minutes for role play
15 minutes for debriefing
25 minutes for large group reflection.

Exercise 3: 'Family culture/Family relationships'

Aim
To explore a range of different kinship arrangements which open up ways of addressing cultural diversity

Instructions
Form into groups of about five depending on the size of the class group. Each group is given one of the following situations to discuss:

Many Western European and white American families function with the principal that the key organizing relationship in the family is the spouse or quasi spouse relationship. Discuss the advantages for family relationships of living within a cultural system which privileges, as the key organizing relationship within the family, the:
(a) mother–son relationship;
(b) brother–brother relationship;
(c) mother–grandmother relationship.

Where several groups have been formed, each group should discuss only one of these.
Additional prompts (to be used if the group is stuck or off-task):
'What are the advantages in this for children / boys / girls?' 'At different ages ?'
'What are the advantages for relations between men/ women?'
'What are the advantages for the spouse relationship?'

'What are the advantages for the child–parent relationships, the child–grandparent relationship?'
'What might these arrangements lead to as themes in family life?'

When the task is completed there should be feedback from each group, both of the content and of some of the process. Class discussion can then see how these ideas relate to the culture of origin of class members.

Timings
10 minutes for setting up
20–25 minutes for small group discussion
30 minutes for large group discussion

Annotated references

Barn, R. (Ed.) (1999) *Working with Black Children and Adolescents in Need*. London: British Agencies for Adoptions and Fostering (BAAF)

This collection by Black authors provides articles about practice which directly address 'racial' and ethnic identity in children and young people. It has a useful chapter on communicating with and assessing Black children and also has focused chapters on work with nurseries and with children in the care system.

Di Nicola, V. (1997) *A Stranger in the Family: Culture, Families and Therapy*. New York, London: Norton

This book draws on a family therapy framework to provide a refreshingly different and engaging perspective on cross-cultural work with families. A creative use is made of cultural family narratives in developing theory/practice links. The book offers a frame of reference on which to base intervention strategies and therapeutic positions. Topics given consideration include culture, cultural narratives, language, cultural identity and cultural/family transitions.

Dwivedi, K. and Varma, V. (Eds) (1996) *Meeting the Needs of Ethnic Minority Children. A Handbook for Professionals*. London: Jessica Kingsley

A collection of articles which, with one notably bad exception, provides useful food for thought about working with children therapeutically in a number of different contexts. This book is going into a second revised edition.

Kakar, S. (1978) (1981) *The Inner World: A Psychoanalytic Study of Childhood and Society in India*. New Delhi, London: Oxford Indian Paperbacks

This is a classic book which looks at the development of Indian children as a distinctive product of the culture in which they are nurtured. Drawing on many aspects of myth, rituals, fables and the arts, it illuminates the social structures which construct the psyche in a way which provides a highly convincing refutation of the idea of a universal psychology.

Scheper-Hughes, N. (Ed.) (1987) *Child Survival*. Dodrecht: D.Reidl

This is a collection of papers from around the world about child abuse that treats culture in a realistic way, showing the relationship between the treatment of children, culture and economic realities. There are chapters on population, fertility and social trauma and the effects of social disruption and catastrophe on child treatment. The section on 'child saving' treats problems and dilemmas in social intervention with an even-handed look at the relationship between culture and treatment of children without transposing 'psychology' as a universal belief system.

Other useful modules

- Adult Mental Health
- Neuropsychology
- Learning Disabilities
- Health Psychology
- Primary Care

Chapter 10
ADULT MENTAL HEALTH

Elizabeth Bennett and Maxine Dennis

Introduction

The social and political context of psychological problems and practice is an integral part of this module. Some important elements of that context are: the historical development of psychology; colonization and its consequences for Britain today; immigration and its effects, racism and its effects and the responses of modern psychology.

Historical development of psychology (and psychiatry)
The development of these disciplines during periods of slavery and colonialism means that the centrality of racism to the structures of psychology and psychiatry cannot be underestimated (Milner, 1990; Karenga, 1992; Howitt and Owusu-Bempah, 1994; Fernando, 1991,1995; Littlewood and Lipsedge, 1997). 'The discipline of psychology does not exist in a historical vacuum; on the contrary, it is influenced by, and in turn influences, society in a reflexive way.'(Nadirshaw, 1999).

Colonization and its consequences for Britain today
The history of colonization has had a major impact on all relationships between Black and White people. This impact is evident in the minds of the colonizer and those colonized (Tan, 1993) and in the fabric of institutions. The effects of colonization have surfaced in, for example, attempts to prove the genetic inferiority of Black people, as in the 'IQ debate' (Eysenck, 1971; Rushton, 1990; Hernstein and Murray, 1994), which is somewhat discredited, though still ongoing. However, many less blatant forms of discrimination remain.

Immigration and its effects
The migration of Black and minority ethnic peoples to Britain has had an impact on both the way they are viewed and how they view themselves. Trainees need to be aware of migration patterns and the various reasons for the presence of Black and minority ethnic people in Britain (Fryer, 1984; Hiro, 1992). (See also the Introductory Module.)

Racism and its effects

The effects of racism permeate all public service institutions, economic structures, media images and people's self-perceptions: 'the power within racism ensures that the application of race thinking invokes assumptions of inferiority-superiority, justifying exploitation and the allocation of individuals, their cultures, etc. to positions on a hierarchy' (Fernando, 1991, p. 27). (For a fuller discussion, see Patel and Fatimilehin (1999) and the Introductory Module.) If clinical psychologists are to work well with Black and minority ethnic clients, they will need to recognize the potential significance of the experience of everyday racism for mental health itself, for uptake of services and for individual therapeutic relationships.

The experience of everyday racism can have an impact on mental health, sometimes described as the 'hidden injury,' which may include depression, school refusal, etc. (Littlewood and Lipsedge, 1997). However, 'while racism can have devastating consequences for the individual, this has to be seen in the context of social consequences and the socio-political forces which perpetuate racial inequalities' (Patel and Fatimilehin, 1999, p.61).

Patel and Fatimilehin (1999) argue that the experience of social hypervigilance is not uncommon, and has important implications for the uptake of services by Black and minority ethnic people and for therapeutic relationships. This hypervigilance is frequently pathologized although it can be construed as an adaptive and purposive response to a hostile environment, especially when discrimination is subtle. White professionals, in their clinical practice and in their contributions to models of service provision, need to respect this and acknowledge that trust must be earned, rather than expected. Thomas (1995) highlights how hypervigilance may also be present in a therapeutic setting.

Racism is not only confined to relations between groups of people based on discernible characteristics like skin colour. There is a growing body of literature that talks about 'the new racisms' within and between certain groups and nations, rather than seeing racism solely in terms of a Black/White divide (Phoenix, 1999). However, others suggest that the central issue remains one of power and oppression and that 'debates on semantics' can act to obscure this (Owusu-Bempah and Howitt, 1999).

Responses of modern clinical psychology

Patel and Fatimilehin (1999) argue that most analyses of the 'problem of racism' have come from those who have suffered racism and that 'the social, political and academic marginalization of the issues of racism has tended to absolve non-minority ethnic people of the responsibility to examine their contributions to social injustice and to instigate change' (p.60). Within clinical psychology there has been a significant shift towards accepting this responsibility, with more attempts to integrate these issues in practice. However, there are pitfalls in this process, for example, some feel that the area is 'too complex' or there is fearfulness about 'doing the right thing' which can lead to inaction or paralysis. Defences employed to manage such feelings can include a 'failure to think' (Cooper, 1997), which can result in lip service being paid. 'Race' and culture can also be marginalized as a 'special issue'. Awareness of these pitfalls can help convert them into steps along the way towards a truly anti-racist practice.

DEMOGRAPHY AND EPIDEMIOLOGY

Introduction

Research into the mental health of Black people has a history of blatant racism (Cochrane and Sashidharan, 1996). Subtle racism still pervades the discipline and is manifested in a number of conceptual and methodological problems, including:

- Ethnic or 'racial' categorization of research samples. Stanfield (1993) suggests that the majority of literature on 'racially' defined populations is rooted in fallacies of homogeneity or of monolithic identity.
- Research projects are undertaken largely by White workers, tending to focus on areas where Black and minority ethnic people experience particular problems. There is a lack of empirically grounded research on mental well-being or the psychological resilience of minority groups that partly reflects the general focus of psychiatric and psychological research on pathology, rather than health.
- The Eurocentric bias in research means that the experience of the White population is accepted as normal, and that any deviation from this norm, in either raised or lowered incidence of particular problems, is explained in terms of either cultural or 'racial' pathology. For example, genetics and abnormal family structures are cited in the raised incidence of diagnosed schizophrenia in African-Caribbean men, while lower levels of depression in women of Pakistani origin are seen as indicative of an inability to express psychological problems or as the result of these women being hidden away by relatives.

Guidelines for ethical mental health research involving issues of 'race', ethnicity and culture (see Patel, 1999) will be useful in critiquing any existing research findings.

Research findings

In-patient psychiatric services
Comprehensive surveys carried out in 1971 and 1981 (e.g. Harrison *et al.*, 1988; Littlewood and Lipsedge, 1988 and King *et al.*, 1994) were based on rates of admission and psychiatric diagnosis (see Boyle, 1999 for a critique of the practice of diagnosis). The major findings were:

- There was an excess of diagnosed schizophrenia among Caribbean-born people.
- For all other diagnoses combined the admission rates of the Caribbean born were substantially below those of the native born.

- For those born in South Asia overall admission rates were lower than those for White British born.

Findings of significantly raised incidence of diagnosed schizophrenia in African-Caribbean men has fuelled a long running debate, with many of the explanations offered proving to be untenable. Cochrane and Sashidharan (1996) give detailed accounts of these arguments.

Findings from treatment-based research are summarized below:

- The elevated rate of diagnosed schizophrenia appeared to be unique to Britain.
- The relative risk appeared to be even greater among African-Caribbean men born in the UK.
- African-Caribbean men with diagnosed schizophrenia were significantly more likely to be detained under a Section of the Mental Health Act and to have had a 'non-standard' pathway into care (i.e. police involvement was *more* likely, direct referral from GP *less* likely) than were White people.
- There was growing evidence of a poorer course and outcome in Britain's African-Caribbean population.
- African-Caribbean men were likely to receive higher doses of neuroleptics, given intramuscularly, more likely to be put on depot medication at an early stage and more likely to receive ECT.

There has been rather less research on need, demand and utilization of services among people from South Asia. Major findings are summarized by Webb-Johnson (1991). The following points are drawn from this and from Cochrane and Sashidharan (1996):

- Treated prevalence rates of schizophrenia were similar to those in the White British population. However, prognosis was better for South Asians, with fewer re-admissions and less disability at follow-up.
- Admissions for other problems were lower. There is some evidence from community surveys that this may accurately reflect need. The exception to this is the increased risk of suicide in young, married Indian women.
- There is evidence of under-utilization of services by those of Pakistani and Bangladeshi origin.
- Community surveys looking at alcohol-related problems among Sikh men have found that alcohol problems occur at similar rates among Sikh men and White British men, but are rare among Hindus and Muslims.
- There is evidence of low uptake of aftercare services: for example Day Services and Clinical Psychology services.

Primary Care services
(See the Primary Care Module for a more detailed discussion.)

There is concern that there may be considerable unmet need for psychological support among Black and minority ethnic people.

- There is no substantial group variation in registration with GPs (Cochrane and Sashidharan, 1996).
- Men and women of Pakistani origin, and men of South Asian and African Caribbean origin consult their GPs more often than other groups, (Cochrane and Sashidharan, 1996).
- African-Caribbean people are just as likely as White people to consult their GPs about psychological (non-psychotic) problems, but are less likely to receive medication (Nazroo, 1997).
- White British women are most likely and African-Caribbean and South Asian women are least likely to be diagnosed by their GP as having psychological disorders (Cochrane and Sashidharan, 1996).

Community surveys
Nazroo (1997) reports on the findings of the Policy Studies Institute's Fourth National Survey of Ethnic Minorities, concluding that all previous studies of ethnic variation in mental health have to be regarded with some caution. Almost all of these were based on treatment statistics, and often only on data from hospital admissions. The primary limitation of these data lies in the possibility that pathways into care for different ethnic groups, rather than differences in rates of illness, may have influenced the pattern of findings reported.

Nazroo considers possible methodological difficulties of the PSI survey, but concludes that the following findings can be accepted with some confidence:

- **African-Caribbean group:** there was no evidence that African-Caribbean men were diagnosed as having higher rates of psychosis than White men.
- African-Caribbean women had diagnosed rates of psychosis twice as high as those for White women, although this difference did not quite reach statistical significance.
- The African-Caribbean group were diagnosed as having a 60 per cent higher rate of non-psychotic depression than the White group.
- **South Asian group:** actual rates of illness in this group were more difficult to assess because of differences between South Asian and White people in the performance on the instruments used to assess mental illness.
- If it is accepted that this difficulty invalidates many of the findings, then the best estimates would come from rates identified for non-migrant groups which are identical to those for the White group for both depression and psychosis.
- If, on the other hand, it is accepted that the differences between White and South Asian groups estimated by the study are genuine, the overall pattern is of relatively low rates of mental ill health in the South Asian group.

- **Demographic and socio-economic factors:** differences in rates of mental ill-ness among different ethnic groups might not be a consequence of dimensions of ethnicity *per se*, such as culture or biology, but of the differences in demographic and socio-economic profiles.

  Generally, differences in pathways into care and type of treatment received, according to ethnicity, does appear to be a robust finding, and one which should concern clinicians. Mental health clinicians need to be familiar with the various national research findings, their identified methodological shortcomings, and the hypotheses put forward to explain the findings. Of equal importance is knowledge of local variations in admission rates, pathways into care and treatment received according to ethnicity.

THEORY

Introduction

Much of the writing and research in this area has been led by American scholars. From the 1950s through to 1970 during the civil rights Black movement, social scientists described a psychosocial conversion process among Black Americans which involved a redefinition of themselves from 'coloured' to 'negro' (each an imposed group identity) to a self-designated identity as Black(s). In the 1970s some theorists applied this phenomenon to individuals rather than the social movement (for example, Cross (1971) and Helms (1984)). Others have extended these theories to Black and White identity development (Atkinson *et al.*, 1989; Cross, 1995; Helms, 1995; also see Introductory Module).

In Britain, a comparable movement to define the effects of racism and oppression on Black and minority ethnic communities is in its infancy. Analyses relevant to Britain will need to consider the more covert kinds of discrimination which characterize the experience of Black and minority ethnic people in this country.

Much of the literature addressing the Eurocentrism of psychological theory takes as its starting point the need to make adjustments to established theories in order to make them applicable to the 'other'– Black and minority ethnic people – rather than an acknowledgement that a paradigm shift may be necessary if psychology is to have any relevance outside of the culture in which it has, thus far, been constructed (see Introductory Module).

There have been various relevant developments, notably the cross-cultural approaches of Sue and Sue (1990), the multicultural approaches of Katz (1978), the transcultural approaches of d'Ardenne and Mahtani (1999) and the intercultural therapy approach (Kareem, 1992), which address theoretical as well as practice issues in relation to therapy in a multicultural, multiethnic society.

There has been some questioning of mechanistic attempts to learn about other cultures in order to become 'culturally sensitive'. This should not preclude attempts to find out about cultures other than one's own, but this generalised and abstract learning should go hand in hand with learning from the particular person one is working with and will mean moving from the position of 'expert' to one of novice/inquirer. Boyd-Franklin (1989) and D'Ardenne and Mahtani (1999) note how de-skilling this process can be.

Relevant concepts

Common stereotypes

SOUTH ASIAN PEOPLE

Common stereotypes have been used to explain the under-representation of people of South Asian origin in mental health services. Some of these are considered by Webb-Johnson (1991), including:

- **Stigmatization of mental illness.** The stigma of mental health is a global problem and to over-emphasize its impact on the Asian community is to take a 'victim-blaming' approach.
- **'Somatization' of mental distress.** There is no conclusive evidence to suggest that people of Asian origin are more likely to 'somatize' than any other group. Explanations for this stereotype include: GPs are perceived by Asian people to treat only physical complaints and these are therefore presented; Eastern traditions use a more holistic model of the self, health and illness, where problems may not be seen as affecting either the mind or the body in isolation. (See also Introductory and Primary Care Modules.)
- **'Asians look after their own'.** The stereotype of the extended Asian family which is able to provide emotional support to its members is not borne out by evidence collected among people of Asian origin living in the UK (Webb-Johnson, 1991).

AFRICAN-CARIBBEAN PEOPLE

- Differential treatment received by African-Caribbean men is often explained by mental health professionals as attributable to the greater 'dangerousness' of this group of users. This perception is not borne out by any body of empirical evidence, but does result in oppressive treatment regimes (Littlewood and Lipsedge, 1997; Dutt and Ferns, 1998) and indeed represents a clear example of racism within the mental health system, where there are systematically differential responses and inequitable outcomes for different groups (Ridley, 1995).
- African Caribbean people are frequently viewed as 'non-psychologically minded', hence the reluctance of primary and secondary care professionals to refer them for psychological therapies.
- Intellectual ability is still questioned (Rushton, 1990; Hernstein and Murrey, 1994) and 'stereotype threat' is shown to have an adverse effect on academic achievement (Steele, 1999). Perceptions of intellectual competence are linked to judgements about the appropriateness of different kinds of treatment.

Conceptual issues in therapy

There is a range of views on the relevance of Western psychotherapeutic models to Black and minority ethnic clients. For example, Cochrane and Sashidharan (1996), citing Jayasuriya *et al.* (1992), say that treatment practices such as psychotherapy and counselling are heavily laden with Western beliefs and value systems, which privilege the philosophy of individualism, the right to self-determination and the desirability of independence and assertiveness.

Littlewood and Lipsedge (1997), on the other hand, recognize that Western notions of 'maturity' in psychotherapy include the key concepts of individuation, autonomy and a non-somatizing, psychological approach to distress, but argue that in Britain today we are not concerned with providing psychotherapy for 'some hypothetical Third World community' but for a proportion of citizens in Britain now, who are undeniably disadvantaged, but emphatically not a group of people who have 'some sort of exotic system of psychological and personal development' (p.289).

Models of mental health

Ridley (1995) points to four main models in the area of mental health and outlines the 'unintentional racist implications' of each:

Deficit models

Here, minority ethnic people are viewed as having deficits in two broad areas:

- genetic/constitutional deficits: for example, in terms of IQ (Jensen, 1969; Rushton, 1988), and in terms of personality deficit and abnormal character and behaviour, (Kardiner and Ovesey, 1951);
- cultural deficits: for example, inferior culture or breakdown of culture under the weight of oppression.

The Medical Model

The focus here is on viewing psychological problems as diseases where symptoms and syndromes are identified and the illness within the individual treated. This model includes a tendency to overpathologize the individual and to overlook the effects of racism, discrimination and poverty on mental health.

The Conformity (or socio-cultural) Model

Here, individual behaviours are understood in relation to the normative or standardization sample of a population, including:

- *Etic models:* culturally universal or generalized, where the criteria for interpreting behaviour always remain constant, regardless of the cultural context of persons being judged.
- *Emic models:* culturally sensitive or specific models, where valid interpretation of behaviour rests upon a person's indigenous cultural norms.

The Biopsychosocial Model
This attempts to look at the whole person, including their physical health, inter-personal and social competence, psychological and emotional well-being, within their social and economic context (Lewis *et al.*, 1993).

PRACTICE

Major models of therapy

It has been suggested that one useful way of categorizing psychological models is along a content–process continuum (personal communication, M. Boyle, University of East London). Professor Boyle posits that learning theory represents the 'pure process' end of the continuum with psychodynamic theories at the 'content' end. The position of learning theory may be explained by the fact that it did not arise out of clinical work and that theories developed in the course of clinical work have a tendency to establish norms, the norms of the clinicians, and to create 'others'– clients who do not meet these norms. It could perhaps be suggested that primarily process-based theories may be more universal in application, while content-based theories are likely to be more culture-specific.

The philosophies on which therapies are based provide another categorization, for example, a differentiation of rationalist and constructivist/constructionist therapies (Mahoney, 1993). Rationalist therapies are primarily normative, starting from the premise that there is 'one true reality'. Constructivist approaches arise out of the increasingly widespread awareness that the belief systems and apparent 'realities' each of us lives in are socially constructed rather than 'given', and so can be constructed very differently in different cultures (or subcultures), times and circumstances, though they still appear 'true' and necessary to those who live by them (Neimeyer, 1993).

The more rationalist approaches inhabit a reality constructed during the 'modern', scientific era of White European and North American, primarily male-dominated, thinking and therefore could be considered to have relevance mainly to those whose realities have been constructed within that same culture and time. Anderson (1990) points out that it is very hard, in a world shaped by many realities, to maintain the position that satisfactory adjustment to one reality constitutes mental health, while unsatisfactory adjustment is a form of illness. However, since all therapeutic approaches are developed and refined within clinical settings, where clinicians add their own culture-specific content in the form of assumptions, beliefs and prejudices, there tends to be a drift towards 'accepted' content in all approaches.

Systemic approaches
Within systemic approaches over recent decades, there has been some movement away from more content-based approaches, such as structural and strategic, towards those which focus primarily on unpredetermined processes, for example, narrative approaches (Eron and Lund, 1996). However, the stance of 'neutrality', central to early systemic approaches (e.g. the Milan School) which

attempted to avoid the introduction of therapist bias, has been questioned on ethical grounds, resulting in the reintroduction of 'content' in the form of recognition of power imbalances within family systems and between families and therapists (McGoldrick, 1994). Particular contents are also inevitably introduced by therapists, who will bring their own culture-specific assumptions about family functioning and directions for change.

In recent years, many systemic therapists have been informed by the ideas of social constructionism. Within this philosophy, no one version of reality or set of values and beliefs is seen either as representing the 'true reality' or as privileged above any other, and therapists are encouraged to adopt a stance of curiosity and 'not-knowing', rather than one of expertise, and to work collaboratively with clients to develop alternative options, rather than to impose a psychological package of treatment (Anderson and Goolishian, 1992). Continual questioning of therapists' assumptions is required (Partridge *et al.*, 1995; Weingarten, 1998).

Cognitive and cognitive behaviour therapy

CBT's roots in Learning Theory are primarily process-and environment-based. Early cognitive additions were also process-focused in that they described the role of various types of information-processing in psychological problems. However, CBT has become progressively more content-laden, and thus more culture-specific. For example, the 'core schemas' often identified may have very different meanings for members of subordinate groups than for members of dominant groups. One 'underlying' schema frequently identified is: 'I must be liked by everyone', viewed by therapists as 'dysfunctional'. For people who have had no experience of being valued, who have been derided and excluded (and this often applies to members of subordinate groups), it is functional to be aware of the opinion of others and, possibly, to court others' good opinion and avoid their displeasure. The meanings of core schemas are largely ignored. In mainstream CBT thinking, beliefs are seen as reactive to early negative experience, as 'leftovers' which interfere with an individual's capacity to respond positively to their current environment. When beliefs are seen as purposive, as an individual's guides to negotiating life, their meanings become crucial in the therapeutic process.

Concerns about the failure of CBT with certain types of client have led to new developments in the field, including an increasing focus on self-organizing and self-protective processes in personality development, these being seen as embedded in interpersonal and social system dynamics (Mahoney, 1993; Neimeyer, 1993).

Schema-Focused Therapy (Salkovskis, 1996) has recently been developed specifically in response to the needs of people with 'long-standing characterological disorders', who have failed to respond to traditional cognitive approaches. It has also been informed by the constructivist movement within the cognitive sciences. These newer developments are important for their recognition of the importance of personal meaning and the social construction of belief systems, and a move away from a normative approach. Padesky and Greenberger (1995) and Hays (1995) both provide useful guides to clinicians on multicultural applications of CBT. Thus far, there is a dearth of research investigating the relevance of the model across cultures, despite the strongly empirical stance of this school.

Psychodynamic approaches

The psychodynamic approach is an umbrella term often used when referring to psychoanalytic approaches derived from Freudian concepts. Freud's concept of the unconscious mind was put forward in the late 19th century. 'He understood the unconscious mind to be a highly structured form of subjective reality, analogous in logic to the emotional world of infants and children, which continues to be active in adulthood' (Pajaczkowska and Young, 1997). Freud's original approach formed the basis of a number of major schools of thought (for example Klein, Jung and Adler; Independents such as Fairburn, Winnicott, etc.). A detailed exploration of such is beyond the scope of this module.

Freud's (1915) original organization of the mind was to divide it into the unconscious and the conscious. His later development of the structural theory of the mind (Freud 1923) brought with it both an emphasis on the strengthening and increase of the independence of the ego from the superego. This would mean a greater focus on individual responsibility and less emphasis on the parental, family, community and society internalized influences (superego). It has been argued that translating such an approach cross-culturally without due attention to a range of beliefs and traditions seriously questions its applicability (see Nobles, 1971; Perez-Foster, 1996).

The racist depiction of Black people within the early psychoanalytic writings is a major source of concern about its applicability (Frosh, 1997). The universal meanings attached to words, actions and events is another area of concern. Much criticism has also been levelled at the psychodynamic approach, mainly in that it has been limited in its attendance to cultural experiences and environmental factors (Littlewood and Lipsedge, 1997).

Leary (1997) states that prior to the mid-1960s Black people were seen as the enigmatic other and attempts were made to explain the 'alien' other. After the 1960s the impact of 'race' and ethnicity in the treatment dyad was discussed, especially the role of the Black therapist (Curry, 1964; Gardner, 1971). However, the emphasis has been placed on the Black therapist and client to provide greater understanding of ethnicity as if they are its sole possessors.

Fanon (1967, 1986) and Kovel (1984) have made important contributions in the struggle for psychoanalysis to take 'race' and cultural issues seriously and to offer a real contribution to the area.

Seminal texts include Fanon (1986), Kovel (1984), Rustin (1992) and Davids (1997). These authors provide an object-relations perspective to thinking about and understanding 'race' and cultural issues. They attempt to provide a dynamic explanation and understanding of how 'Blackness' and 'Whiteness' is perceived, understood and what constitutes the role of the therapist.

There may also be quite a split between theory and how it is applied in practice, where attention to the ethnicity and culture of both therapist and client would be necessary for a more authentic and non-pseudo therapy to take place (see Perez Foster *et al.*, 1996; Mohamed and Smith, 1997). Clearly, there is more attention needed in developing the theory and its application in individual and group psychotherapy (Dalal, 1993).

PRACTICE

Practitioners may well be able to use the methods and techniques of any of the major approaches in 'culturally competent' ways which are respectful of difference. While therapies can become blinkered and excluding through processes of in-group confirmation, they can also become more flexible and inclusive, given the preparedness of therapists to reflect constructively on their practice.

Assessment (see also the Primary Care, Child, Adolescent and Family and Older Adults modules)

1.   Assessment is not a neutral process, and the attempt to be 'neutral' is thwarted by the very presence of two (or more) individuals with different experiences and different world-views in the room. It is also where initial engagement with the client(s) takes place and is therefore vital for the establishment of a good working alliance. Therapists need to be aware of what they and the client bring to the assessment situation, for example, pre-transference issues (Curry, 1964) and world-views (Sue and Sue, 1990; Brown and Brown, 1995).
2.   How clients gain access to services (Moodley and Perkins, 1991) has repercussions for how they perceive the setting and the psychologist as the broker of the system.
3.   Black and minority ethnic people are often stereotyped as not being psychologically minded and therefore likely to respond to chemical, rather than verbal, interventions. Trainees need to be aware of how such stereotypical images may inform the recommendations they make following assessments.

Psychometric Assessment (see also Neuropsychology module)

The onus is on the clinician to be clear about the purpose and utility of psychometric assessment with any particular individual. Marsella and Kameoka (1989) argue that for valid and reliable assessments of psychopathology across cultures, linguistic, conceptual, scale and norm equivalence factors need to be attended to. Trainees need to be aware of when their use of psychometric testing is genuinely informing their work with the client and when it may act to bolster discriminatory practices.

Intervention

Ethnic matching
This is a complex notion, which can appear very crude when translated into practice. Each individual's identity is multifaceted, each facet having a different

salience in different contexts and to prescribe a 'match' on the basis of, for example, skin colour or ethnicity may not be appropriate. Services should aim at being able to provide clients with choice about the therapist(s) they work with. In practice this is often not achievable and it too has its complexities, e.g. how do we view the request of a White client to work only with a White therapist? How do we respond to the Indian woman who says that she does not want to be seen by an Asian therapist? All clinicians should aim at developing their capacity to work in culturally competent ways.

Use of interpreters
Trainers should explore with trainees the blocks to working effectively with interpreters and the steps necessary to enable this process. See also the section on working with interpreters in the Introductory Module.

Addressing 'Race' and Racism in Therapy
Therapists are responsible for initiating the exploration with the client of difference, ethnicity and racism, both in terms of the possible impact of racism on the client's mental health and its impact on the therapeutic relationship. Many differences (in ethnicity, age, class, gender, sexuality, access to resources, family history) will operate in any dyad, and many may be relevant to the therapeutic endeavour. Here, the focus is on Black/White difference, bearing in mind that this crude dichotomy only poorly represents the realities of a meeting between two multi-dimensional people.

For a Black client, seeing a Black psychologist has potential advantages – the expectation of being understood, of not being stereotyped or being viewed as 'exotic'. However, there can be difficulties too, which will need to be addressed. These might include the client's expectations, and the therapist's impulse, to create a political alignment, for example, 'engaging with the client against the system'; the client viewing the therapist as having 'sold out' to the system and occupying a privileged position in relation to the client; and the client seeing the therapist as 'not good enough', perhaps because of internalized racism.

White clients seeing a Black therapist may privilege 'professional' above 'colour' and therefore minimize the importance of any difference, or they may question the therapist's capacity to understand, or may be openly hostile. Davids (1992) presents an analysis of some of the dynamics in this dyad, from an object–relations perspective.

Between a White therapist and a White client, ethnicity and racism are rarely spoken about (Mohamed and Smith, 1997) except when the White client expresses openly racist views. It is worth considering whether putting 'race' on the agenda might make a useful contribution to therapeutic effectiveness in these dyads.

While White therapists have a responsibility to make it possible for Black clients to talk about racism and difference, there is a danger of 'dehumanizing' Black clients by assuming that all their difficulties revolve around being Black or are the result of oppression. The client may not wish certain feelings to be understood and may feel humiliated and disempowered by being pigeonholed as a victim of racism (Thomas, 1992). Black clients may also resist talking about their experience of racism to a White therapist, either out of compassion, e.g. not wishing to offend an apparently well-intentioned White person, or out of fear that they may antagonize the therapist and thus jeopardize their treatment. Ridley (1995) also describes eight 'racially related' defences therapists may employ when working with a Black/White difference.

Spirituality and religion in therapy

The area of spirituality or religious belief is generally invisible in mainstream psychological literature. The dominant position of Western culture allows its members to accept secularism as the norm and thus to discount the importance of spirituality or religion in people's lives. A shift to the view that secularism is just a position, specific to certain peoples at a certain time in history, requires that psychology rethink its approach to this area of human life.

There are examples of the use of religious and spiritual traditions within the context of therapy: for example, Buddhism (de Silva, 1993); Hinduism (Kakar, 1982); Black Christian churches (Smith, 1996); Nation of Islam/Black Muslims (Akbar, 1996; Owens, 1980). (See also the Introductory Module for further references.)

Within the trainee group there is likely to be a range of religious and spiritual beliefs, and this can be used as a resource for exploring some of the complexities of working with difference.

Traditional healers

Clients may approach traditional healers for help with psychological or emotional problems. Knowledge of traditional healing practices can be useful and it may at times be possible for psychologists to work in partnership with such healers. Lago and Thompson (1996) name and describe a number of these traditional healers. However, readers should be aware that the names and descriptions provided may not match the experience and knowledge of clients, and it is important that assumptions are not made without finding out from the client how they view the practices and relevance of any particular type of healer.

SERVICE DELIVERY

(See also the Professional and Organizational Module)

Introduction

The development and delivery of mainstream services has, until very recently, been provider-rather than user-driven which has meant that the acceptability of services to potential users and their families as a key element in service planning has been largely overlooked (Cochrane and Sashidharan, 1996).

If a particular service is perceived by Black or minority ethnic people as inappropriate or unacceptable, they are presented with a choice between making themselves more appropriate, i.e. acculturating, or not using that service. The attempt to acculturate may result in unhelpful contacts, while the choice not to use services can be explained away by service providers on the basis of stereo-types such as 'Black and minority ethnic people prefer to deal with mental health issues within their own communities'.

The introduction of clinical governance could have profound implications for the development and delivery of culturally competent mental health and psychological services. On the one hand, its emphasis on 'evidence-based practice' could restrict the development of creative approaches. The therapies which have a recognized evidence base are those that have been developed within a Western psychological paradigm and researched using White Western clients. Their relevance or appropriateness to other groups of people is, thus far, untested. Innovative approaches, which acknowledge other world views and draw on a wider range of models of psychological functioning, may not be considered in the commissioning process.

On the other hand, clinical governance also requires that services be more locally accountable to the population they serve. The National Service Framework for Mental Health (1999) advises that 'involving service users in the service planning process can help to develop more acceptable and culturally sensitive services' (p.51). If this is translated into a requirement for genuine dialogue with the community in which mental health services operate and with service users, then 'good practice' will come to encompass some of these more innovative approaches.

Legislation

The Mental Health Task Force Report (Department of Health, 1994) called for services that were 'more responsive to the needs of people from different ethnic and cultural backgrounds'. In 1991 the Care Programme Approach (CPA) was introduced and in 1994 Supervision Registers were made part of the CPA for those seen as a risk to themselves and/or others. *Health of the Nation* (Department of Health, 1992) outlined specific targets for Black and minority ethnic people. *The National Service Framework for Mental Health* (1999) reinforces earlier statements, advocating that 'mental health services need to develop and demonstrate cultural competence' (p.44).

These various initiatives can, at times, be seen to conflict with each other. The introduction of the CPA was in part a response to the system's need to identify individuals who could be held responsible and accountable when things went wrong. At that time there were many media stories of 'big, Black and dangerous' psychiatric patients being a danger to the public at large. Taylor and Gunn (1999) provide a useful analysis of this phenomenon. Sashidharan and Commander (1998) state that there has always been an uncomfortable overlap between psychiatric practice and the maintenance of social order, in the assessment of mental health needs.[1]

---

1. Patel and Fatimilehin (1999) point out that 'one common misconception is the notion that racism is more evident in psychiatric practice than elsewhere in the mental health system. Clinical psychology, counselling and other psychological health professionals are as responsible as psychiatrists in the perpetuation of various forms of racism' (p.63).

Models of service delivery

Moodley (1993) raises the issue of whether the only way to achieve fully accept-able services is to create new and ethnically separate services. Evidence from the US suggests that such services are better at engaging minority ethnic clients but do not necessarily produce better outcomes (Flaskerad and Hu, 1994). Moodley also points out some of the potential dangers of this approach, for example, there are too many minority groups to provide services exclusive to each at a realistic cost; in many cases suitably qualified staff may not be available or may not wish to work in an ethnically separate unit; such services could easily become mar-ginalized and there would almost certainly be local and national political oppo-sition on the grounds of cost.

Dutt and Ferns (1998) suggest that service provision is best achieved through a twin track approach of developing culture-specific services at the same time as adapting existing mainstream services to ensure that they are more culturally appropriate for Black and minority ethnic communities. In practice, there are culture-specific services set up in the voluntary rather than the statutory sector. While many of these are excellent, they generally have lower levels of funding than equivalent statutory services, are often viewed as 'lower status' and are vul-nerable to withdrawal of funding. They also very rarely include clinical psy-chologists in their staff teams.

Community psychology approach

The inclusion of this section does not imply that community psychology is a sub-speciality exclusive to adult mental health. Rather, a brief overview is provided of the theoretical and practice issues which are relevant across specialities. Com-munity psychology approaches may have particular relevance to service provi-sion for Black and minority ethnic clients since they:

- Move away from an individualized view of distress to one which sees psy-chological problems in their social and political context.
- Explicitly consider the role of material disadvantage in the creation of mental health problems.
- Emphasize user-and community-led service development initiatives.
- Use therapeutic (or empowerment) approaches which utilise the resources of a community, rather than rely on the expertise of professionals.

Bostock (1991, 1998) defines community psychology in terms of its concern with how social environments perpetrate psychological suffering. Holland (1988; 1996) advocates the view that preventative work in mental health must make its central task the transformation of passive receivers of mental health services into active participants in the understanding of and solutions to their own and their neighbours' distress. Fryer (1998) adds a more individually focused perspective.

Orford (1998, see also Orford, 1992) sees the task of community clinical psy-chologists as helping people to:

- Understand the connection between the social and economic reality of their lives and their states of health and well-being.
- Join with others with similar realities to give voice to this understanding.
- Engage in collective action to change these realities.

Community psychology is seen as being practised at many different levels, through clinical intervention with individuals, families and groups; through involvement with local groups and communities; through ecological interventions, i.e. contributing to changes in the environment, and through action at the organizational or political level in the development of policy and planning. (Koch, 1986; Holland, 1988; Bostock, 1991, 1998; Smail, 1995).

Other useful models of service delivery

Many of the approaches, or projects, described in the previous section can be seen as alternatives to mainstream provision. The SHARE Directory, published by the King's Fund (see Introductory Module reference list) provides details of a range of alternative mental health provision.

Jennings (1996) describes the example of services developed in partnership between statutory agencies and Black voluntary sector organizations and their local Black communities. She describes the task of these partnerships as developing more effective services and working across different perspectives, ideologies, values and cultures to develop something that is an alternative to the status quo.

'Just Therapy' is a reflective approach to therapy developed at the Family Centre in New Zealand. Waldegrave (1990a) explains that the approach is termed 'Just' because it indicates a 'just' approach to the client group, using a form of therapy which takes into account gender and cultural, spiritual, social and economic contexts; because the approach attempts to demystify therapy so that it can be practised by a wider range of people whose skills are based on community experience or cultural knowledge, and because it is just, or simply, therapy, leaving out the jargon and conventions of many professional approaches and, Waldegrave maintains, removing a Western cultural bias.

LEARNING OUTCOMES

Trainees should demonstrate:

1. An ability to critically appraise psychological models employed in AMH as they relate to issues of 'race' and culture.
2. An awareness of the complexity of the issues involved in the use of psychometric assessment in AMH.
3. An awareness of service delivery issues as they relate to ethnic and cultural diversity, including an awareness of national and local policy and issues specific to psychological services.

Suggested exercises

Exercise 1: Personal awareness

Aim

Increased awareness of one's own ethnicity.

Instructions
Divide into pairs, interview each other as follows and then discuss as a large group:

- How would you describe your ethnicity?
- What do you see as the advantages and disadvantages of your experiences within your ethnic/cultural group?
- How do you think clients perceive you in terms of your ethnicity?
- How do you think this may affect your therapeutic relationships?

Timings
15 minutes in pairs
30 minutes for large group

Exercise 2: Case discussion and role play

Aim
An opportunity to think about and practice working clinically with a difficult situation during a placement.

Instructions
Role play in groups of three or four with a client (White English), trainee therapist (half of the groups have a dominant group therapist, half have a non-dominant group therapist) and observer(s), using referral provided. Discussion in small groups, then in large group.

Referral: A 28–year-old single, unemployed man is referred by his GP, suffering from anxiety and panic attacks. He previously worked for many years as a motor mechanic. At the beginning of the first session, he says he was expecting to see a male/female doctor (opposite to the sex of the trainee). In explaining his sense of loss (of job, of community), he says his neighbourhood has changed, there are now too many ... (people of the same ethnicity as the trainee).

- How would you negotiate this first meeting?
- What feelings would it generate in you?

- Do you feel you can work with this client?
- What support would you expect from your supervisor and the organization that you are working in?

Timings
10 minutes for role play
10 minutes for small group
30–40 minutes for large group

Annotated reading list

Cochrane, R. and Sashidharan, S.P. (1996) Part 3 in: *Ethnicity and Health: Reviews of Literature and Guidance for Purchasers in the areas of Cardiovascular Disease, Mental Health and Haemoglobinopathies*. Report 5. NHS CRD, Social Policy Research Unit, University of York

This is essential reading. It provides a comprehensive review of the literature up to 1995 covering: demography and epidemiology; a critique of research methodology; the treatment of Black and minority ethnic people within psychiatric services and in Primary Care; discussion of the Eurocentrism of psychiatric concepts and practice and an analysis of current thinking on service delivery. The section on epidemiology should be read in conjunction with Nazroo (1997) – see below.

Dutt, R. and Ferns, P. (1998) *Letting through the Light*. A Training Pack on Black People and Mental Health. London: Race Equality Unit, Department of Health

Aimed at social workers but relevant to clinical psychology. It is practice-focused and each section contains case studies, exercises and good practice suggestions.

Nazroo, J.Y. (1997) *Ethnicity and Mental Health: Findings from the National Community Survey*. London: Policy Studies Institute.

Provides a detailed report of the mental health section of the Fourth National Survey of Ethnic Minorities (PSI, 1993/4). The survey was community-based and comprised a large nationally representative sample. Its findings challenge many of the ideas which have become almost truisms among mental health professionals.

Rawaf, S. and Bahl, V. (1998) *Assessing Health Needs*. London: Royal College of Physicians

This text has chapters on many areas of health and mental health. It provides research data and a range of suggestions about service provision.

Ridley, C.R. (1995) *Overcoming Unintentional Racism in Counseling and Therapy. A Practitioner's Guide to Intervention*. Multicultural Aspects of Counseling, Series 5, Thousand Oaks: Sage,

Provides information on addressing racism within a clinical setting. Written for practitioners and provides specific case examples. Note in particular: Chapter 1, Minority clients as victims; Chapter 3, Definitions of racism; Chapter 4, Models of mental health; Chapter 6, Defensive racial dynamics.

Other useful modules:
Primary Care
Older Adults
Psychosocial Rehabilitation/Long-term needs
Neurosychology
Research

Chapter 11

OLDER ADULTS

Graham Gibson, Vaman Lokare and Kate Tress

DEMOGRAPHIC FACTORS

The existing data for demographic characteristics of the elderly population in Britain are sketchy and the 1991 census fails to provide a breakdown of ethnicity by age. However, large numbers of people now over the age of 65 have a different country of birth than Britain, and have therefore gone through a process of migration.

However, the Fourth National Survey of Ethnic Minorities in Britain, conducted by the Policy Studies Institute (Modood *et al.*, 1997), does provide some useful data. A very high proportion of Asian elders (age 60+) live with a son or daughter compared with 31 per cent of Caribbean elders and only 13 per cent of White elders. Modood *et al.* also report that a large number of minority ethnic people in middle age do not have a parent in this country owing to migration patterns; however, of those who do, 22 per cent of South Asians are reported to care for a parent, while 8 per cent of Caribbeans do so. It is also noted that this pattern of care for a parent by middle-aged children is similar for White and South Asian groups, except that in the Asian group the parent is more likely to be cared for at home.

When it comes to mental health issues, the absence of ethnic monitoring across the NHS until relatively recently means there is a dearth of readily available information before 1994. Studies by Manthorpe and Hettiaratchy (1993), Norman (1988) and Chaudhury and Au (1994) are useful. There are also studies dealing with the health of the minority ethnic elderly in relation to diabetes (Raleigh *et al.*, 1997), coronary heart disease (Balarajan, 1996) and mortality rates (Balarajan, 1997). There are reports from studies carried out in the country of origin of the different groups which may aid us to some extent in the better understanding and planning of services (e.g. Tout, 1993).

THEORY

Although in an American context, Markides and Miranda (1997) provide some useful discussion of issues regarding theory and concepts of relevance to the mental health of ageing populations of minority ethnic origin. The social construction of ageing has particular relevance to thinking about the ways in which one becomes an elder within a given community. The different life expectancies in countries around the world can create different assumptions and expectations of the age at which one becomes old or feels old.

The roles of the older person within a given cultural group may differ, and values associated with ageing may be affected by values held within the dominant culture (Koyano, 1989; Logue, 1990; McGoldrick *et al.*, 1982; Palmore and Maeda, 1985; Shiang, 1986). The language used in different communities to describe old age can reflect the position older people are ascribed within those communities. The degree to which old age is problematized is variable, as is the sense in which it confers status, power or disempowerment.

The idea that the extended family system will inevitably care for its older members needs to be re-examined. The isolation of elders is an increasing problem, whether or not elders are living with their families. It is often the case that children, whose parents have invested in, both financially and emotionally, have been in conflict about adopting the values of their Western education and have embarked on a destiny separate from that of their family and sometimes their community. This can lead to a situation where elderly parents, rightly or not, feel alone and abandoned. The stress for elders living in one society, yet with vivid memories often increased in age of the past society, can take its toll in the form of psychological difficulties. Without understanding these issues, elders from minority ethnic groups seeking psychological help can easily mistakenly be described as 'confused' or in extreme instances labelled as 'mad' depriving them of appropriate help, thus further marginalizing them.

Maintaining identity

Acculturation is the process of maintaining an identity with one's own culture of origin while adapting to the dominant culture. Living together and reacting with the dominant community may have helped to bring about some form of integration. Yet much of it could be superficial when one considers that many immigrants and settlers have within their communities of origin their own religion, culture and beliefs. For some communities such as Bangladeshis, the older generation, particularly women, have not become comfortable in using English and integration for them has been limited. This includes sometimes major limitation even on communication within families, where children and certainly grandchildren may not share a common language with the elders.

Issues about the continuation of marital relations into older age, both at the social and the intimate level, are culturally influenced and shaped and will have a major bearing on clients' expectations both of family relationships and of the kinds of issues they would expect a psychologist to discuss with them. The status of widowhood (increasingly likely with age) also needs to be understood within the relevant cultural frame.

Displacement

Many of the elders who migrated to Britain in their youth cherished the thought of returning home to their country of origin in old age. Some have achieved this, but many in their old age say regretfully that they cannot go back. This can be because there is no one left there, as in the case of political refugees, or because close family, particularly children, have all emigrated. For many older adults, there is a dilemma about returning to their home on the one hand, versus remaining in Britain where the next generation is settled. Isolation increases as friends die and members of the next generation become increasingly preoccupied with their own families. As advancing age brings with it physical restrictions, the adaptability required for living within a dominant culture decreases. Possible difficulties with recent memory can leave distant memories intact. This could mean the exile is re-exiled, traumas of the refugee experiences are relived and displacement is re-enacted. Stresses and psychological problems within the elderly population can also be conceptualized as a tension between the wishes and hopes associated with the original migration experience and the restrictions imposed on them by the realities of membership of a minority group.

Preparation for death

This is closely tied in with philosophy of life, religion, culture and life experiences. Different approaches, attitudes and beliefs about death and the after-life vary in different minority ethnic groups and, of course, among individuals. Similarly, the anticipatory periods of mourning range across a spectrum from suppression and denial to acceptance and elaborate preparation. The possibilities for incorrectly attributing certain preparatory stances towards death and pathologizing them within a diagnostic framework need to be carefully addressed. The importance of cultural information, and the necessity for the psychologist to carefully check its relevance for the individual client and family, should not be underestimated. Parkes *et al.* (1997) provide a useful account of major world systems of beliefs and rituals around death and bereavement although, as with many such texts, their examples should not be taken as definitive and should be checked out carefully with the client or family.

METHODS OF TEACHING

1. Lectures on theoretical topics.
2. Videotaped material, for example television programmes about older adults experiencing racism, growing up in the UK, the dearth of National Health Service and Local Authority provision for different cultural groups.
3. Role plays, for example playing an older person from the trainee's own culture with a view to exploring trainees' assumptions.
4. Trainees to do a family of origin exercise/family tree in order to look at their own cultural heritage with a particular focus on roles and relationships of older people in the family.
5. Visits to cultural centres and day centres to learn from older adults about their issues. This can help the trainee to understand the breadth of cultural differences, including those found in routine day-to-day activities.

6.   Discussion of vignettes of interaction or stories from clients to explore issues pertinent to older adults from minority ethnic groups.
7.   Every effort should be made to enable trainees to interview a family with older adults of a different colour, ethnic background and religion from their own, with a view to helping trainees learn about a culture different from their own.
8.   As part of the clinical placement requirements, trainees should work with a minimum number of clients from different cultural/ethnic backgrounds to their own.

PRACTICE

Assessment

1.   Awareness of possible referrer bias, cultural stereotyping (see Wilson and MacCarthy, 1994).
2.   Where there is a lack of shared understanding between the trainee and client/family about the nature of the presenting problem, there should be an appropriate use of compromise to further the therapeutic endeavour. This may require an appreciation of the power relationships within the family and between the client/family and the professional network.
3.   Developing a critique of psychometric assessment in populations on which they are not standardized, and where standardized, examining the tools for their cultural relevance (see also the module on Neuropsychology for a more detailed account).
4.   Assessment to include a consideration of the wider networks around the client.

Interviewing skills

1.   Being able to understand, respect and address individual and cultural differences during a therapeutic session. This includes developing a method for acquiring knowledge about the family's or client's culture.
2.   Developing skills and awareness about working with a family when not all the members speak the trainee's language, thus working with an interpreter. Being aware of issues when a younger person or child has been used to interpret for an older adult.
3.   Exploring with the client or family their cultural and familial beliefs about the presenting problem and about old age, including religious precepts where relevant.
4.   Becoming aware of the social, political and spiritual implications of asking particular types of questions: e.g. sexual functioning, questioning male/female roles, dependence in old age, questions relating to immigration status, inappropriate use of interpreter or family member to discuss personal/sensitive questions.
5.   Examining prompt material used in reminiscence work for its cultural

specificity, and broadening the range of such material. Encourage clients to bring their own material.

Intervention

1. The adjustment of existing intervention approaches in a culturally sensitive way.
2. The exploriation with clients/families of how psychological interventions might be reformulated and accommodated as a healing process which is culturally relevant for the particular client.
3. The integration of psychological and social interventions, e.g. use of community resources as a site for meeting clients.
4. The production of culturally meaningful written communications to older adults and their families.

SERVICE DELIVERY

1. Making trainees aware of the need for delivery of a culturally competent service to older adults within their own locale, including the need for the staff profile of the service to reflect the community it serves.
2. Developing an awareness of the need to address racism, as it affects referral, service delivery and therapeutic outcomes.
3. Liaising with other professionals and voluntary agencies who are attuned to the needs of older adults from specific ethnic groups.
4. Finding out ways to both use (without exploiting) and support existing community resources aimed at the welfare of older adults, e.g. co-working so as not to 're-invent the wheel' or imply that new services will be better than existing ones.
5. Learning about the process of consulting and being accountable to potential service users for meeting the needs of older adults.
6. Exploring how to make the service accessible to the local community and to all sections in it, e.g. basing part of the service in suitable outreach locations including the use of home-based work.
7. Understanding different methods for the promotion of clinical psychology services to all communities.

LEARNING OUTCOMES

1. The trainee will be able to develop an understanding and acknowledgement of their own beliefs, assumptions and attitudes about old age and cultural difference.
2. The trainee will have an understanding of the different ways of carrying out an assessment which is appropriate to their clients' culture.
3. The trainee will be able to use his/her understanding of the racism experienced by people to have a fuller appreciation of the problems being experienced by clients.
4. The trainee will have an appreciation of ageing, attitudes to ageing and

family life-cycles across different cultures.

5.   The trainee will be developing the sensitivity and flexibility which are conducive to working with families from ethnicities different to their own.

6.   The trainee will have an understanding of the personal therapeutic and professional issues when working with cultural difference. They will also have the confidence and competency to help alleviate the difficulties encountered.

7.   The trainee will have an appreciation of the clinical relevance of individual differences, life experiences, responses to illness and responses to therapeutic interventions, within the context of culture.

Suggested exercises

Exercise 1 'When I am old'

Aim
To orientate the participants to old age and to link this experience with their own culture.

Instructions
Everyone is asked to sit silently and mentally add 40 years on to their own age and to think about what will be happening in their lives and relationships then. If they wish they can make notes or doodle or perhaps draw a picture of what they might look like. Once they have done this they are asked to think in silence about a song, story, poem or film from their own culture (or family?) about old age. They should try to link the second part of the task to the first. The group should then choose a way of feeding back their thoughts and feelings to the larger group for further discussion. Once there has been a good airing of the themes, trainers should lead a discussion about how they will find out what people from cultures other than their own might think about in relation to old age.

Timings
At least 10–15 minutes for the first part of the exercise
Approximately 10 minutes for the second part
At least 25 minutes for feedback discussion
Approximately 15 minutes for trainer-led discussion

Alternatively, the exercise can be conducted over more than one session.

Exercise 2 ' I had a dream'

Aim
To enable trainees to think about different ways in which members of cultural groups, other than the dominant culture, might have arrived in this country. To further their understanding of how dreams might have been fulfilled and how they were thwarted and what dreams are still alive.

Instructions
Imagine that you are asked to tell those members of your family, who are not living where you are now, what it is like. If you have never 'moved', imagine that you did and try to tell your family what your new place is like. Focus first on the hopes you have for the life you are leading in your new place. Then focus on the difficulties you are facing being a stranger in this place.

Discuss in pairs.

Now imagine that your grandmother or grandfather (or other older family member) came with you to this place, and then describe what it is like for them to be here.

Discuss in pairs.

Select four items that belong to an older member of your family which you think might have special significance to them, things they would not want to lose or that they might want to keep with them wherever they lived. Why did you choose those four items and how would you explain to a person from another culture why they are important?

Discuss these ideas in pairs.

Timing
25 minutes for the exercise
20 minutes for feedback to the large group

Exercise 3 'Finding out'

Aim
To help trainees develop a number of different ways of finding out about older people from a culture other than their own.

Instructions
Trainees are to get into groups of four and brainstorm a number of different ways of finding out about older people in a cultural community other than their own.

Possible areas to 'find out' about:

- customs
- possible positions in the family
- ways in which respect is shown to them
- possible rituals in relation to being in the oldest generation
- fables, myths and stories about old age in the culture they have chosen
- institutions, if any, for elders in the culture
- anything else that interests the group

The group should then discuss the advantages and pitfalls of finding out in each of the ways raised. This could either be in the form of a debate or a general discussion.

If it is possible to integrate this exercise over two sessions of teaching, trainees should spend the time between the first and second sessions 'finding out'. They should bring back to the group the result of their endeavours, including an account of the successes and difficulties encountered in the methodologies they chose.

Timing
The first part of the exercise could be approximately an hour, or longer if part 2 is not feasible.
The second part of the exercise could be two hours or conducted as an assignment.

ANNOTATED REFERENCES

(Contributor: Afreen Huq)

Arean, P.A. and Gallagher-Thompson, D. (1996) Issues and recommendations for the recruitment and retention of older minority ethnic adults into clinical research. *Journal of Consulting and Clinical Psychology*, 64, 5, 875–880.

The available literature indicates that treatment of mental disorders offsets mortality, morbidity and poor quality of life in senior citizens. This article discusses successful techniques for recruiting and retaining older adults in research studies, a matter which is relevant for clinicians as well.

Chaudhury, S. and Au, A. (1994) The usage of the Mental Health Service by the elderly from ethnic minorities. *PSIGE Newsletter*, June, 50, 40–43.

Useful for service provision considerations.

Manthorpe, J. and Hettiaratchy, P. (1993) Minority ethnic elders in the UK. *International Review of Psychiatry, 5*, 171–178.

Highlights factors that may lead to higher risk of psychological morbidity in older immigrants.

Markides, K.S. and Miranda, M.R. (Eds.) (1997) *Minorities, Aging and Health*. Thousand Oaks: Sage

Chapters 11 and 12 focus on mental health issues.

Redelinghys, J. and Shah, A. (1997) The characteristics of ethnic elders from the Indian sub-continent using a geriatric psychiatry service in West London. *Aging and Mental Health, 1*, 3, 243–247.

This is a cross-cultural comparative study that examined the demographic, social and clinical characteristics of Indian sub-continent origin elders with mental illness. This particular service was well established and designed to be sensitive to needs of ethnic groups, by specifically employing bilingual workers and an Indian Community Psychiatric Nurse (CPN), and locating its dementia day hospital and CPN base in the community close to this group. Seventeen per cent of the patients in the study were of Indian origin compared to 7 per cent in the general population (Ealing Council, 1995). Compared with indigenous elders, ethnic elders were younger, had more children, had more people living in their household and were more likely to have schizophrenia. There were no differences with regard to use of health and social service resources between the two groups.

Silveira, E.R. and Ebrahim, S. (1998) Social determinants of psychiatric morbidity and wellbeing in immigrant elders and whites in East London. *International Journal of Geriatric Psychiatry, 13*, 801–812.

The outcome of the study appears to support a 'multiple jeopardy' theory of ageing in minority elders in East London.

Other useful modules
Neuropsychology
Adult Mental Health

Chapter 12

LEARNING DISABILITIES

Sandra Baum, Zenobia Nadirshaw and John Newland

Introduction

This module aims to develop the knowledge, skills, attitudes and values relevant to the professional practice of psychologists who work with people with learning disabilities from Black and minority ethnic backgrounds. It takes a life-span developmental perspective and focuses on personal and societal reactions to these groups, exploring their marginalized role and devalued status. It also offers a framework for understanding the lives and experiences of Black and minority ethnic learning disabled people as a doubly disadvantaged group in society, in terms of the processes by which these groups and their carers find themselves in subordinate positions and at the receiving end of little or no appropriate services (Nadirshaw, 1997, and in press). This is commonly referred to as 'double discrimination' (Baxter *et al.*, 1990).

THEORY

The Mental Health Foundation (1996) estimates that 2 per cent of the UK population, over one million, have learning disabilities. The majority of these cases are mild, and fewer than 50 per cent of these will ever have been identified by educational, or health, or other authorities as impaired intellectual ability. Within the general population, it is estimated that 4 in 1,000 people (over 200,000 people) have severe learning disabilities, of which 50,000 are under 16 years of age. Proportionally more males (54 per cent) than females (46 per cent) are affected. Studies suggest that up to 25 per cent of those with severe learning disabilities are profoundly affected, often with multiple disorders.

Despite the fact that at least three million people from mixed and minority ethnic backgrounds are living in this country, no national data exists for the incidence and prevalence of learning disability among the Black and minority ethnic communities (Emerson and Hatton, 1999). Local studies, however, have provided useful but controversial information. Azmi *et al.*'s study (1996) in North West England found the prevalence rate of severe learning disabilities in children and young adults between 5 and 34 years of age to be approximately three times greater in the Asian than in the non-Asian communities. This picture is consistent with the relatively young age profile of the Asian population as a whole. Comparing these figures with other case registers confirms, at least on a small scale, an increased prevalence of learning disabilities (including severe learning disabilities) among the Asian communities. Theories commonly advanced are: marriages among first cousins (consanguinity); a higher incidence of syndromes (for example rubella) that cause disabilities and general effects of social and educational deprivation, poverty, environmental pollution, lack of knowledge about and unfamiliarity with methods of genetic counselling, and poorer ante-natal services and maternal health care (Baxter, 1998).

Unfortunately, no such figures exist for the African-Caribbean communities although a recently funded Department of Health project refers impressionistically to high levels of autism in learning disabled African-Caribbean children (CVS, 1998). Field studies in this project describe a process whereby there has been an increased awareness of autism (and its diagnosis) in the general population as a whole with the consequence that a significant number of Black Caribbean communities are coming forward for guidance and support regarding this condition. Epidemiological data in the general Black population suggest that increased life expectancy of this population, ageing parents and family/carers, increased survival rates of children with severe and complex disabilities are likely to increase the demand for residential provision in the next two decades.

At the heart of every service is a professional ethos and ideology. The concepts and ideas of normalization and social role valorization (Wolfensberger, 1983) have had a profound impact upon the way services are organized, delivered and managed. The overall principles are based on the belief that people with learning disabilities (like other devalued people) have the same rights as others and should be socially accepted and valued like other non-handicapped people. The argument being that learning disabled people must be encouraged to adopt the culture, expectations, attitudes and behaviours of the 'dominant' society. This presupposes many judgements: for example, that the current values held within mainstream British society are worth aspiring to and that these values are pertinent, appropriate and useful to *all* individuals. The pressure to 'fit' into the dominant norms and value systems, with very little choice to stand out and be counted, is a reality for many learning disabled, including Black, people. It appears that value is conferred only on people who look, behave and perform within an established norm (Ferns, 1992). The damaging effects on Black and minority ethnic learning disabled people that relinquishing their 'differentness' (of diet, clothing, appearance, lifestyle, family grouping) brings is not truly understood. The goals selected via the individual programme planning system are a good example of this pressure. Decision making and authority still arguably rest mainly in the hands of White people who on the whole cater to the needs and wishes of the 'dominant' society's values and belief system. Service providers need to be aware of this.

PRACTICE

Trainees need to relate the above to the history of oppression and discrimination experienced by learning disabled people (Williams, 1989) and the resulting devaluation that occurs in Black and minority ethnic learning disabled people and their carers. Some of the effects are:

- The colour blind approach which treats 'everyone the same' thereby denying them suitable and relevant services according to preferred identified need.
- Discrimination, which may lead to the exclusion from appropriate treatment and interventions provided within mainstream service provision.
- Negative attitude towards Black staff and carers (Azmi *et al.*, 1996).
- Stigmatization, loss of self-esteem, confusion in identity and group belongingness, stereotyping and labelling.

Trainees need to critically evaluate the normalization/social role valorization principle using Ferns's (1992) anti-racist perspective and assess the impact of it on the lives of Black and minority ethnic people with learning disabilities and their carers.

LEARNING OUTCOMES

Trainees should:

- Explore the issue that 'double discrimination' is not the result of neutral, objective intentions in the human and welfare system but the result of selective experience and interest of institutions and organizations.
- Explore how many Black and minority ethnic learning disabled people become trapped in a disadvantaged and inequality cycle as a result of the triple disadvantage of disability, poverty and racism.
- Develop an awareness of the general inequalities in health for Black and minority ethnic groups and to be clear of what they are and how they arise in the Black and minority ethnic learning disabled person's life.
- Be aware of the psychological impact and its consequences on the Black and minority ethnic learning disabled person (for example, the effects of labelling and oppression) and the resulting devaluation that occurs as a member of an oppressed group
- Be able to critique the core themes and principles underlying normalization and social role valorization using a race equality perspective.
- Develop an interest in pursuing inclusive research at individual and organizational levels. For example, the barriers to access as experienced by Black and minority ethnic learning disabled people and their carers; levels of knowledge and attitudes about learning disability issues (including genetic counselling); the empowerment and experiences of Black staff within statutory and non-statutory organizations.

SERVICE POLICY AND SERVICE DELIVERY

Theory

After many years of neglect, the debate on community care is slowly beginning to recognize the potential significance of ethnicity in formulating policy and the need for both policy and action to respond to the multiethnic nature of British society. *The Health of the Nation* document (1995) and *Signposts for Success* (Department of Health, 1998) gave recognition to the fact that 'people from different cultural backgrounds may have particular care needs and problems'. Local health and local authority commissioners and service providers were charged with addressing the specific needs of this client group. However, actual practice in many areas still remains colour-blind (Nadirshaw, 1991a, 1997, 1998a and in press).

There is general agreement among service providers that there is a low uptake of services by families and people with learning disabilities from Black and minority ethnic communities (Begum, 1995). Barriers to service uptake and utilization include language and communication difficulties, lack of appropriate information and translated materials, lack of sensitivity to cultural and religious needs, racism in service delivery and negative past experiences on the part of the learning disabled person and their family.

Recently, there has been greater emphasis placed on making services more accessible and applicable by, for example, employing Punjabi-speaking members of community teams (Ellahi, 1992) and also by asking people who use services to write about their experiences, the things that need to change and their efforts to create change (Thompson, 1991). Additionally, there are practical guides for good practice in addressing 'race' and disability issues for statutory and voluntary organizations (Begum, 1995) and checklists for health service providers to become sensitive to the range of needs of Black and minority ethnic people with severe learning disabilities (Nadirshaw, 1997 and in press).

The needs, wants and wishes of this group based on their own unique life circumstances and aspirations are frequently not addressed, often leading to marginalized and segregated 'specialist' services. This results in mainstream service providers on the whole remaining unconfident and unskilled in working with families whose norms, circumstances and experiences may differ significantly from their own. Nadirshaw (1998b) highlights the deficiency contained within the community care framework for Black and minority ethnic learning disabled people. For example, Black families are not conversant about their rights within this legislation. They have no real understanding of the community care management process, the criteria used for eligibility for services or about the divide between the health and social care context of service provision and roles of learning disability team members.

Practice

It is important for trainees to understand how the needs of Black and minority ethnic learning disabled people become marginalized, segregated, ignored or assumed to be the same as their White peers. 'Diversity' and 'difference' become compartmentalized and classified as 'special'. Their needs are not 'special', only different. Services must recognize and positively value that 'differentness' (Nadirshaw, 1998a).

Since no national data currently exist about the characteristics and circumstances of Black and minority ethnic families in Britain, the need and demand for such services remains hidden and unacknowledged. Trainees could conduct small-scale studies within their local catchment area to explore how the need and demand for services to the Black and minority ethnic learning disability population within the local population could be matched.

Trainees need to understand the lack of real impact of community care legislation and its process of assessing needs. Black and minority ethnic learning disabled people and their carers, like other groups, may not truly appreciate the importance of the process, the distinction between purchasers and providers, the different rules and responsibilities of the statutory sectors, their rights within the complaints process and procedure, etc. In view of this, trainees may need to practice and rehearse the skills of advocacy with individual families or with the Black voluntary sector in their local communities.

Learning outcomes

1.   Trainees to be aware of the practical guides and checklists for good practice in addressing 'race' and disability issues for statutory and non-statutory sectors (Begum, 1995; Nadirshaw, 1997).
2.   Trainees to have an awareness of the barriers to service utilization for Black and minority ethnic learning disabled people and their carers as a result of:
     •   Lack of information about available services
     •   Irrelevant and meaningless procedures of many existing day and residential services
     •   Suspicion/fear/stress related to using services (Baxter *et al.*, 1990)
     •   Lack of understanding of the community care assessment of need (Nadirshaw, 1998b)
3.   Trainees to be aware of the role, responsibility and impact of health and social services departments and the voluntary sector in developing appropriate and sensitive services for this group: for example, staff training, 'user friendly' day and residential and respite services, better identification of need, demand and supply, staff and support for Black groups (Ahmed and Webb-Johnson, 1995).

ASSESSMENT

Theory

Traditional procedures for assessing people with learning disabilities have been criticized in recent years, for example, by defining what is lacking in social competence and skills rather than emphasizing the positives (Brechin and Swain,

1988). The inadequacies of such assessment procedures become even more apparent when applied to Black and minority ethnic people with learning disabilities. Such assessments are often based on White British norms and may include 'racial stereotyping, inappropriate cultural approaches and language' (Baxter, 1998; Nadirshaw, 1991b in press).

Assessment procedures now adopt a holistic approach which takes into consideration all aspects of the person's life and their specific needs, while facilitating satisfying life-styles and relationships (Brechin and Swain, 1988; Pitt, 1987). Clearly, assessment procedures must take into account the specific needs of Black and minority ethnic people with learning disabilities and recognize the impact that these procedures may have on families.

Practice

- It is important that all assessment procedures are critically evaluated for stereotypes and cultural bias within the interviewing and psychometric testing situation.
- It is essential to recognize the part that racism plays in Black and minority ethnic people's lives and how this may impact on the assessment procedure.
- People with learning disabilities who are bilingual or cannot speak English should be given the opportunity to speak in their preferred language to find out their views and opinions.
- Trained interpreters should be used whenever possible with families whose first language is not English to ensure that everyone can express their opinion without being misunderstood.
- Families and the person with learning disabilities should be asked about their past experience of assessment and what their understanding is of this procedure. Families should be encouraged to talk about themselves, their cultural background and their needs. Assumptions about what is 'best' for them should be avoided.

Learning outcome

To be able to carry out a holistic assessment of the needs of a person with learning disabilities which takes into account the impact of a person's ethnicity and culture (see Groth-Marmat, 1990).

PRE-SCHOOL CHILDREN WITH LEARNING DISABILITIES

Theory

The prevalence of learning disability among minority ethnic children (particularly Asians) appears to be higher than among White children (Akinsola and Fryer 1986; Emerson *et al.*, 1997). The literature on Black and minority ethnic pre-school children with learning disabilities tends to focus on the implications for the family rather than on the child. The emphasis on the family, which is similar to extant work within White populations, fails to address the additional stresses faced by Black and minority ethnic families. Quine and Pahl's (1989) study of how families respond to a child with severe learning disabilities is useful, but the stressful effects of direct and indirect racism are not examined. Similarly, Azmi *et al.*'s study (1996) indicates that Asian carers' stress levels are three times greater than that reported in other studies of carers with learning disabled people. Davis and Russell (1989) provide a comparison between physical and learning disability in an Asian community. Beh-Pajooh (1991) provides an analysis of social relationships within an integrated playgroup. Overall, the clinical psychology literature within the area is scant.

Practice

How parents are told of their child's learning disability at birth can affect their perceptions and expectations of their child's development and their attitude to learning disabilities (Fatimilehin and Nadirshaw, 1994; Shah, 1998). The skills of psychologists would be useful in working within antenatal services and genetic counselling to reduce the risks of certain abnormalities.

The need to consult with both experienced professionals and local organizations (typically in the voluntary sector) is critical. The avoidance of a priori assumptions is essential. An examination of the referred family structures and functions should be part of the preliminary assessment, with the quality of the family support services being within the purview of the assessment. Attitudes towards the learning disabled child and their condition need to be explored (Fatimilehin and Nadirshaw, 1994).

The assessment methods for individual children may use play as the medium. There are a significant number of culturally bound items within most assessment materials and these should be identified and the results qualified. For example, the use of culinary equipment is culturally dependent. Assessments involving dolls are likely to require prior thought and preparation. Given that psychological assessments may be conducted within the home environment, specific sensitivity should be exercised in both arranging and conducting domiciliary appointments.

When considering the range of potential psychological interventions, the following should be observed:

- The way in which the family relates the presence of a disabled child to other areas of their life (e.g. religious observance) should be incorporated into the decision-making process.
- The effects of the intervention should be monitored not only in terms of family functioning but also in the delivery (or not) of services. For example, there may be higher rates of psychological distress in Black and minority ethnic families as a consequence of poor uptake of locally provided respite services that are not responsive to cultural needs.
- An intervention which focuses only on the parental relationship may miss

the wider context. One parent may disagree with using an inappropriately provided service, while the other may not. However, an intervention aimed at providing a suitable respite service may significantly ameliorate the perceived dysfunctional parental relationship.

Learning outcome

To examine a commonly used assessment for pre-school children and identify culturally ambiguous items. Explore the impact of removing these items on the assessment.

THE SCHOOL AGE CHILD WITH LEARNING DISABILITIES

Theory

Baxter *et al.* (1990) provide a comprehensive chapter on issues concerning the school age child from Black and minority ethnic families. It concentrates on assessment procedures, education, home–school liaison, respite care and transition to adulthood, highlighting the following:

- The Advisory Centre for Education (1989) recommends that authorities should ensure that a 'competent bilingual professional' is involved in the assessment proceedings throughout, all materials used should be translated and meetings should be arranged where parents who have children with learning disabilities can meet to discuss common concerns.
- Two major concerns about educational services offered to children are: the misplacement of Black and minority ethnic children in special schools or other segregated services such as special units; and, inappropriate service provision owing to the lack of appreciation for an individual's different cultural and social needs. The curriculum content may not reflect minority cultures and teaching pupils in English may add to their learning disabilities. Racist stereotypes and overt racism may be common in schools and should be recognized. Educational services could ensure that all teachers are trained in the anti-racist approach and that Black and minority ethnic teachers are proportionally represented in all schools.
- To increase home liaison contact, all information and communication should be translated into relevant languages. Also, Black and/or bilingual home–school liaison teachers provide an invaluable resource to schools and are crucial in building links with parents.
- In respite care schemes throughout Britain, Black and minority ethnic families are less likely to be involved than their White peers. Some of the reasons for low take up of services are information and communication difficulties; parents' concerns about how Black children will be looked after and the availability of Black carers and professionals to service schemes.
- Baxter *et al.* (1990) argue that during the 'adolescent period' there may be a conflict of expectations between White staff and Black and minority ethnic

parents as to what is appropriate behaviour. Families may expect children to ease into adulthood by taking on responsibilities from an early age rather than adopting 'carefree rebellion' sometimes associated with the White majority culture. Leaving home and living independently also need to be considered sensitively (Chevannes and Tait, 1997; Azmi *et al.*, 1997).

Practice

When working with Black and minority ethnic school age children and their families, psychologists should seek the assistance of bilingual co-workers to advise and support parents, and to encourage them to become more involved in their child's education, as appropriate. Psychologists should always be aware that information and communication difficulties might be an important factor in parental under-involvement in school activities and put them in contact with relevant schemes and organizations to redress the balance. Clear advice should be provided on the process of statementing as a statutory requirement to parents who may not understand the complex and highly bureaucratic assessment and review procedures. Parents may believe that 'special' education means 'better quality' than that in general schools.

Learning outcomes

1. To have an awareness of some of the barriers and obstacles that may prevent Black and minority ethnic parents from being involved in activities and organizations in the education environments.
2. To gain knowledge about local schemes and organizations which can support parents and provide services for respite care, home–school liaison and transition to adulthood initiatives (Reading/CVS, 1998; Reading, 1999).

ADULTS WITH LEARNING DISABILITIES

Key themes are considered in this section.

1. Sexuality and sex education

Theory

The particular needs of Black and minority ethnic people with learning disabilities in relation to sexuality have received little attention in literature. Many ideas presented in the form of sex education are culturally insensitive, particularly to Muslims (Compton, 1989), and do not reflect the values and experiences of Black and minority ethnic people. Baxter (1994) highlights the historical and social assumptions relating to sexuality and Black communities, exploring issues of racism and sexual stereotyping. She also reviews the values and dangers of cultural information, offering suggestions for improving professional practice in teaching and counselling people with learning disabilities and their families from Black and minority ethnic communities.

Practice

Some issues to consider in clinical practice are as follows:

- The influence of culture in relation to attitudes about premarital sex, marriage, parenthood and the role and function of the family must be addressed when working with people with learning disabilities and their families from Black and minority ethnic communities. For example, sometimes it may be important to consult extended family members on issues such as counselling and on matters regarding sexual relations, particularly as conventions may exist about what is discussed outside the family or between men and women. Religious requirements of modesty may make it necessary to have counsellors of the same sex (Baxter, 1994).
- Sex education materials may not necessarily reflect the experiences and values of Black and minority ethnic people, perpetuating inappropriate approaches in the treatment of sexuality with this client group (Baxter, 1994).
- There will always be a range of diversity of individual viewpoints in relation to sexuality. Christopher (1980) suggests openly asking what a person's views are on various subjects such as birth control, while acknowledging that their religion may be particularly important in shaping their views.

Learning outcomes

Trainees should demonstrate:

1. Awareness of the relationship between racism and sexual stereotyping and how they shape perceptions, attitudes and behaviour in relation to people with learning disabilities.
2. An ability to be culturally sensitive and inoffensive in relation to sexuality when teaching and counselling people with learning disabilities from Black and minority ethnic families.

2. Challenging behaviour

Theory

A small number of people with learning disabilities may exhibit behaviour which is so challenging that services may have extreme difficulty in meeting their needs. Black and minority ethnic people may have additional difficulties which contribute to their behaviour being labelled as 'challenging'. First, they are less likely to be heard, understood or have their needs and wishes responded to by service providers. These problems may be compounded by language difficulties. Second, owing to cultural differences non-verbal behaviour may be misread as challenging. Sometimes, the experience of being racially harassed or stigmatized by the local community because of ethnicity and having learning disabilities may cause extra problems for families. Finally, in Britain, Black and minority ethnic people are often viewed stereotypically as a threat. Black people are at a higher risk of being diagnosed as having a challenging mental illness with a large proportion being misdiagnosed, their normal signs of distress being misinterpreted as mental illness (Littlewood and Lipsedge, 1982). Within services for people with learning disabilities these views and images result in Black and minority ethnic people being labelled as posing a challenge to the service system (see Baxter *et al.*, 1990, for a fuller discussion).

Practice

It is important to understand the reasons for a person's challenging behaviour and to gain insight of the situation from their perspective. Psychologists must be aware of the prevalence of stereotypes and the likelihood that people from Black and ethnic communities who are described as challenging are more likely to be subjected to a 'pathological' perspective, as though there were something inherently wrong with them, rather than to a contextual perspective that examines the wider system and contexts within which the behaviour is operating.

Learning outcomes

In relation to Black and minority ethnic people, trainees should be able to:

1. Interview a person who is labelled as challenging, as well as their family. They should be able to identify whether they experienced any of the above additional difficulties that led to their behaviour being seen as challenging.
2. Conduct a functional analysis of a person's challenging behaviour, which takes into account the impact of a person's 'race' and culture.

3. Advocacy

Theory

Advocacy involves speaking up for and supporting a person or issue to the benefit of the individual or groups of individuals concerned. Several forms of advocacy are necessary and important to safeguard the interests of people with learning disabilities. Citizen advocacy and self-advocacy are particularly important.

In relation to citizen advocacy and people with learning disabilities from Black and minority ethnic communities, the following issues must be addressed:

- There should be appropriate matching of advocate and partner. Black and minority ethnic people may be better able to represent the interests of Black and minority ethnic service users.
- Recruitment drives through the ethnic press and media should be encouraged to increase volunteers from Black and minority ethnic backgrounds.

Information and images about schemes to aid this process should reflect all service users' ethnic backgrounds.

- Schemes should recognize and build an informal advocacy, which may already exist in Black and minority ethnic communities. Community teams could actively develop links with the Black voluntary sector.
- Where organizations have 'Black advocate/White partner' schemes, there needs to be an awareness and acknowledgement of problems that the advocate may experience and challenges to any racism experienced by the advocate.

In relation to self-advocacy the following issues must be addressed:

- Services need to ensure that there is separate time and space for self-advocacy groups for Black and minority ethnic service users (Black People First, 1994).
- Service users may need to develop general skills of self-confidence and assertiveness.

Practice

- Black people who become advocates for White people may face difficulties, including racism. These problems must be acknowledged and the organization must provide appropriate support (Baxter *et al.*, 1990).
- Experienced and committed advocates may still encounter problems when faced with powerful professionals who may not appreciate the issues confronting Black and minority ethnic people when they use and access services for people with learning disabilities, including the system of community care plans. (Nadirshaw, 1998b).

Black, minority ethnic and White advocates should receive training in racism awareness, anti-racist principles and on how to obtain views of Black service users (McIver, 1994).

Black and minority ethnic service users should be encouraged to speak up for themselves and any intervention programme should always include developing self-confidence and assertiveness skills.

- Co-ordinators of citizen advocacy, advocates and service users should be involved in the teaching of clinical psychologists.

Learning outcome

Trainees should demonstrate an awareness of what citizen advocacy and self-advocacy are and the importance of considering 'race' and culture when matching advocate and partner.

4. Bereavement

Theory

For the majority White British cultures, dying and bereavement are sometimes viewed as a personal, private affair involving close family and friends. These expectations may not be similar for all communities, with marked cultural differences, beliefs and expectations existing regarding bereavement (Baxter *et al.*, 1990).

In relation to people with learning disabilities, the commonly held view is that they do not have similar emotional needs to others. Their feelings are often ignored or misinterpreted and their grief is not acknowledged (Oswin, 1981). People from Black and minority ethnic groups who have learning disabilities may have additional difficulties during this period, particularly if they attend local statutory and voluntary facilities, where there might be a danger that their rituals, beliefs and traditions will not be respected. These issues may be exacerbated if, as a result of bereavement, the person with learning disabilities has to move away from the family home, particularly when they come from a culture where living away from one's family and community is unusual and rare. For these families 'there may be strong family ties, a feeling of responsibility as well as personal experience of racism and aberration in society' which may exacerbate the usual fear of seeing one's relative move to alternative accommodation (Baxter *et al.*, 1990).

Practice

Sensitivity to the bereaved person's beliefs and traditions at this time is imperative. Detailed information from the person's family (or significant others who are sensitive to the person's culture) should be gathered regarding established routines, norms and experiences to maintain as much continuity as possible.

Trainees should ask families and the person with learning disabilities to describe what has happened to them, their understanding of what death is and what their rituals are for grieving. This information will be important to ensure practical support for the bereaved person with learning disabilities to mark their mourning by engaging in culturally and personally meaningful activities.

Learning outcomes

Trainees should demonstrate an ability to:

1. Be culturally sensitive when supporting people with learning disabilities and their families from Black and minority ethnic communities in relation to dying and bereavement.
2. Liaise with statutory, voluntary or private agencies which provide services for the bereaved person with learning disabilities to ensure that they understand and can support the beliefs, traditions and rituals of the person during this period.

OLDER ADULTS WITH LEARNING DISABILITIES
Theory

There is a paucity of published research relating to the provision of psychological service for Black and minority ethnic older people with learning disabilities. These complex issues are not just those of possible marginalization within an already marginal service for older people with learning disabilities, but also incorporate the additional psychological stress from both direct and indirect forms of racism.

At the basic level, respect and concern for the individual should be expressed in consideration of linguistic and cultural factors especially when psychological assessments are employed. Using interpreters does not obviate the need for more sophisticated procedures. For example, Sakauye (1990) showed that the paraphrasing done by interpreters often leads to confusion and miscommunication. The consequences are more pronounced for Black and minority ethnic older people given that many individuals will be living with others (possibly relatives) who are currently providing support. The same carers will potentially have a significant influence in the outcomes. Given that values, religious beliefs, assumptions about the causation of diseases, and attitudes about medication and other health interventions all vary greatly, these factors need to be carefully investigated and weighed in developing the therapeutic alliance, in generating hypotheses and in the psychological formulation.

Practice

Trainees should be aware of the changing nature of cultural values and norms of the older person. The older person from Black and minority ethnic backgrounds may be aware of the loss of identity and their status in the family and will require emotional support.

Learning outcome

Trainees should be able to state three assumptions commonly employed in psychological formulations relating to Black and minority ethnic older people with learning disabilities and demonstrate how their validity can be assessed.

Suggested exercise

A care manager telephones your community team. She is looking for respite accommodation for two young people (one brother and one sister) who are 18 and 21 respectively, who would prefer to be placed together. Both are described as having severe learning disabilities and as 'coming from Pakistan'. The brother has a hearing loss and respiratory problems.

The sister displays difficult behaviours such as throwing objects around the floor when demands are made of her. The parents are 'going home' for three to four months as the maternal grandmother has just died. They have sought the help of Social Services via a friend who speaks English. The children have never received any statutory care. The care manager asks the community team for an opinion regarding the care needs of these two young people.

Questions to consider:
- What information might you need as a member of the learning disabilities team?
- What assessment would you carry out to assist the care manager in identifying the best resource and service provision?
- What problems might you encounter in undertaking the above?
- How would you and the community learning disabilities team help the parents? If not, why not? And if so, how?

Instructions
In small groups, read the vignette above and discuss the above questions for 20 minutes. As a large group, discuss the answers based on the aims of the exercise.

Aims
To enable trainees to explore:

- Stereotypes and assumptions about people 'from Pakistan.'
- Advantages and disadvantages of using a trained interpreter in conducting an assessment at home.
- The role of the psychologist in the assessment of the children's needs
- To identify the care plan and what additional 'extras' might be needed

Endnote
The module highlights the relative lack of inclusive research in the area, arguably a reflection of the status accorded to Black and minority ethnic learning disabled people and their families. It seeks to ensure that psychologists themselves do not become another barrier within service structures. It concludes with the need for further and more detailed understandings of the complex interplay between the activity of the psychologist and the organizational structure which itself may be subject to institutionalized racism.

Acknowledgements
With thanks to the publication by Baxter, C., Poonia, K., Ward, L. and Nadirshaw, Z. (1990). *Double Discrimination. Issues and Services for people with Learning Difficulties from Black and Minority ethnic Communities.* King's Fund/Commission For Racial Equality, December – a major contributor to our ideas. Also to Rosey Singh, Clinical Psychologist from the Eastbourne Community NHS Trust.

Chapter 13

PRIMARY CARE

Sue Gibbons and Yasmin Mullick
in consultation with Barbara Daniels

Introduction

The primary care system is the first point of access into the health system for the majority of the population. In a recent survey of African-Caribbean and Asian users of mental health services in England and Wales, Wilson and Francis (1997) reported that GPs were the first point of contact with mental health services for 53 per cent of respondents. Therefore, it is particularly important that primary care services recognize and address the diverse needs of the different ethnic groups who come into contact with their services.

However, Mahtani and Marks (1994) report that people from Black and minority ethnic groups do experience considerable psychological distress but health professionals, including psychologists, find it difficult to meet their needs. They also report that research shows an under-representation of Black and minority ethnic people in referrals to clinical psychologists. A survey into access to mental health care in an inner-city area in the UK, the West Birmingham Health District, found that Asian people and African-Caribbean people with mental health problems are less likely to be identified and referred to specialist mental health services than White majority people (Commander *et al.*, 1997).

DEMOGRAPHIC DETAILS AND RELEVANT RESEARCH

GP consultation rates

Two recent nationwide studies, The Fourth National General Practice Morbidity Study based on 1991–92 consultations and the Health Education Authority's 1994 Health and Lifestyle Study, both report significantly higher levels of consultations with GPs among members of minority ethnic groups. There were raised levels of consultation among all minority ethnic groups for 'signs, symptoms and ill-defined conditions'. This may reflect difficulty in communication of psychological distress rather than over-use of services (Smaje, 1995).

The higher level of GP consultations among minority ethnic groups has largely been understood and treated within a 'somatization' framework. However, Krause's (1989) study on Punjabi people living in Bradford offers a different explanation of somatic symptoms. The study describes distress referred to as 'sinking heart', where a Punjabi understanding is based on culturally specific ideas about the person, the self and the heart, whereby the physical, emotional and social signs of distress are expressed and interpreted as a whole. This model can be applied to understand other cultures.

Health of the Nation

The Government's White Paper, *Health of the Nation*, sets out five key areas for national targets, two of which were to reduce:

- suicide rates where there is a higher rate amongst women of Indian origin, particularly those aged 15–24 where the standardized mortality ratio for suicides is nearly three times the national rates and in those aged 25–34 where the rate is 60 per cent higher (Raleigh V. S. *et al.*, 1990; Ethnicity and Health, NHS Centre for Reviews and Dissemination, 1996);
- higher rates of cardiovascular disease in South Asian and African-Caribbean populations in the UK. In particular, South Asian groups are at higher risk of coronary heart disease and Afro-Caribbeans are at greater risk of stroke (Ethnicity and Health, NHS Centre for Reviews and Dissemination, 1996).

Selective epidemiology

1. Non-insulin dependent diabetes mellitus is more highly prevalent among minority ethnic populations. The mortality rates from diabetes by selected place of birth in England and Wales (1979–83) showed the highest rate among those from the Indian sub-continent (Balarajan and Busulu, 1990).
2. Tuberculosis is significantly higher in minority ethnic groups (Balarajan and Busulu, 1990). Among women from the Indian subcontinent, mortality from the disease from 1979 to 1983 was ten times higher than the general female population.
3. Sickle cell disorders are most prevalent in African and Caribbean populations, while sickle beta thalassaemia also affects people originating from South Asia, Southern Europe and the Middle East (Smaje, 1995).
4. There are high rates of smoking among Indian and Asian men (Ethnicity and Health, NHS Centre for Reviews and Dissemination, 1996).

THEORY

Concepts

Assumptions and prejudices exist about different racial and cultural groups and mental health. Knowledge of these, particularly from a medical perspective, may be helpful in understanding the perspectives of members of the Primary Health Care Teams (PHCTs) and the experiences of some clients: for example, the assumption that South Asian clients somatise their distress (Beliappa, 1991).

It is important to acknowledge that there may be very different issues facing individuals within any minority ethnic group, rather than viewing them as a homogeneous group: for example, UK residency status, language differences, whether they are first, second or third generation in this country, and of course individual differences. The trainee will need to explore these with the client, rather than making assumptions on the basis of ethnicity. It is important to explore with the client their particular needs, for example, attention to confidentiality issues within tightly knit communities.

An awareness is needed of the social construction of concepts used to describe people's emotional states such as depression and anxiety. Different cultural beliefs contribute to varying understandings or constructions of distress or problems. For example, Beliappa (1991) comments that in some Asian cultures, emotional disturbances are traditionally described as 'sorrow', 'anxiety' or as a 'burden', rather than being classified as 'mental illness' as in Western cultures and that 'the absence of an equivalent South Asian term for 'depression' raises interesting questions on certain assumptions about 'normality'.

The concepts widely used are likely to be those of the dominant culture group and therefore require scrutiny in application to minority ethnic clients. Trainees could consider with their clients their own understanding of these terms in relation to the individual, their family, their community, their culture and the dominant culture. Is the client's understanding of terms the same as or different from the trainee's? What impact do these different understandings of a widely used concept have upon the individual?

An awareness of cultural differences in the expression of and response to distress will allow greater understanding of clients from different cultures by members of the PHCT and, therefore, will enable a more flexible and appropriate service to be provided.

Some clients may use traditional healing methods common in their own cultures. A lack of respect for treatments which do not fit within the Western model is a form of prejudice and can lead to racism. Knowledge of these methods can help practitioners to understand the perspective and experiences of clients from different ethnic backgrounds, enabling a more flexible and appropriate service to be provided.

Issues to consider

Eurocentrism of psychological theories

Most, if not all, theories used within clinical psychology have been developed in Europe or North America. For example, Maslow's hierarchy of needs places self-actualization at the top of the hierarchy that defines psychological well-being. This hierarchy is based on Western cultural assumptions related to the primacy of the individual within society in contrast to other cultures that may place affiliation and spirituality higher up in an equivalent hierarchy.

Kleinman (1987) indicates that most cross-cultural psychiatric research focuses on biological determinants for psychiatric disorders, viewing social and cultural factors merely as influencing the content of the disorder. For example, the experience of delusions of a person diagnosed with schizophrenia would be understood to be biologically based, while the content of the beliefs could be understood within a social or cultural context. Kleinman asserts that most recognized cross-cultural psychiatric research, such as that carried out by WHO, is conducted along these lines. This, he claims, leads to severely biased and at times fallacious conclusions about the psychological well-being of people, particularly those from non-Western cultures.

Knowledge of different cultural practices is needed to aid formulations and possibly interventions, particularly those practices with medical applications, around major life stages such as birth, puberty, marriage and death. For example, consider female circumcision, male circumcision, funeral and burial practices in different cultures; some Orthodox Jews forbid contraception and abortion unless the woman's life is at risk; chewing pan is practised in many Asian communities.

Racism and racist practices
These are likely to occur at different levels within the system: for example, by individual practitioners, and through practice policies within the Health Authority/Trust. Refugees have been refused the right to register at practices, receptionists may speak louder or lose patience with those who speak little English. Teaching or training for the practice team on anti-racist practices might be appropriate: for example, in respectfully managing patients who speak little English or who do not understand Western health care systems, or in managing racism from patients to members of the practice team.

Homogeneity
People from minority ethnic backgrounds are often treated as a homogeneous group where individual ethnic differences are ignored. Apart from being racist, this policy does not enable the client's needs to be recognized and met appropriately.

Ethnocentrism
Inappropriate assumptions are made about the needs of people from different ethnic groups on the basis of majority experience.

Primary Health Care Teams (PHCTs)
As standard good practice, the ethnic make-up of the practice team should ideally reflect the ethnic breakdown of the population serviced by the practice. The trainee can develop an understanding of the relationship between the patient and the health worker in terms of their cultural differences: for example, what assumptions or prejudices might the patient or the health worker have about each other, and how might these influence the working relationship?

Even a PHCT reflecting the ethnicity of the practice population may not necessarily adhere to culturally sensitive or anti-racist practices, particularly when working within wider structures with institutional racism prevailing such as the local health authority or the NHS. It is also important to be aware of opportunities for racism and discrimination among members of the PHCT.

The primary health care system

The primary health care system in the UK is one of many possible models of health care provision. For users from different countries, understanding of this system may be limited and expectations may be very different. For example, in this country the PHCT is the gatekeeper to specialist services (secondary or tertiary care), while in some African countries, users have direct access to specialist services without needing to be referred.

Relevant models of service delivery in primary care

There is a general lack of psychological models which address issues of 'race' and culture, and which are appropriate to a primary care setting.

Partnership model

This is important for developing close informal links with GPs and other members of the Primary Health Care Teams, facilitating working relationships characterized by approachability, informality and good communication. There is an opportunity for co-constructing a model of health appropriate to the local population (Donnison and Burd, 1994).

Prevention model

This is based on a philosophy of care rather than a psychological theory. The main focus is on professionals working proactively to identify patterns of health care needs and factors which contribute to them. Primary prevention projects have been defined by Gill Edwards (1989) as 'programmes designed to ... counteract psychosocial, ecological or socio-cultural causes of mental health problems at the level of at-risk groups, local communities or society as a whole'. A primary care prevention model addresses health problems at the earliest possible stage, or works on the contributory factors: for example, addressing poor housing conditions to prevent the development of numerous illnesses, stopping smoking campaigns, antiracism campaigns to counter-racism and racist attacks, educating patients on diet and fitness (examples of such projects include Hunt, 1989; Holland, 1991). This model allows health practitioners to identify the needs of particular Black and minority ethnic groups and to target appropriate health care and prevention strategies.

Multidimensional model (Kat, 1994)

Primary care as the initial response to a person seeking help is placed in a unique position where the 'mind–body split', or the conventional distinction between physical and psychological ill-health, is most easily broken down. This places primary care practitioners in a position where they can work together to meet the patient's needs appropriately, without recourse to viewing complaints as solely physical or solely psychological. This model may be particularly appropriate for patients from cultures which do not recognize a 'mind–body split' (e.g. Krause, 1989).

Consultation model

This model is based on a theoretical systemic model of working (e.g. Jones, 1993; Huffington and Brunning, 1994; Cambell *et al.*, 1991) in which a multiplicity of views and ideas are equally valued. The client is encouraged to bring a partner, relative or friend to the session to invite different views on the problem. The psychologist may work with a 'team': this consists of one or more colleagues, who could be GPs or other health professionals. The team discuss their ideas and hypotheses about the client's difficulties and context in front of the client to enable the client to choose from a wider pool of perspectives. This model has been successfully used by clinical psychologists and GPs working collaboratively.

PRACTICE

Assessment

Use consultations with the referrer (e.g. the GP pre-assessment) to learn as much as possible about the unique needs of the client. This might include information collected about language differences, the person with whom the client usually attends and how the client communicates with the referrer. While gathering information, the trainee can become familiar with and use the available resources in the GP practice. There will be information about whether the client needs or has used interpreters, linkworkers or advocates.

A trainee should develop a way of working which entails comprehensive assessments. A wide-ranging assessment will ask about or be open to hearing about social and economic conditions, family organization, effects of culture, 'race' and other factors which bear upon the way the client conceptualizes his or her condition or difficulty. Objective assessment measures should be culturally valid if at all possible, or used judiciously if not (see Neuropsychology Module). Formulations should clearly indicate a focus on the individual within their socio-economic and ethnic context. The impact of racism on their physical and psychological health should also be part of the formulation.

Interviewing

Interviews may at times require the use of interpreters. Follow guidelines about the use of interpreters when interviewing and seek training in working with interpreters (see Tribe, 1991 and the Working with Interpreters section in the Introductory Module). When involved in seeing a family, a trainee should gather information on the family's understanding of how the referral arose and their expectations. Being clear about the role of a psychologist and asking whether the family wants the clinical psychologist to liaise with other significant people, for example a local healer, is advisable.

Intervention

Direct work

As Primary Care psychology usually provides short-term interventions, trainees need to consider when Black and minority ethnic clients would benefit from longer-term therapy. Working collaboratively with the client allows a joint negotiation for the length and focus of the intervention. In addition, the trainee should be aware of the assumptions that are made behind offering a particular model to Black and minority ethnic clients, e.g. insight-orientated versus behavioural. They should bear in mind that it has been documented that people from minority ethnic groups are more likely to be prescribed medication rather than any of the 'talking therapies' (Webb-Johnson and Nadirshaw, 1993; Littlewood and Lipsedge, 1989).

There needs to be an awareness of assumptions of psychological models used or the models held to be most universal. Most Western models assume notions of individualism which are not necessarily shared by non-Western cultures. The wide range of clients in the primary care population requires a wide range of psychological interventions (refer to Introductory Module).

There is a need to be aware not to pathologize nor idealize (e.g. as exotic) individuals from a different culture. There is also a need to become aware of the therapist's role: who one has 'become' for the client (e.g. healer, teacher, friend, elder).

And finally, awareness of the client's notion of what constitutes success or change, particularly in the time-frame offered in Primary Care: for example, the 'colonizing effect' where a White therapist formulates and determines 'success' for the Black client.

Indirect work

Consultations with the GP before and after psychological interventions provide the trainee with an educative forum regarding the patient's distress and psychological health. This can increase the referrer's understanding of issues related to race, culture, gender, sexual orientation, etc.

Trainees can develop a role in working with specialist staff such as health advocates who enable people from Black and minority ethnic groups to secure the services they need and ensure these are provided in ways that are appropriate for the client. For example:

- helping the practice to think about whether they make best use of their resources. For example, are health advocates respected as professionals and allowed to advocate for clients and to educate Primary Health Care team members?
- working alongside a clinical psychologist. A trainee could help health advocates clarify their role and help them to publicize and assert their skills and knowledge.

As members of the PHCT, trainees are in a position to use their observational experience to contribute in reflecting on the group processes, to comment on the effectiveness of team-working and to help think about increasing accessibility for Black and minority ethnic groups. The trainee can facilitate the use and availability of resources in the Practice by compiling a leaflet (including different languages) of mental health services in the local community for Black and minority ethnic groups. This would allow the patient to have a choice in how they access services rather than solely relying on a referral by their GP.

SERVICE DELIVERY

Many people do not understand the relationship between primary and secondary health care unless they have had experience of it. Many inner-city GP practices have a high number of new immigrants and refugees and, therefore, a system needs to include an induction to the Primary Care system. This induction may apply generally to Black and minority ethnic groups and more specifically to refugee groups.

Knowledge of the ethnic make-up of the local population served by the practice will guide trainees in developing their knowledge about the possible needs of particular groups. For example, knowledge of whether there are refugees living locally could highlight some understanding of legislation on entitlement to health care and local GP practices with regard to refugee communities. For particular groups of clients, becoming registered at the practice might be problematic: for example, owing to racist practices; or if people do not hold residency status, the practice might refuse them or only allow them temporary registration.

A more equitable service can be given to clients where the members of the PHCT and/or the languages spoken reflect to some extent the ethnic make-up of the local population. This enables a person to have some choice in who they see and also makes the service feel less alien to someone who is not from the White majority group.

The building or setting may be experienced as more or less welcoming to all users. For example, reflecting different cultures through pictures displayed, magazines, notices in community languages, whether the reception staff reflect the ethnicities of the local population or of the White majority group. Information supplied by the practice may or may not be available in the languages spoken by the local population.

Trainees can develop an awareness of traditional healing methods of different cultures common in the local population. For example, through consultation with practitioners of traditional healing methods and by thinking about how these methods can link in with Western methods used in the Practice. Trainees can also familiarize themselves and gain knowledge from other primary care professionals – for example, health visitors, district nurses and school nurses – of specific traditional practices (e.g. birth practices, feeding and weaning practices).

Psychological research within the practice can examine the quality of the service provided by the PHCT (e.g. looking at the psychological service offered to patients from different ethnic groups). Ethnic monitoring can be set up to ensure that issues of equal access relating to ethnicity are attended to as well as client satisfaction studies.

Trainees can contribute to an audit project, looking at accessibility to an on-site clinical psychology service at the GP practice, by examining the data for Black and minority ethnic clients who get referred to the service and comparing the data to the local ethnic demography.

LEARNING OUTCOMES

1. Trainees will show an understanding of their own ethnicity and be able to develop an understanding of their own ethnocentric biases. They will also acknowledge the biases of others and how these impact upon how they perceive a client's psychological difficulties and how they might influence what intervention a client may be offered.
2. Trainees will show an awareness of the areas within the primary health care system where racism or unequal access to services is liable to occur. They should also make observations and offer thoughts about appropriate interventions. If working alongside a clinical psychologist, they may discuss ways of addressing these issues.
3. Trainees will be able to demonstrate, through their psychological formulations, an understanding of how issues of 'race', culture and social and economic variables influence the presentation of the presenting problems.
4. Trainees will have had at least one experience of working with a client of a different culture from their own in the primary care setting, and will be able to reflect on their experience, thinking about issues of 'difference', and how they showed an awareness of these.
5. Trainees will have had at least one experience of working with an interpreter, preferably in a primary care setting, or, if not, in any clinical setting or a role play scenario.
6. Trainees will show an appreciation of the roles of community groups or voluntary organizations in providing services in conjunction with the primary care services.
7. Trainees will have an understanding of the dynamics present within a PHCT and the personal implications of this for themselves as trainees. They will be able to make observations and reflections about issues to do with power and how decisions are made within a team.

Suggested exercises

Exercise 1

Aim
To examine racial and cultural stereotyping as used by trainees and wider society and expand trainees' beliefs away from these stereotypes.

Instructions
Divide into small groups and assign each group a client referred for stress by the GP. Clients (all aged 28) include:

- Pakistani Muslim female, divorced
- Bangladeshi male, married
- White English male, single
- African-Caribbean female, lives with partner
- White Irish woman, single

Imagine two scenarios for which the client might be referred:

(1) Based on stereotypical ideas about the reason for referral

(2) Based on non-stereotypical ideas about the reason for referral

Take each imagined scenario and devise questions that you would ask the referrer. Notice if the questions asked from each scenario are the same or different.

General feedback and debriefing

Timings
15 minutes for each scenario
15 minutes for devising questions
15 minutes for feedback

Note for trainers
Monitor the feelings generated from the discussion about racial and cultural stereotypes, particularly in mixed ethnic working groups.

Exercise 2

Aims
1. To examine how a General Practice makes itself accessible and appropriate to people from Black and minority ethnic backgrounds.
2. To think about issues from the different perspectives of the PHCT.

Instructions
A General Practice has a high proportion of African-Caribbean patients. A meeting is organized to discuss the idea of employing an African-Caribbean counsellor.

Trainees to volunteer to role play the participants of the meeting: for example GP, practice nurse, psychologist, practice manager, potential service user, representative from a Black women's voluntary group, health visitor. Remaining trainees to adopt the role of observers. 'Observers' to pay attention to negotiation amid power imbalance: e.g. statutory and voluntary, ethnicity, gender, professional status.

Observers comment on the process.

Role play participants (in role) to comment on their participation.

De-role and final comments.

Timings
15 minutes for role play
15 minutes for comments on participation
10 minutes for final discussion

Other useful modules
- Child, Adolescent and Family
- Adult Mental Health
- Older Adults

Annotated references

Muhammed, S. (1991) Improving health services for Black populations. *Share*. London: King's Fund Centre.

This article examines ways of addressing the health needs of Black populations at the organizational level of health authorities and purchasing consortia. While it does not focus specifically on primary care, it offers suggestions on how to include the health needs of Black populations in the planning and development of health care services which includes the issues related to racism.

Mahtani, A. and Marks, L. (1994) Developing a primary care psychology service that is racially and culturally appropriate. *Clinical Psychology Forum, 65*, 27–31

This article looks at how a primary care psychology service in Tower Hamlets has accommodated the needs of the Black and minority ethnic groups in the local community. The authors raise issues and describe interventions of direct work and indirect work through their work on primary health care projects in the community. Easy to read and provides a helpful reference list.

Hopkins, A. and Bahl, V. (Eds.) (1993*) Access to Health Care for People from Black and Ethnic Minorities*. London: Royal College of Physicians

This book examines the problems of access to health services by Black and minority ethnic groups and sets out the principles and offers practical help for purchasing and providing appropriate health care. There are useful chapters specifically on issues in General Practice, health promotion, access to mental health services and physical disease incidences among minority ethnic groups.

Smaje, C. (1995) *Health, 'Race' and Ethnicity. Making Sense of the Evidence*. London: King's Fund Institute

This book reviews the literature available from a range of disciplines concerning the health of people from ethnic minorities, their use and experience of health services, and the history of attempts to address their needs in health policy. The strength of this book is in the critical commentary it provides on the material it summarizes.

Balarajan, R., Yuen, P., Soni Raleigh, V. (1989) Ethnic differences in General Practitioner consultations. *British Medical Journal*, October, *14*, 598–660

This article compares consultation rates to GPs by age, ethnicity, gender and socioeconomic class. Ethnic differences were greatest at ages 45–64, when consultation rates in people of Pakistani, Indian and West Indian origin were much higher for both men and women compared with White people. This has implications for the workload of general practices.

Murray, S.A. and Graham, L.J. (1995) Practice based health needs assessment: Use of four methods in a small neighbourhood. *British Medical Journal*, June, *3*, 1443–1448

This article examines four complementary methods used to define health needs in a community. These are: rapid participatory appraisal, postal survey, analysis of routinely available statistics and collation of practice-held information. The article is useful in comparing different qualitative and quantitative methods and their suitability for assessing different health needs and exploring potential service provision. Although there is no attention given to ethnicity, it gives a good picture of the benefits and methods of researching the health needs of a community.

Chapter 14

PSYCHOSOCIAL REHABILITATION (LONG-TERM NEEDS)

Mayuri Senapati and Anne Goodwin
With contributions from Ken Bledin, Herby Pillay
and Mair Thomas

Introduction

Psychosocial rehabilitation services can be perceived all too often as the end of the line for people whom the health care system has so far failed to help. Because mental health services in the UK have not been designed around the needs of Black and minority ethnic people, and there may be inadequate understanding among service providers of the complex issues being faced by individuals in distress, we might expect these people to be over-represented among those clients/patients whose needs cannot be adequately addressed within the primary or secondary (acute) care services. They may also have already dropped out through frustration at the inability of statutory services to meet their needs.

Models of psychosocial rehabilitation take account of the importance of context or the social environment in determining people's quality of life. For this reason, the approach should be easily able to recognize and take account of issues relevant to Black and minority ethnic people, including the impact of racism on their social functioning. However, such models have evolved within a system which manages difference all too often by labelling people as psychotic and, as such, making it difficult to address the difference between the largely White professionals who have developed such models and the Black and minority ethnic people who require the services.

DEMOGRAPHIC DATA

Caution is required in considering demographic data, as most studies have been carried out within a framework of psychiatric classification which has fundamental limitations from a psychological perspective (see Boyle, 1990). In particular, since cultural stereotyping and racism play a part in the social construction of mental illness, the appropriateness of diagnosis of Black and minority ethnic people can be called further into question (Fernando, 1995b). Nevertheless, it is important for trainees to have some knowledge of the literature which identifies prevalence of mental illness, rates of relapse, and factors contributing to use of services across cultures in Britain.

In many studies, a disproportionate number of people with a diagnosis of schizophrenia come from a minority ethnic background, with rates among African-Caribbeans reported as between 2.4 and 18 times higher than White people (Bhugra *et al.*, 1997). The Black Caribbean community is particularly over-represented in terms of diagnosis of severe mental illness, hospital admission, section rates under the Mental Health Act and occupation of secure beds (The Sainsbury Centre for Mental Health, 1998). However, Black and minority ethnic people have been found to be under-represented among those with non-psychotic disorders (Ineichen, 1980).

A high rate of schizophrenia in relation to White people has been found among Asian people only over the age of 30, and particularly older females, suggesting that factors involved in the aetiology of the disorder operate differentially over the life cycle for different ethnic groups (Bhugra *et al.*, 1997). Having received a diagnosis of schizophrenia, African-Caribbean people appear to be at greater risk of relapse than either Asian or White people (Bhugra *et al.*, 1997; Birchwood *et al.*, 1992). Unemployment appears to be a significant contributory factor (Bhugra *et al.*,1997). Perkins (1995) found that African-Caribbean, African and Asian people were more likely than White people to be long-term mental health service users.

Black and minority ethnic people may be particularly likely to fall into the category of those who do not engage well with services. People may be suspicious of services due to negative past experiences of psychiatric care, other statutory services, and/or contacts with the criminal justice system. Additionally, where compliance with anti-psychotic medication is given a central role within the package of care, those who are uncomfortable with this model, either because of the physical side effects of medication or psychological issues around power and control, may feel alienated from services. Recent research from the Sainsbury Centre (1998) found that 'for many Black users a key reason for non-engagement is quite literally a fear that involvement with mental health services will kill them. In evidence, examples of several deaths in hospital and prison were given, some related to over-prescribing of psychiatric medication, others to aggressive restraining techniques.' Services may not be meeting the needs of Black and minority ethnic people because of racism within the mental health workforce, lack of knowledge of different traditions among mental health workers leading to insensitive practice or services being out of touch with current issues for Black and minority ethnic communities.

THEORY

In the context of psychiatry, a traditional view of rehabilitation is that people who experience severe mental health difficulties have fixed disabilities and that these disabilities are solely reflective of the cognitive and social deficits attributable to the 'illness'. Bennett (1991) provides a more 'adaptive' view of rehabilitation that aims to move away from the 'throughput' image of rehabilitative interventions as attempts to help the individual to make the 'best of a bad job'. The ideas of Wolfensberger (1972) and his colleagues (Wolfensberger and Glen, 1983) on 'normalization' have significantly influenced the development of psychiatric rehabilitation theory. Utilising the ideas of 'normalisation', Bennett's notion of rehabilitation emphasizes the dynamic interaction between a person's disabilities and the attitudes, expectations and tolerances of their social environment.

Two other related but distinct concepts that have influenced the development of rehabilitation services are deinstitutionalization and community care. Deinstitutionalization proposes that the majority of the disabilities of 'patients' in long-term institutional care, for example in asylums, arise from the institutional practices that occur within these organizations. Therefore, rehabilitation programmes are geared towards moving people out of institutional environments and 'resettling' them into the wider community. Psychologists need to consider the effects of institutionalization together with the specific issues (e.g. institutional racism in the wider community) that arise for Black and minority ethnic people.

The philosophy of 'community care' focuses on providing appropriate care and support for people with serious mental health difficulties in the community. The onus therefore is shifted from the 'disabled' person having to learn to 'resettle' in the community to the service providers having to develop community services in a way that enables the 'disabled' individuals to live meaningful lives outside of institutions. Service providers therefore have a responsibility to define the minority ethnic groups and to consult and to provide appropriate services for them.

Another set of research that has influenced psychiatric rehabilitation services is the family intervention or the Expressed Emotion (EE) research (Kuipers and Bebbington, 1988; Leff and Vaughn, 1981; Kavanagh, 1992). The researchers claim that constructs such as 'hostility', 'over-involvement', and 'critical comments' (on the carer's part) are associated with increased relapse rates in the 'patient'. The clinician devises intervention packages, such as psycho-education programmes or Family Management Programmes (Falloon, 1988) to enable families to reduce the levels of EE and thereby reduce the rate of relapse.

A clear critique of the Family Management Programme is elaborated by Johnstone (1993). Although she does not mention the cultural and racist implications in the possible construction of the West Indian family as 'hostile' or the Asian family as 'over-involved', she does draw attention to the 'enormous contradiction and confusion' that exists in the family management literature on the issue of pathologizing families where a family member has been given the diagnosis of 'schizophrenia'. In the context of the existing stereotypes in the diagnostic processes and procedures applied to the Black individual, this kind of family management programme that pathologizes the family as having a role in maintaining a possibly misdiagnosed 'illness' can be perceived as being insensitive. In relation to Black and minority ethnic families who may already have been pathologized by society, psychologists need to be skilful in dealing with what may be seen as 'double pathologization'.

Psychosis

The past ten years or so have seen significant changes in the models of psychosis which predominate within psychiatric services. It is now much more acceptable to look for the meaning within phenomena such as 'auditory hallucinations' and 'delusions' which involves setting a person's beliefs in the context of their current and past life experiences. Within such a context, clinicians should be more readily able to take account of experiences of oppression and racism in their formulation of an individual's difficulties. There is also now less emphasis on persuading sufferers to accept a medical explanation of their difficulties in order to receive services. This should facilitate clinicians working alongside people from cultural and ethnic backgrounds different from their own. The crucial factor is for sufferers to come to an understanding of their problems which is functional for them and one which enables them to take up the help that they need rather than one that fits in with dominant models within health services.

Independence

The fundamental goal of most rehabilitation interventions seems to be to enable the individual to function more independently. Trainees need to be aware that the notion of independence as synonymous with healthy adult functioning, is a cultural belief common to White European societies and is not necessarily viewed in the same way by clients from Black and minority ethnic communities where interdependence, or dependability might be more valued. Rehabilitation services need to grapple with the range of ways in which clients may manage the fact that their difficulties cause them to be dependent on others for aspects of their lives which are generally managed autonomously or in a more empowered version of interdependence.

Valued social roles

A successful outcome of rehabilitation is deemed to be engaging in valued social roles. Obviously what is valued is influenced by personal preferences and the cultural context of the individual. The multiplicity of 'communities' to which we all belong and the various roles that we occupy need to be acknowledged. When considering valued social roles for Black and minority ethnic people who use rehabilitation services, there is a need for sensitivity about the specific community which is most in accord with their beliefs as well as their need to find a way of positioning themselves in relation to White majority people and the community of people who do not use services (Perkins, 1995).

Assimilation, rehabilitation and the Black client

The difficulty with the ideas of assimilation and integration inherent in rehabilitation practice based on normalization is that despite their 'appealing face validity and surface logic' (Baldwin, 1985), they do not emphasize enough the potential in asserting the 'unique culture' (Emerson, 1990) of the devalued group. In the context of 'race' equality, it is not clear how these principles can be fairly applied to the predicament of the individual who is marginalized both on the grounds of being Black and on the grounds of being labelled as long-term

mentally ill. For instance, implicit in the principle of assimilation is the requirement for differentness or 'stigmata' to be reduced, thereby enabling the devalued
individual to 'attain more valued membership in society'. The question that
arises here is, how do you (and indeed why should you) 'reduce' the differentness that distinguishes the Black way of being from other ways of being as a
means of attaining valued social status?

It is important to contextualize the 'mad' experience within its personal,
socio-cultural and political context. Inherent in the process of contextualizing is
the empowering potential, both for professionals and clients alike, to challenge
and confront oppressive psychiatric practice that pathologizes madness as an
individual's deficit. This issue of the wider community owning up to collective
responsibility with regard to the 'mad' experience of some in society is power-
fully emphasized by Coleman (1999) in his book *Recovery: An Alien Concept*.
Coleman relates the story of the practice within aboriginal culture where if
someone becomes mad, the whole tribe comes together to discuss what the tribe
has done to cause the person to be mad. He goes on to say, 'when someone goes
mad in our culture (Western), it is off to hospital with them. It is not a gathering
of the local community that gets together to decide what is wrong with the community. It is a ward-round made up of so-called experts who get together, often
without the person concerned being present, who decide both what is wrong
with the client and how it will be treated' (Coleman, 1999).

Medication compliance as promoted by bio-driven rehabilitation

The agenda for 'treatment', as implicit in the traditional rehabilitation model, is
to minimize presenting symptoms through compliance to medication. People
labelled as severely mentally ill (SMI), and particularly Black people labelled
thus, are often a disempowered section of the community with little real economic and political choice. As with other disadvantaged groups, they may feel
less well placed to question or challenge the agendas of psychiatry in the context
of seeking appropriate help. However, the fact remains that medication compliance is not necessarily synonymous with enhanced mental health of the Black
client who, because of the crude stereotype of being potentially dangerous or
violent, is liable to receive higher doses of neuroleptic medication (Thomas,
1997). In this sense, medication compliance programmes (alias psycho-education
groups, often facilitated by clinical psychologists) can be seen as psychiatry's
'white glove' for controlling the unwanted in society through pathologizing mad
behaviour as biological. The direct adverse effects (often described as side
effects!) of neuroleptics have been well documented by reputable psychiatrists as
equivalent to brain damage (Breggin, 1993). Often the effects of treatment are for
many worse than the 'illness' being treated (Coleman, 1999). The not-so-hidden
truth about neuroleptic drugs is that they do not cure, but maintain the client in
a state of side-effected stupor (and therefore less able to be 'violent'), and maintain the psychiatric system in its inability to attain social justice for those deemed
(or doomed) as mad. Therapeutic doses of neuroleptics (Thomas, 1997) could
very well have a role in symptom control and enable 'personal recovery', if
strategically used (Coleman, 1999). Yet it is the misuse, not the use, of these

potent chemicals that continues to be rife. In this context, the Black client continues to remain most vulnerable to this misuse of psychotropic drugs delivered
with such impunity by those in positions of control, and some psychiatrists
themselves hold that 'the use of high doses of medication in particular groups,
particularly young African-Caribbean men, has almost certainly contributed to
the sudden death of a number of young Black men over the last ten years'
(Thomas, 1997).

Social recovery as promoted by bio-driven rehabilitation

'Social recovery' from 'schizophrenia' as defined by Warner (1994) is measured
by 'social functioning' which, according to Warner, is a combination of a range
of features, including working ability, capacity to care for basic needs, abnormal
behaviour causing distress to others, criminal activity, number of friends or
sexual functioning

The importance of 'social recovery' in rehabilitation theory is reflected in the
considerable success of social skills training in rehabilitation practice. The success of course is in terms of uptake of the idea of social skills training by those
involved in rehabilitation. In reality, when success is measured in terms of
empirical outcome for those being rehabilitated, there is very little evidence that
skills training improves the quality of life of the person deemed in need of rehabilitation. The promoters of skills training ascribe the limitations of this method
to 'the generalisation problem' (Shepherd, 1978 cited in Pilling, 1991) or the 'difficulty in transferring of skills to the living environment' (Liberman *et al.*, 1986).

Coleman (1999) provides a powerful critique of the skills-training-focused
ideas for 'social recovery'. He argues that far from an individual social skills
deficit, there are complicated factors well beyond an individual's control such as
the state of the economy and prevalent stigma that influence whether or not an
individual with a 'psychiatric history' is enabled to access economic independence. As for sexuality and friendships, the relationship between these dimensions of human expression in the context of the direct effects of over-medication
has never been made clear (Coleman, 1999). He makes the point that 'the effects
of medication in itself causes much of the social dysfunction and most certainly
disables many clients to an extent that they will find it near impossible to start
and maintain the social contacts that will lead to friendships forming'. 'Social
recovery' when applied to the Black or minority ethnic client has in it the iatro-
genic potential of becoming a tool for institutionally validated racial oppression.

De-medicalization of 'madness'

Recent years have seen a radical move within clinical psychology towards de-
medicalizing the experience of madness (Boyle, 1990; Bentall, 1990). One of the
central propositions of these developments is the idea that experiences, traditionally explained in terms of 'long-term mental illness' are really on a continuum with, and do not differ qualitatively from 'normal' cognitive processes
(Bentall, 1990; Chadwick *et al.*, 1996). Experiences such as delusional beliefs, far
from being 'empty speech acts, whose informational content refers neither to self
nor world' (Berrios, 1991, p. 12), can be explained in terms of the client's position

in the social universe (Bentall, 1990). This meaning-focused perspective of 'madness', in moving away from the abnormal/deficit-driven illness model, offers an alternative view that the content and theme of experiences such as delusions and hallucinations are significant, carry personal meaning and relate to the individual's experience of social living.

For the Black or minority ethnic client, the 'toxic experience' of surviving in a racist society cannot really be meaningfully separated from the experience of being labelled as severely mentally ill. In this context, therefore, the foremost task of rehabilitation programmes would be to 'improve insight' of service providers to the impact of racism on the experience of madness.

Cognitive behaviour therapies (CBT) and psychosis

Although not all clinical psychologists practising CBT for psychosis employ similar techniques, there is a consensus among most practitioners that 'treatment' should pay attention to the individual context in which symptoms are experienced rather than 'schizophrenia' per se (e.g. Chadwick *et al.*, 1996). It is also emphasized that the symptoms associated with psychosis are not qualitatively different from 'normal' experience. The need for a collaborative and empathic approach to therapy which pays attention to the emotional content of the sufferer's experience is highlighted by most of the proponents of CBT for psychosis (e.g. ibid.). This way of working with psychosis offers an autonomous psychological perspective that attempts to free psychosis from the reductionist psychiatric diagnostic processes. However, CBT for psychosis suffers from the similar limitations that are inherent in the general cognitive perspective (Coyne, 1982). As Johnstone (1995) points out, highly complex problems presented by most clients are not amenable to 'simplistic solutions'. 'Psychotechnologies' (Gournay, 1995), such as cognitive behavioural techniques, are derived from essentially Westernized, positivistic models that do not really position the client's distress in his or her political and social reality.

> In the midst of all this jargon and theory, the person himself or herself ... the lived experience of disorder, dysfunction or disability is lost ... if we turn to the only people who are truly experts in the experience of mental distress, the users themselves, and ask what helped in their own rehabilitation, we do not find them calling for more cognitive behavioural techniques ... two rather different themes emerge ... one is meeting someone who was finally able to see them and relate to them, as a person with difficulties rather than a patient with an illness, and to offer not techniques but a human understanding and compassion.
>
> Johnstone, 1995, p.28

CBT theorists have yet to come up with a way of confining racism into schemas, thereby enabling Black and minority ethnic survivors of mental health problems to counter these with equally potent anti-racist schemas.

Ownership at the helm of a different kind of 'long-term' caring

For recovery to become meaningfully associated with rehabilitation, one needs to split open the myth of 'long-term mental illness' and initiate equal dialogue where the lived experiences of the service users obtains a central place. Coleman (1999) describes this as the process of reclaiming 'ownership'. It is standard practice in psychiatry to accept that the professional practitioner, usually the psychiatrist or the psychologist, has a specialist understanding of the client's experiences by virtue of their professional training. Their self-styled ownership of this mythical expert knowledge gives the professional practitioner unwarranted power over the client (Coleman, 1999). Therefore, if Black or minority ethnic clients challenge the diagnosis of 'long-term mental illness' and refuse to accept the offered treatment, they would be labelled as lacking insight, again empowering the professional to impose more custodial means of 'taking care'.

PRACTICE

Individual work

The issues of power and of sensitivity to other cultures, which apply to all areas of therapeutic intervention, are also of relevance to psychosocial rehabilitation. Perhaps particular sensitivity is required when working with people diagnosed with a 'mental illness', as they will be also disempowered through the process of this labelling.

Professionals working with people who experience psychosis can have particular difficulties in relating to the psychotic experience. This difficulty is compounded when there are language barriers between the client and the professional. Interpreters are likely to require specific training and support to work with people with psychosis. Additionally, there are cultural differences in modes of expression within the English language, which may facilitate or impede communication with people at times of stress or distress.

Family work

While working with families applying traditional behavioural family therapy approaches, professionals need to be mindful of the differences in family values (the client's) from the White Western culture within which this therapy was developed. Attention should be given to the identification of the appropriate individuals to include in a family meeting, and the appropriateness of different modes of communication in the presence of an outsider. Also, cultural issues will influence a family's willingness and ability to care for a relative at home, and the nature of the support they would require to be able to do so.

Indirect work and multidisciplinary team work

Psychologists in psychosocial rehabilitation do much of their work indirectly through other staff. As staff attitudes can have a major impact on the functioning of those people who use services, trainees need to be able to anticipate the attitudes of other members of the multidisciplinary team to Black and minority ethnic people and how they will respond to racism when this is experienced within the workforce. They also need to think about ways of enabling colleagues to take account of issues of power, racism and culture in planning and delivering care. This issue may be particularly present in discussions around compliance with medication. In some regions, White trainees may find themselves in the minority in a multidisciplinary team with a high proportion of Black and minority ethnic people among the staff, or vice versa. Trainees need to consider the implications of this for themselves, particularly in relation to their own attitudes, beliefs and position in the team and within the wider society.

Service development

Services need to be accessible both geographically and psychologically to people from Black and minority ethnic communities (Perkins, 1995). In many cultures, including White European-based ones, contact with psychiatric services, and particularly the long stay psychiatric hospitals, is considered to be stigmatizing. Making services accessible requires attention to where and by whom individuals may be seen, the design of buildings, the use of literature in a range of languages, the ethnicity of the staff team, the use of positive images of Black and minority ethnic people, etc. Additionally, the use of advocates to bridge the gap between service users and providers can help to make services more accessible.

Trainees need also to be aware that the slow pace of change within institutions is partly due to their (often unacknowledged) function in providing society with a way of keeping 'difficult' and 'different' people out of mind. This function will be even stronger in providing a place for people who are different from the majority on more than one level, e.g. ethnicity, culture as well as mental health problems. This may particularly impede the process of planning services that genuinely meet the needs of Black and minority ethnic people.

SERVICE DELIVERY

Consciousness raising

Szivos and Griffiths (1990) define consciousness raising as a strategy for social change which 'takes place on the level of group or social action and involves a positive assertion of value outside the ethnocentric value-system espoused by the mainstream culture'. The dominant culture in the West understands and explains the experience of unusual mental states such as 'psychosis' within the illness or deficit model. Perhaps in this context rehabilitation back to the 'norm' makes sense. Consciousness raising on the other hand could be applied to advocate the validation of (rather than rehabilitation from) the 'mad' experience. This may be achieved by creating a political space where people with a diagnosis of 'long-term mental illness' in general are enabled to 'own' (Coleman, 1999) their experiences, the incarceration surrounding these experiences, and explore the consequences of living marginalized lives, often managed by powerful others. The role of any professional seeking social justice for the Black or minority ethnic client receiving long-term mental health 'support' would be to politically support and personally nurture the potential in every Black client for the reclaiming of 'ownership' to happen (see Coleman, 1999, p. 69).

In order to make any meaningful impact on service provision for Black and minority ethnic clients, rehabilitation programmes will have to actively acknowledge the effects of power and oppression manifested in the form of racism that is so insidiously connected to the process of labelling and maintaining a Black individual as mad.

Rehabilitation services for Black and minority ethnic clients need to be explicitly committed to creating a therapeutic space where, as in intercultural therapy, a real acknowledgement of the social reality of 'race' and racism is made. Professionals, by virtue of carrying the responsibility of power, ought to initiate dialogue about discrimination and persecution (Thomas, 1997) and thereby create an ethos where people's experiences are talked about in the context of their social and political realities.

Black user empowerment

Like the survivor movement in mental health, a growing number of Black-led services (e.g. Nafsiyat in London, Awaaz in Manchester, Black Carers' and clients' project in Brixton), have empowered Black users in various ways. Rehabilitation services could learn from the experiences and knowledge bases of these organizations by direct consultations and adoption of their race equality ideology.

Sassoon and Lindow (1995) identify two strands to Black user empowerment. First, the 'reactive' aspect deals directly with the impact of inequality through advocacy, legal representation and training projects built upon the Black client's consultancy and negotiation skills. Second, the empowerment process is 'innovative': from outside of the system, innovative Black projects provide a 'safe base in which consciousness around Black identity and its relationship to the psychiatric experience can be explored' (Sasoon and Lindow, 1995). This idea is similar to the idea of consciousness raising as advocated by Szivos and Griffiths (1990) discussed above.

Medication and informed consent

The controversy over the long-term use of psychotropic drugs has been articulated in the rehabilitation literature (see Pilling, 1991). Specifically, the long-term efficacy of psychotropic medication, the methods of administration and prescribing, the adverse effects of psychotropic medication and the reinforcement of the medical model have been the focus of some concern (Pilling, 1991). Earlier in this module, it has been pointed out how symptom relief or clinical recovery can actually create social disability. Pilling (1991) in *Rehabilitation and Community Care* asserts that medical treatment remains an important part of most rehabilitation programmes and 'a broad based multi-disciplinary, multi-agency model of rehabilitation is the most important corrective to the abuse of the medical model'. Perhaps there is mileage in this view that the cause of the oppressed can be adequately represented in a model where power is less monolithic. In a multi-agency model however, we need to note that power, responsibility and accountability is not equally distributed. In the case of Black and minority ethnic clients, justice is hardly likely to be achieved if the multi-agency model does not make explicit the specific strategies to be implemented to eliminate the misuse of medication. Compliance to medication has to be essentially based on informed consent rather than 'persuasion' and 'encouragement'. Informed consent would mean making the adverse effects literature, and the limited efficacy literature available to all clients and multi-agency service providers. One suggestion is that there could be greater involvement by user movements in relation to neuroleptics and their usage.

LEARNING OUTCOMES

Trainees should:

1. Be aware of how their own ethnic and cultural background impacts on how they may be perceived by clients and other service providers. Be aware of own limitations and biases in the understanding of others.
2. Develop some understanding of how institutional structures can develop to protect professionals from facing difficult feelings around difference, leading to loss of the significance of the individuality of the service users, and of how this dynamic is particularly strong with psychiatric services, and especially so for people perceived as 'different' on multiple levels. Trainees should understand how in this context racism is more often than not implicated in the social and emotional difficulties experienced by individuals from minority ethnic communities.
3. Be able to take account of cultural background and values in formulating the difficulties of clients and in setting goals for meaningful change.
4. Be aware of how the service structures in which they work contribute to and work against their accessibility to Black and minority ethnic people. Develop strategies to enable themselves to identify and challenge structural inequalities based on 'race'.
5. Be aware of the relevant theories and models of psychosocial rehabilitation and their application to work with Black and minority ethnic people. Develop a critical analysis of the current theory and its limitation in this context.

METHODS OF TEACHING

1. Critical presentation of theoretical topics in the form of lectures and reading material.
2. Discussion and debate facilitated by people with first hand experience of the psychiatric system, for example representatives from 'survivor' and/or user movement groups (Hearing voices network, Mind).
3. Experiential learning through role playing of personal experience (using diversity in terms of gender, sexuality, race, age, class and culture within the group).
4. Interactive learning through the use of workshops and small group discussions on themes raised above.

5. Recommended reading of relevant fiction and non-fiction that highlight the Black British experience (an up-to-date reading list could be compiled. See Introductory Module, annotated Reading).

Suggested exercise

Exercise

Scenario
You are the key worker to a 31- year-old Indian woman given 'primary diagnoses' of postnatal depression and schizo-affective disorder. Your client is a housewife and lives with her husband and four young children, the youngest being two years old and the oldest seven. She became very withdrawn six months after the birth of her third child and later presented 'bizarre' behaviour: for example, running out of the house into the garden for no apparent reason, believing that her husband's family were plotting against her and believing that evil spirits had cast a spell on her life. The client is on a depot medication and has been refusing to take her injections as well as oral medication, saying it interferes with her ability to look after her children and enjoy an 'awake' life. Her husband refuses to let her come off her medication and has been using a lot of pressure to ensure that she takes it. He is convinced that if she stops taking her medication she will 'become mad again'. The client is entirely dependent on her husband who is the accepted head of the household and controls management of domestic affairs at all levels except immediate childcare, cooking, cleaning and other menial chores. The children present as healthy, happy and relate well to both parents.

Questions to consider:
1. Diagnoses or misdiagnoses? How could the multiple diagnoses have arisen for this client and how would you use your critical analyses or deconstruction of these in the clinical setting?
2. How would you understand positioning of power within the marital relationship from a non-Eurocentric, feminist perspective?
3. If the 'terrorist' in this family is madness, how would you get the husband on your side (or would you?) in order to help this woman experiment with coming off medication?
4. What difficulties might you encounter in attaining the trust of your client?
5. What diffficulties might you encounter when presenting the case to your medically-led multidisciplinary team (who all value and like you)? How would you maximize support for yourself and manage your team's responses and potential conflict over this case?

Instructions
Present above vignette with the questions and encourage small group discussions followed by presentation to the whole group and then end with a final whole group discussion. Discussions should be time limited: e.g. 10 minutes for initial presentation of the vignette, 15 minutes for the small group discussion, 20 minutes for whole group feedback and discussion. Factual information about medication withdrawal (neuroleptics) and civil rights (to refuse medication) in the context of the Mental Health Act should be made available to trainees.

Aims
1. To explore strategies of managing the understanding of deconstructed diagnoses, particularly in relation to minority ethnic clients, and identifying ways in which clients can be enabled to live and hope beyond the confusion of multiple diagnoses.
2. To explore strategies of confronting racism and cultural insensitivities in mental health settings and acting as a clinical psychologist in a predominantly medicalized multidisciplinary context.
3. To explore assumptions of power balances/imbalances in relation to a minority ethnic family.
4. To explore some of the limitations of the White, middle-class female empowerment model.

Annotated references

Bentall, R.P. (1990) (ed.) *Reconstructing Schizophrenia*. London, New York: Routledge

This book is an invaluable compilation of the ideas of clinical psychologists writing on the issue of madness from a non-medical perspective. The issues addressed include the problematic conceptualization of madness as a disorder, the role of biology in psychotic behaviour and the contemporary management of madness through behavioural, cognitive and family management perspectives.

Boyle, M. (1990) *Schizophrenia – A Scientific Delusion?* London: Routledge

This book offers critical analyses of psychiatric theorizing about schizophrenia as a scientifically established disease. The arguments developed in the nine chapters are crafted with exquisite logic and present a historical, political and philosophical analysis. The final chapter offers an alternative to the 'theoretical confusion' generated by the politics of psychiatric diagnosis. Highly recommended.

Coleman, R. (1999) *Recovery An Alien Concept?* Gloucester: Handsell Publishing

An excellent presentation of the concept of recovery so lacking within the traditional understanding of 'mental illness'. The author utilizes personal experience of the psychiatric system to suggest that 'recovery can be a reality ... for the great majority of those who enter the psychiatric system'. The book offers a compelling argument against the disempowering shackles of traditional psychiatry and puts the possibility of personal recovery at the centre of its discourse. The discourse is characteristically of passion and hope. A must-read for trainees interested in working in this area.

Thomas, P. (1997) *The Dialectics of Schizophrenia.* London/New York: Free Association Books Limited

This book takes its perspective from biological, psychological, social and economic positions, regarding these of equal value. An argument is made for understanding clients' experiences in the context of their life history and social and cultural factors.

Fernando, S. (1995) (Ed.) *Mental Health in a Multi-ethnic Society. A Multi-disciplinary Handbook.* London: Routledge

This book is an invaluable contribution to the understanding of mental health issues in a multidisciplinary and multiethnic context. The range of issues addressed includes a political analysis of the social realities of 'mental illness', a fairly comprehensive analysis of the legal aspects of mental health care, ways of empowering mental health system users and a solution-focused 'way forward' within and outside of the psychiatric structure. The authors represent the various professions involved in mental health service delivery and their stance is contemporary and community care orientated.

Chapter 15
HEALTH PSYCHOLOGY

Lih-Mei Liao

Introduction

This section offers some considerations and suggestions as to how clinical psychology trainers might integrate 'race' and culture issues into the teaching of health psychology. However, there are important limitations to be considered. The first concerns the problem of defining health psychology within clinical psychology. In the past, clinical psychologists have tended to view health psychology as a specialism within their own discipline. However, there is now formal recognition that health psychology is a separate discipline drawn from a knowledge base which is distinct from that of clinical psychology. The former Special Group in Health Psychology has gained divisional status within the BPS. The focus of health psychology is on research, primary prevention and the development of population based interventions. On the other hand, 'health psychology', as practised by clinical psychologists in medical settings, tends to focus on individual therapy in secondary care contexts. Many 'health psychology' modules within clinical psychology training are more aligned to what used to be termed 'behavioural medicine' and now known as 'clinical health psychology'. It is difficult to address how to teach 'race' and culture issues in a clinicial specialism which itself has not been clearly defined.

Another problem in producing this module relates to the fact that 'clinical health psychologists' work in such diverse medical settings that might each be considered a specialism with its own special set of issues. For example, the special knowledge and skills required for working with clients with cardiovascular disease may be quite different from those required for working in the context of disfigurement. Likewise, consideration of 'race' and culture issues will differ in those contexts. For instance, diabetes is prevalent among some Asian populations and special knowledge about dietary practices and physical activities and their modification may need to be developed. This, however, may be much less relevant to those working within the context of pain management, or sexually transmitted disease. Thus, this section can only draw out broad parameters and cannot address micro skills or specific knowledge required for each of the wide-ranging medical settings in which clinical health psychologists currently work.

DEMOGRAPHIC DETAILS

Health outcome and risk patterns differ according to broad social categories (see Ahmed, 1993):

- Socio-economic status (e.g. heart disease is more prevalent in lower income groups compared to higher income groups).
- Sex (e.g. women live longer than men but report more ill health).
- Age (e.g. cancer becomes more prevalent with age).
- Ethnicity (e.g. British babies born to mothers whose country of birth is Bangladesh have lower average birth weight than those born to White British mothers).

Demographic factors interact and produce different permutations. For example, men are more at risk of coronary heart disease than women but this difference tails off after the age of 55. The different patterns may reflect genetic factors, reporting artefacts, social causation, or all of these.

THEORY

It is common for clinical health psychologists to look to the academic discipline of health psychology to fuel the development of psychological interventions with clients experiencing health problems. In their application to health-related problems presented by clients from minority ethnic backgrounds, there are some points to consider:

1. There have been relatively few opportunities for minority ethnic communities in Britain to define research questions in health psychology.
2. There has been relatively little published research that examines the illness experience of people from minority ethnic groups in Britain.
3. There is relatively little published research that examines the health-related perceptions (e.g. attitude to breast screening) of minority ethnic communities, though there is rather more information on the distribution of health-related behaviours (e.g. smoking prevalence) among different social groups.
4. There have been relatively few psychological interventions targeting health issues concerning minority ethnic communities; those that have taken place have tended to be a-theoretical, thus not feeding back into theory development within health psychology.
5. Health psychology in Britain focuses on individual factors (e.g. the relationship between the individual's health beliefs and smoking behaviour), often at the expense of institutional factors (e.g. limited occupational choice, reduced access to health services). The dominant view of personal control and responsibility over health outcome may not adequately reflect the socio-political disadvantages that can cause poorer health among British minority ethnic communities.

This is not to say that there are no universal beliefs and experiences in relation to health and illness. However, clinical psychologists would need to be aware of the limitations of their models when applied to minority ethnic clients and would need to explore them with individuals.

PRACTICE

Several levels have been identified whereby clinical psychologists can work towards enhancing the well-being of minority ethnic clients in general medical settings. The potential for each of the following suggestions for development would depend on the specific setting and the clinician involved.

Direct psychological interventions

1. Recognize the importance of clarifying meanings and assumptions throughout the consultation process.
2. Explore the referral process (e.g. what is the client's understanding about why they have been referred, and how they, and if applicable significant others, might feel about being referred to a psychologist; what this means in their culture).
3. Explore the client's willingness to engage with the psychological process (e.g. explain that their choice would not affect their medical care) and explain what the assessment might consist of.
4. Examine to what extent, if at all, the client's cultural conceptions about the particular medical diagnosis influence their behaviour in relation to the condition (e.g., arthritis – what is it, what causes it?). It may be appropriate to learn from 'alternative' practitioners (or mainstream depending on whose point of view) involved in the client's health care such as hakims, herbalists or spiritualists.
5. Offer the opportunity for further understanding about the medical diagnosis (e.g. infertility) by giving information with sensitive consideration of the possible impact given the client's ethnic background and for discussion about treatment procedures and choice.
6. Offer to define explicitly and discuss psychological intervention options with client.
7. Relate client's experience to context, of which their ethnicity is a dimension.
8. Definitions of psychological adjustment currently reflect European ideologies so therapist's awareness of own beliefs will be important. For example, where are the therapist's values positioned along the continuum of independence and interdependence, or of closed and permeable interpersonal boundaries?

Making clinical psychology services more accessible to minority ethnic clients with health-related problems

1. Promote the need for easily accessible interpreting services.
2. Promote the need for easily accessible translation services and the distribution of information.
3. Network with community groups to increase awareness of and ways of accessing psychological services within general medicine.
4. Monitor the above interventions systematically.

Working with other health professionals

1. Discuss the health risk-taking and illness experience of individuals within their cultural context through multi-disciplinary case studies or seminars.
2. Develop multi-disciplinary interventions where appropriate (e.g. psycho-educational groups for Asian clients with diabetes, involving dieticians, physicians and chiropodists).
3. Contribute to clinical audit activities where possible: e.g. investigating minority ethnic clients' satisfaction with the health care processes.

Contributing towards institutional changes

1. Carry out service delivery research: for example, explore specific needs for psychological care among minority ethnic client groups and promote service developments accordingly.
2. Carry out theoretical health psychology research with minority ethnic populations. This might involve the use of alternative methodologies to examine cultural constructions and spiritual beliefs about health and illness, cultural variations in health-related behaviours and what might underpin them, perceptions of health care processes, preferences for alternative methods of health care, and so on.
3. Disseminate knowledge and experience where possible.
4. Debate the issues in mainstream health psychology in this country.

LEARNING OUTCOMES

Trainees should be able to:

1. Identify inequalities in health care processes and health outcome, and make use of the contextual information in problem formulation with clients from minority ethnic groups.
2. Identify limitations of the prevailing theoretical models in health psychology in order to apply them thoughtfully with clients from minority ethnic backgrounds.
3. Discuss research questions in the psychology of health and illness that are pertinent to minority ethnic people.

4.   Adapt their psychological knowledge and intervention techniques to enhance the health and well-being of clients from minority ethnic backgrounds.

METHODS OF TEACHING

The following methods may be helpful:

1.   Pre-reading of articles, books and handouts.
2.   Guided discussion of conceptual issues.
3.   Interactive teaching methods to teach skills (e.g. workshop format) incorporating small group work, role play using vignettes, feedback and so on.
4.   Presentations of individual cases and discussion.
5.   Presentations of larger scale interventions (e.g. local initiatives) and discussion.

Suggested exercises

Exercise 1: Self-reflection

Aim
To increase awareness of the experience of minority ethnic clients within the medical context

Instructions
Divide into pairs or do the exercise on an individual basis.

Cast your mind back to your last consultation with a same-ethnicity doctor (if trainee has had no such experience, think in terms of a friend or relative).

Take 10 minutes to answer the following on a piece of paper (not collected):

• What were your thoughts and feelings in anticipation of the consultation?
• What were the characteristics of the interaction (e.g. attentiveness, brevity, guilt)?
• To what extent were you able to communicate your problems/needs?
• To what extent did your doctor respond to them?
• How would any of the above be different if you had perceived your doctor to have been ethnically different from you?

Exercise 2: Case discussion

Aim
To practice psychological skills in a medical context, with an awareness of issues of 'race' and culture.

Scenario
Referral: A 49-year-old Black woman who has recently been diagnosed as having non-insulin dependent diabetes is referred by her White British consultant for psychological support. In the letter, the referrer mentions that she has not been managing her dietary regime and that this might be due to her depression, but that she risks further deterioration in health with continued poor management of her condition.

Instructions
Divide into small groups of four to six.

Assuming that you are a White British clinical health psychologist, discuss in the next 20–30 minutes:

• What issues would you want to explore?
• How would you address your difference?

If your client comes along because she has been sent and she does not know what psychology is, how would you explain health psychology and what your role is in her health care?

Exercise 3: Large group discussion

Aim
To practice formulating research questions on health issues in relation to minority ethnic people.

Scenario
There is a small fund for research on a health-related topic with the local Asian population and your department is very keen to bid for a project. You are a White British trainee and you have taken up the challenge to do some groundwork as part of your placement experience.

Instructions
Divide into small groups of six to eight.
In 30 minutes, outline a project taking into account some of the following points; then feed back to the large group to defend your suggestions.

Points to consider:
- How would you select a relevant topic (taking your own interests into account)?
- What theoretical models would your explore in your project?
- What literature would support your work?
- How would you ensure that the project is viable?
- What research methods would you choose considering that minority ethnic participants are typically under-represented in postal survey type projects?
- How would you recruit participants?
- How would you deal with language barriers that may arise?
- How would your project benefit your participating community (directly or ultimately)?
- How would you disseminate your results?

Annotated references

Ahmed W.I.U. (1993) (Ed.) *Race and Health in Contemporary Britain*. Buckingham: Open University

An excellent general introduction. As well as being a good source of information on the health outcomes of Black and minority ethnic populations in Britain, this book provides a good exposure of racist practices within the health care services and critically analyses specific health care processes and their underlying ideology.

Blackmore, K. and Boneham, M. (1994) *Age, Race and Ethnicity*. Buckingham: Open University

As the title suggests, this book focuses on the 'greying' of Britain's minority communities, thus addressing an important gap in ageing studies. Health and health care issues of ageing minority ethnic populations are specifically tackled in Chapter 7.

Douglas, J. (1992) Black women's health matters: Putting Black women's health on the research agenda. In H. Roberts (Ed.) *Women's Health Matters*. London: Routledge

In Britain, research in women's health from a feminist perspective has traditionally been based on 'White feminist' ideology. The author argues that the little research that addresses specific health experiences of women from minority ethnic communities also reflects this ideology. Examples are given of researchers failing to ask to what extent racism contributes to the health and well-being of the Black participants.

Lupton, D. (1996) *Medicine as Culture: Illness, Disease and the Body in Western Societies*. London: Sage

This book will be of general interest. It gives a fascinating analysis of the social construction of health, illness and medicine in Western societies, thus exposing many of the assumptions which may or may not be shared by other social groups.

Clark, R., Anderson, N.B., Clark, V.R. and Williams, D.R. (1999) Racism as a stressor for African Americans: A biopsychosocial model. *American Psychologist, 54*, 805–816

In the prolific research literature on stress, studies investigating the extent to which experience of racism could contribute to ill-health are relatively rare. Racism is also conspicuous by its absence from theories about the relationship between stress and well-being. This article outlines a biopsychosocial model for future research into perceived racism. The exhaustive reference list would be a great asset to psychologists in training, teaching, research and practice.

Additional sources for further reading
1. The Health Education Authority Library is an excellent resource.
2. Relevant articles occasionally appear in main medical journals such as the *British Medical Journal* and *Lancet*, and in mainstream health psychology journals such as *Health Psychology, Journal of Health Psychology* and *Psychology and Health*. However, such articles are more often found in multidisciplinary international journals such as *Social Science and Medicine, Community and Medicine, Journal of Public Health Medicine* and *Family Practice*.
3. *Health Psychology Update*. Newsletter of the Division of Health Psychology, British Psychological Society.
4. Government publications.
5. Local studies, e.g. those published by local health authorities or academic institutions.

Other useful modules
Primary Care
HIV/GU-Medicine/Sexual Health
Substance Misuse
Child, Adolescent and Family
Older Adults

Chapter 16

HIV/GU-MEDICINE/SEXUAL HEALTH

Oliver Davidson

Introduction

The psychologically intimate area of human sexuality and sexual health provides fertile ground in which emotionally charged constructs such as sex and death interact with 'race' and culture issues. Clearly, an individual's attitude and behaviour regarding their sexual health is strongly mediated by influences arising from their cultural background.

There is much importance in the human experience of sex, pleasure, morality, fertility, pregnancy, guilt, joy, passion, fear, shame, sexually transmitted infections (STIs), HIV/AIDS, and HIV-related death. However, people's experience of their own sexual health is greatly determined by cultural and sub-cultural factors such as gender, age, education, socio-economic status, politics, religion, nationality, language, geographical origins and ethnicity. 'Race' and ethnicity can play a very significant role, but they can in turn interact with sub-cultural factors such as sexual orientation and personal lifestyle to create the complex social foundations underlying human sexuality and sexual health.

Although the main focus of this module is on 'race', ethnic, gender and religious influences, it is important to keep in mind how these interact with other cultural and sub-cultural factors contributing to a person's overall sexual identity.

DEMOGRAPHIC AND EPIDEMIOLOGICAL DETAILS

In the UK there has been an absence of ethnicity information in routine surveillance of HIV and sexually transmitted infections data, due in part to the concern over possible misinterpretation, misuse and controversy that the publication of such epidemiological information might precipitate (Fenton and Johnson, 1997). Ethnicity data needs to be collated and utilized in a sensitive and responsible manner (Bhopal, 1997). However, this must be balanced by the growing need to assertively override the fear of sensationalist misuse that such data gathering attracts (e.g. De Cock and Low, 1997). Information can and must assist the people being studied, not solely be held against them.

While the HIV/AIDS epidemic has developed within the gay male population in the UK as in most of the Western world, it is becoming increasingly clear that the second social group most affected by HIV and AIDS in Britain appears to be the heterosexual African communities, particularly those having recently arrived from Africa and now residing in large urban areas such as London (Bhatt, 1995). Although ethnicity data has been poorly recorded in the past, recent reports argue that the age adjusted relative risk for reported cases of AIDS in the UK for 1994–95 was 20 times greater for African adults in the UK and 355 times greater for African children in the UK, compared to non-Africans living in the UK (De Cock and Low, 1997).

Data on ethnicity have not routinely been collected for STIs here in the UK. In the USA, surveillance data suggest rates of STIs and HIV/AIDS are disproportionately higher among people from minority ethnic groups (CDCP, 1994; Ellerbrock *et al.*, 1991). However, a few reports are now being published that attempt to document the influence that ethnicity may have on STI incidence in the UK. One study reported that the incidence of gonorrhoea in south London was found to be over eight times higher in 'Black' populations compared to 'White' populations. These findings were independent of age and gender, and the differences persisted after adjustment for socio-economic status using Jarman indices (Low *et al.*, 1997). Although the study attempted to collect ethnicity data in accordance with the 1991 census categories, inconsistencies in ethnic monitoring within the GUM clinics forced the authors to use only three broad categories (White, Black, other and unknown). The authors, therefore, caution against making distinctions within the ethnic categories, but none the less assert that large inequalities in STI incidence do exist between ethnic groups, and that these need to be taken seriously by the communities themselves.

The only nationwide study to examine sexual attitudes, behaviours and lifestyles was the National Sexual Attitudes and Lifestyles Survey (NATSAL) carried out by Johnson *et al.* (1994). There were very few respondents from Black and minority ethnic backgrounds in this research, but this was addressed in the next version of the survey carried out in 1999. Preliminary work directly aimed at sexual health and minority ethnic people in the UK has only been developed recently. Examples include the qualitative ExES Study (Exploring Ethnicity and Sexual Health) which examined sexual attitudes and lifestyles of five minority ethnic groups in central London (Elam *et al.*, 1999), the Mayisha Study which assessed HIV-related knowledge, attitudes and behaviour in five African communities in central London (e.g. Fenton *et al.*, 1999) and a study by Mahtani *et al.* (in preparation) which examined the medical and psychological priorities of minority ethnic attenders at a London GUM clinic.

There is a complete lack of ethnicity data in the epidemiology of psychosexual problems related to HIV, STIs and sexual dysfunction in the UK. This relates to the overall lack of ethnicity data for sexual health in general, as discussed above, but also probably reflects the relative lack of priority given to psychosexual problems in the past. While there are many anecdotes and clinical impressions regarding psychosexual problems in different ethnic groups, none have been tested through NHS service monitoring systems or, more importantly, through community-based prevalence surveys.

THEORY

Concepts

The most important clinical issue to remember is that a psychologist should *never assume anything* about a service user merely on the basis of their ethnicity. There are no rules governing the manner in which a service user's attitudes towards sexual issues are predetermined by their ethnicity, religion, gender, sexuality, politics or country of origin. We cannot assume anything about the degree to which health service users are influenced by their cultural background. Service users should be considered individually, in the context of their own separate systemic influences. Although their ethnic background may well have significantly influenced their psychological development, we cannot presume in what manner. People may choose to interpret such backgrounds in whatever manner they choose. Ethnic stereotypes are in no way useful when considering the psychological concerns of an individual service user.

It has been argued that there is a history of racist research and teaching surrounding ethnicity and health, including sexual health. There have been many attempts to demonstrate racial variations in disease states (among other things), but there is a growing demand towards the responsible use of ethnicity and health research to provide an assessment of the needs and inequalities of different ethnic groups and to help guide practical resource allocation to help act upon any inequalities (Bhopal, 1997; Fenton and Johnson, 1997).

Recent data suggests that there are significant differences in the incidence of HIV and STIs across different ethnic groups in the UK, and although many of these differences can be attributed to confounding variables such as age, sex or socio-economic status, strong trends remain even after these factors are taken into account.

Potential cultural factors

An individual's cultural belief can influence the attitudinal relationship between sexual response and psychological well-being. A number of issues may be relevant when working on sexually related issues with service users from different cultures.

1. The family as a social unit

In comparison with contemporary Western society, many cultures do not hold the individual as the most important social unit, and the concerns of the extended family hold priority over the individual when decisions are being made regarding a particular individual's behaviour. This could be especially relevant when issues related to sex, sexual functioning, STIs and reproduction are concerned. The importance of an individual's attitude towards these sexual issues may therefore be surpassed by the concerns of the whole family and its reputation in the community. For example, an individual who is asked by the health service to contact recent sexual partners following the diagnosis of HIV (or even an STI) may place the reputation of their family in higher regard than their responsibility towards their own health or that of their partners.

Another implication is that when an extended family lives together, perhaps in a small dwelling, the close proximity of sleeping and accommodation may impact upon a couple's ability to enjoy privacy and sexual intimacy.

Sex can be constructed in terms of personal enjoyment or fulfilment in some cultures. However, sex can also be viewed more in terms of reproduction potential, given the social status that fertility and children can possibly bring upon an individual or family. This was, of course, traditionally an important issue in European societies, and in some cases still is, but it has also been argued that the Industrial Revolution, the development of contraception technology and the changing role of women have all influenced the meaning of sex in developed countries.

There can be a number of factors associated with arranged marriages that impact upon a sexual relationship. Such relationships are often as much an issue of developing a relationship between two extended families as between the married couple. Sexual attraction cannot be assumed to occur in such relationships; indeed, one of the arguments in favour of these arrangements is that they avoid many of the adverse developmental complications of passionate relationships. The woman may be expected not to have had sex before, and therefore to have very different sexual expectations relative to a sexually experienced woman. Given the pragmatic approach to such marriages, the man's ability to sire a child may be immediately under close scrutiny, especially by the family of his new wife, a situation that can help develop a performance anxiety around his sexual functioning.

2. Sources of information and expertise

Information and knowledge regarding the physiology of the human sexual response can vary greatly across different groups, depending upon education and experience. Awareness of sexual biology and sexual physiology can vary widely, with equally differing understandings of what is going on when things go wrong.

Although medicine has become the strongest provider of sexual health information and care in the developed world, it is fair to say that its power base has become lessened through the humanization and accountability demanded of the medical profession by the public. None the less, many people still look towards physicians for advice and guidance on sexual health matters. As distinct from the medical doctor or nurse, the spiritual or folk healer can also play an important role in the treatment of psychosexual problems (e.g. Muslim *hakim*, Hindu *vaid*, and European naturopath). The re-emergence of 'alternative' therapies in the West provides a good example of this. Whatever the case, authority figures such as healers or doctors can play an important role in the 'top down' treatment of sexual health concerns, especially if an expert opinion is required.

3. Gender power issues

There have been many social constructs involving the importance of gender power across time and culture. If the service user comes from a context where the male is expected to play a dominant role in marriage, there may be significant concerns if it is felt that he is unable to fulfil that role. For example, male potency can be seen as very important in providing a sense of male identity and power. If not involved in procreation, male ejaculation can sometimes be considered to drain the mind as well as the body. Consequently, masturbation and nocturnal emissions (wet dreams) can be construed in a very negative light, and in a manner that sometimes seems to hold very little physiological evidence. Examples include:

- *koro syndrome*: a fear sometimes expressed by people of Chinese backgrounds that masturbation, wet dreams and excess sex will cause the penis to retract into the abdomen and cause death.
- *dhat syndrome*: a fear sometimes expressed by people of Hindu and Muslim backgrounds that semen loss is harmful and causes debility and weakness (e.g., Malhotra and Wig, 1975; Paris, 1992). Ayurvedic medical systems consider that semen production occurs in the bone marrow, and some rural traditional cultures in and around the Indian sub-continent attribute significant distress to any unnecessary semen loss (emissions, masturbation, excessive sex)
- *blindness*: a fear sometimes expressed by people of Christian or European backgrounds, particularly male adolescents, that masturbation can result in blindness.

Across all cultures, women and men can have very different roles to play in personal, sexual and family decisions. For example, females may be expected to play a submissive role in some cultures, including decisions over sex and family planning. This continued to be the case in Western society, prior to the relatively recent developments of feminism. In many Islamic cultures, it can be considered inappropriate for women to express interest in or knowledge about sexual matters. It may also be very inappropriate for a woman to talk to a man about such issues. Within a relationship it may be considered inappropriate for women to discuss sex or negotiate a change in a couple's sexual behaviour.

Female Genital Mutilation (FGM) can be a firmly entrenched practice, endorsed by both men and women within a number of African cultures, including those from Somalia, Ethiopia and Sudan. Organized dissent from such practices is becoming widespread in these countries, and the WHO is assisting national and international organizations to eradicate this practice, while the UK has formally outlawed the practice through its Prohibition of Circumcision Act (1985). The Northwick Park Institute for Medical Research set up an African Well Woman clinic in the UK in 1993, believed to be the first such clinic in the Western world to address FGM issues.

Such is the concern over the power of female sexuality that in many cultures male extramarital sexual desire can be attributed to the deliberate seductiveness of women rather than to the individual responsibility of the male. On the other hand, in some east African cultures, the paternal aunts have a very dominant and powerful role over decision making with respect to a family's children, including sex education and guardianship. They are usually brought in to provide sexual education and an understanding of sexual relationships when daughters reach puberty, and they can have automatic guardianship rights over the children of a deceased brother.

Models

Issues such as those outlined above can significantly influence the ability for contemporary Western health models to provide culturally appropriate psychological assessment and treatment services for sexual health concerns. Eurocentric, individual-focused clinical psychology models applicable to sexual health concerns tend to focus on personal empowerment and psychological well-being through the enhancement of individual self-efficacy and internalized locus of control. Such models may not be the most relevant, however, when dealing with people whose culture does not share such individualistic views.

The possibility that people from Black and other minority ethnic groups may not want to utilize services based on such Eurocentric models is empirically important. Preliminary data suggest that some service users from these groups may still want to access sexual health services, and that they may still want to deal with some of the emotional issues associated with their sexual health concerns in the NHS clinic setting (e.g. Mahtani *et al.*, in preparation). For example, it is interesting to consider the way in which Jehu's 'PLISSIT' model of psychosexual therapy may still assist in the delivery of a psychology service for sexual problems across a number of different cultures. This stage model of psychosexual service delivery (whereby different types of therapeutic intervention are administered, as required, beginning with 'Permission' and followed by 'Limited Information', 'Specific Skills' and 'Intensive Therapy') still opens itself to a number of questions when applied across different cultural settings. For example, what actually is permissible sexual behaviour within a certain cultural context? What types of sex education are appropriate for informing different people? Can specific skills-training like Masters and Johnson Sensate Focus work with people who do not share the internal locus of control premise (some argue that it is possible: see d'Ardenne, 1996)? And how appropriate is intensive therapy across different cultural settings?

However, the systemic model clearly lends itself well to this area. Such a model addresses many of the incongruencies outlined above by asking questions such as: what is the context under which the problem is occurring? What are the expectations of the service user? What existing resources can be brought to bear within the service user's life to assist in the problem?

PRACTICE

Interviewing, assessment, intervention, service delivery

In general, psychological assessments are best conducted with a systemic framework in mind. What does the presenting problem mean to the service user and their family? What are their explanations? What would they normally/traditionally do to assist with the problem? What is available in their community to assist in the problem?

There are a few sources of cultural, ethnic and religious information relevant to health service users in the UK with sexual (and other health) concerns from Black and minority ethnic backgrounds. Although these may be of assistance in attempting to appreciate some of the broader aspects of how culture interacts with sexual health, they are forever in danger of making global estimates and hence guide the clinician into making generalized assumptions. It is impossible for a clinician to attempt to keep up to date on all details of every cultural sub-group; attempting to do so will be frustrating and ultimately unsuccessful. Clearly, service users themselves are the best source of information regarding their own specific cultural issues relating to sex. The meaning of sexual health to individual service users is the most important concern. Ask them sensitively. They are the experts.

The use of interpreters for interviews by a clinician unfamiliar with the language of the service user needs to be arranged with care. Service users may be particularly concerned about confidentiality, especially if the interpreter comes from the same discrete ethnic community. If the service has the freedom to provide choice, service users should be consulted on whether or not they would prefer a male or a female interpreter and whether or not they would like the interpreter to come from their own ethnic background.

Rather than imposing a Eurocentric psychology on service users with significantly different views of psychosexual issues, it may be best to liaise with culturally appropriate individuals, groups and organizations that already exist in the service user's community. These individuals or groups can, in turn, work in conjunction with health services, if appropriate. If it is difficult to access such resources, then a more community-based approach may be appropriate. For example, a service can develop the formation of focus/support groups among service users' peers with similar concerns, who can in turn inform the statutory bodies of the manner in which services can best be developed to maximize equity of access across key groups.

It is probably even less appropriate for psychology sexual health staff to be discussing and working on sexual issues with minority ethnic service users of a different gender. For this reason, it is usually best if gender matching of therapist to service user is offered.

The use of advocates (peers of the service user who have more familiarity with the service) may be useful in the sexual health setting. These tend to come from community-based organizations, and a minimal degree of professionalism is essential, particularly regarding confidentiality and treatment options.

SEXUAL HEALTH SERVICE PROVISION

While cultural background issues help shape the aetiology and impact of many individuals' sexual health concerns, they also significantly influence the manner in which the same individual accesses services such as the NHS in order to address these concerns. Outlined below are some of the process issues relevant to service provision.

Some service users may express serious concern over the level of confidentiality governing any information they provide to health staff, both within and outside of the NHS workplace. This may especially be the case with information regarding sexually intimate behaviour or potentially seriously infectious diseases such as HIV, Hepatitis and TB. Services must therefore clarify the influence of the VD Act (last amended 1974) which places confidentiality of service users as a priority, and ensure staff adherence to this.

While NHS staff may view sexual health status as important, many service users may feel they have other concerns that take more immediate priority, including their asylum status, financial and accommodation problems, the safety of family still living abroad, and the health and welfare of family and friends in the UK.

Individuals or couples from cross-cultural marriages (e.g. across differing religions, nationalities, ethnicities, social class, education) may experience particular problems related to their different expectations regarding gender roles and sexual behaviour (e.g. Clulow, 1993). Such differences may manifest themselves in the way that the individual or couple access and utilize the service, and the issues that are raised. Psychologists need to keep this factor in mind when developing and administering services.

Services also need to consider the impact on staff following disclosure by service users of certain cultural sexual practices, in order that staff continue to provide non-judgmental professional services following the disclosure. Examples from some African cultures include female and male circumcision occurring at puberty, along with labia pulling, wife inheritance by a brother following the death of the husband, polygamy, and so on. Such practices may invoke strong personal feelings in health staff, given the strong differences in practice that they themselves may have experienced and learnt. However, it is one of the aims of a health service to provide a non-judgmental health service, and to delineate when it is appropriate to intervene in a cultural practice (e.g. when there is physical/psychological damage perhaps in accordance with British law), and when not to intervene (e.g. if a service user communicates satisfaction with the practice).

LEARNING OUTCOMES

'Race' and culture training in sexual health is based on premises very similar to other settings. Training should be within existing modules rather than as a stand-alone module. By the end of the course, trainees should be:

1. aware of some of the diversity of cultural issues influencing sexual beliefs, sexual behaviour and sexual health.
2. aware of issues relating to the applicability of Eurocentric health and clinical psychology models to culturally diverse people from Black and minority ethnic backgrounds.
3. able to understand and formulate the cultural aspects of a sexual health problem from the service user's point of view.

METHODS OF TEACHING

- Guest speakers. A very interesting source of information is through a speaker representing a particular ethnic/cultural background. Some of these people are working in community-based organizations and can provide quality interactions with health staff in the issues relating to their community.
- Selected reading. Although there is little in the way of published work specifically looking at sexual health and psychology services in the UK, an emerging literature is under way, and publications will flourish in the near future. Keep your eyes open for new publications.
- Small group discussions. These continue to provide valuable insight into the breadth of response from different clinicians, who can discuss their own assumptions, experiences and feedback.
- Role plays. As in all aspects of training, skill practice is essential in the acquisition of professional technique. Live, audio-taped or videotaped role plays with trusted colleagues can be of great benefit, using live case material or vignettes.

Suggested exercises

Exercise 1: The importance of language in communicating sexual health issues

Instructions
Divide group into threes. Instruct them that they must each take a turn as the service user, as the psychologist and as the observer. The service user is then asked to remember an event that has occurred to them in the past that was very embarrassing; they are then asked to recount the event to the psychologist, but they are not allowed to use any words that have the letter 'S' in them. This is a simple way of utilizing English as a 'foreign language'. After a five-minute discussion, the service user is asked to provide feedback to the triad on what it felt like when attempting to describe the event; the psychologist is then asked to feed back what it felt like to be on the receiving end; and finally the observer feeds back on what they observed.

Timings
At least 45 minutes: 5 minutes role play and 5 minutes feedback, in three cycles of 10 minutes each, which should take 30 minutes to complete. Overall group feedback is provided after the small group exercise.

Aims
- To let participants experience what it feels like to discuss embarrassing information to a psychologist, when English is not their first language.
- To let participants experience what it feels like to receive an account of an embarrassing experience from someone whose first language is not English.
- To let participants observe the interaction between a psychologist and a service user recounting embarrassing information when English is not their first language.

Note for trainers
Warn the participants to be careful when thinking of an embarrassing event, and make sure they do not disclose anything too personal.

Exercise 2: Experiencing ethnic differences in the therapist–service user relationship

Instructions
Divide group into threes. Instruct them that they must each take a turn as the service user, the psychologist and as the observer. The role plays involve the first assessment session, and include a Black therapist with a White service user, and a White therapist with a Black service user. Participants choose a role play scenario from a list of provided vignettes, which include the shame of coping with a genital herpes diagnosis, the fear of coping with a HIV diagnosis, the experience and aftermath of having been sexually assaulted, the embarrassment of having been recognized by a friend in the waiting room and the difficulty of discussing sexual functioning with a therapist from the opposite sex.

Timings
At least 45 minutes: 5 minutes role play and 5 minutes feedback, in three cycles of 10 minutes each, which should take 30 minutes to complete. Overall group feedback is provided after the small group exercise.

Aim
To let participants experience the psychological assessment (and initial management) of important issues disclosed by service users who come from different ethnic backgrounds.

Notes for trainers
- Warn the participants that some of the issues raised in the role plays may trigger personal issues for the participants, either through their own experience or through their personal opinions. Ask participants to make sure they do not choose scenarios that may provoke distress.

> - Trainers need to juggle the scenarios around the gender and ethnic background, including religious conviction of the participants.
> - Remind participants that the emphasis is not on generic sexual health assessment but on trying to assess and understand the experience of the service user.

Annotated references

Bancroft, J. (1989) *Human Sexuality and its Problems*. Oxford: Churchill Livingstone

The extensive, basic text on human sexuality, sexual health and sexual problems.

Bhopal, R. (1997) Is research into ethnicity and health racist, unsound, or important science? *British Medical Journal*, 314, 1751–1756

An important article drawing the attention of medical audiences to race and culture issues in health research.

Bhugra, D. and de Silva, P. (1993) Sexual dysfunction across cultures. *International Review of Psychiatry*, 5, 243–252

A key article describing some of the transcultural issues in sexual dysfunction.

Elam, G., Fenton, K., Johnson, A., Nazroo, J. and Ritchie, J. (1999) *Exploring Ethnicity and Health*. London: SCPR

A recent exploration of ethnicity issues in sexual knowledge, attitudes and lifestyles.

Johnson, A.M., Wadsworth, J., Wellings, K. and Field, J. (1994) *Sexual Attitudes and Lifestyles*. Oxford: Blackwell Scientific Publications

The first extensive national survey of sexual attitudes and lifestyles (NATSAL) carried out in 1991, and repeated in 1999 with more emphasis on ethnic representation and sexual health.

Other useful modules
- Health Psychology
- Substance Misuse
- Adult Mental Health

Chapter 17

SUBSTANCE MISUSE

Hermine Graham and Shamil Wanigaratne

Introduction

Substance use and misuse is a historical and present-day fact in every society and country. The cultural, racial and religious structures, as well as the availability of different substances, have created a complex picture of substance use and misuse across communities. Problematic substance misuse has been differently perceived and defined within cultures. This has ranged from being a 'moral degenerate', to being afflicted by an illness, to using substances as a compensatory mechanism (Brickman *et al.*, 1982). Socio-economic and political factors, as well as the existing knowledge base at any given time, have dictated the definitions or more broadly the perception of problematic substance use.

DEMOGRAPHIC AND EPIDEMIOLOGICAL DETAILS

The real extent of substance misuse or problematic drug and alcohol use in the UK is unknown. It is estimated that at least 25 per cent of the general population have used some illicit drugs at some point in their lives, a figure of ten million people between the ages of 15 and 69. Of the general adult population, it is estimated that at least four million people (10 per cent) will have used illicit drugs in the last year, and two million people will have used these drugs in the last month (Baker, 1997). Estimates for minority ethnic communities on the other hand are sparse. The consequences of lack of reliable statistics on substance misuse in Britain have been described as leaving the field open to 'wishful thinking, anecdotal assertions, propaganda, rumour, exaggeration and potentially wildly inaccurate guesswork' (Baker, 1997). Generalizations and misperceptions such as 'most drug users are black people' (Baker, 1997) is an example of this. The Four City Study (Leitner *et al.*, 1993) found that in one location, over half the White respondents had taken illicit drugs compared to only one-third of the Black respondents. The British Crime Survey (Ramsey and Percy, 1996) found that White and African-Caribbean lifetime drug use was identical at 29 per cent.

In estimating figures for substance misuse for ethnic minorities, there is a real danger of generalizations or blanket figures that could have the effect of hindering planning and appropriate service development, rather than helping. While it can be argued that broad-brush general figures are important in a national context, particularly for resource allocation, it can have the opposite effect on appropriate service development for minority ethnic groups in a local context. To be helpful, epidemiological data on substance misuse by minority ethnic people need to provide a fuller picture, with appropriate sensitivities to subtle variations in the picture.

In the absence of detailed comprehensive nationwide surveys, the picture of the needs of Black and minority ethnic groups has to be constructed from small-scale local studies. The following are examples of findings for different ethnic groups.

- Cannabis is the main illicit drug used in the African-Caribbean community in the UK as with their White counterparts (Castleton and Francis, 1996; Mirza *et al.*, 1991; Perera *et al.*, 1993). Crack/cocaine use is emerging as the second most used drug and the most problematic from both the perception of the services and the drug users (Castleton and Francis, 1996; Daniel, 1992; Perera *et al.*, 1993).
- Members of the Somali community in the UK are known to chew a plant known as 'Khat' or 'Qat' that contains a drug with stimulant properties. In a study investigating patterns of Khat use among 207 Somalis living in London, using a particularly culturally sensitive methodology known as privileged access interviewing (Griffiths *et al.*, 1993), it was found that 78 per cent of the sample had used Khat at some stage in their life and 67 per cent had used the substance the week prior to the interview (Griffiths *et al.*, 1997). The figures for Khat use were similar in both men and women and 76 per cent of the sample reported using more of the substance while living in the UK than when living in Somalia.
- Alcohol consumption and alcohol-related problems among both men and women from the African-Caribbean communities in the UK appear to be comparatively lower than that of their White counterparts (Balarajan and Yuen, 1986; Cochrane and Howell, 1995; Haines *et al.*, 1987).
- Among Asian people, there is little data on drug use in the Chinese communities. The few studies on drug use by Asian people have been conducted in areas with Indian, Pakistani and Bangladeshi communities. Obtaining an accurate picture of drug use here is more difficult because of the concept of '*izzat*' or 'respectability' (Khan *et al.*, 1995). This may explain the consistently low level of self-reported drug use in this group (Pearson and Patel, 1998). Studies indicate that cannabis is the main drug of abuse in the Asian community in general (Khan *et al.*, 1995; Sangster, 1997).
- Sikh men were found to consume more alcohol than White men and were more likely to drink alone (Cochrane and Bal, 1990). Cochrane and Bal (1990) and McKeigue and Karmi (1993) found that around 90 per cent of Asian Muslims did not drink alcohol.

THEORY

Concepts, issues and relevant models

There is an under-representation of Black and minority ethnic clients presenting at substance misuse services both in the statutory and non-statutory sectors (Abdulrahim, 1992; Perera *et al.*, 1993; Mirza *et al.*, 1991). The following factors must be examined in order to redress the imbalance.

There is a widely held perception that these services are run for and by White people (Awiah, 1992; Butt, 1992; Mirza *et al.*, 1991; Perera *et al.*, 1993). The perception that services are for White male opiate users is difficult to dispute, as this is the reality in most services. The desire for ethnic specific services has been expressed by participants in a number of surveys (e.g. Khan, 1995), including Asian respondents who would find the discovery by a member of their own community that they misuse substances unacceptable.

Drug services in the UK have evolved around providing services for opiate users (Strang and Gossop, 1994). This has had the unintended effect of making services less responsive to the changing pattern of drug use in the UK. A considerable switch in resource allocation is required to develop services for individuals whose drugs of choice are not opiates (Tippell *et al.*, 1990). For example, tackling the use of Khat in the Somali community would require a very different service than that for opiate users.

The perception that treatments offered by substance misuse services are not appropriate for the particular needs of individuals from Black and minority ethnic groups has emerged in a number of studies (c.g. Perera *et al.*, 1993). Help for psychological problems, practical forms of help, counselling and alternative therapies such as acupuncture emerged as approaches which were more acceptable than a Western medical model of treatment since these individuals did not see their problems as a disease.

Fears about confidentiality have emerged as a factor in most studies looking at minority ethnic groups and substance misuse (e.g. Abdulrahim *et al.*, 1994; Perera *et al.*, 1993). There is a perception that services are linked to the police, Home Office, social services, social security and other authorities, and that just by attending services, these authorities will find out about a person's illegal drug use.

Institutional racism is perhaps the most fundamental reason why individuals from Black and minority ethnic groups do not access services. The perception among service users may also exist that services are intrinsically prejudiced against individuals from Black and minority ethnic groups, based on the individual's own experience of racism in the UK. This may not be an easy perception to shift.

PRACTICE

Useful references for this section include: Cheung, 1993; Rowe and Grills, 1993; Catalano *et al.*, 1993; Vega *et al.*, 1993.

Interviewing
- Use interviewing techniques that match the client's cultural and individual style of communicating. Show some appreciation of the client's own dialect and language-for example: by clarifying terminology used, the use of interpreters and culturally/linguistically appropriate information/leaflets if necessary.
- Acknowledge and, if appropriate, utilize the client's religious and spiritual beliefs.
- Be aware of stereotypes held about drug users and the client's ethnic/cultural group; also the client's stereotypes of the psychologist.

Assessment
- Make an effort to understand the client's cultural orientation and their social, peer and individual perception of substance use.
- Assess the spiritual, social, familial, economic and cultural influences on the client.
- Assess any additional stress factors (e.g. client's peers' perception of help seeking behaviour for substance misuse).
- Take account of the limitations of standardized assessments, measures/psychometrics (i.e. the lack of normative data or appropriate comparative groups for culturally different groups, particularly cultural, linguistic and religious) when administering and interpreting any results.

Intervention
- The application of existing intervention approaches in a culturally sensitive way, giving the client choices is important.

Co-construction of more culturally syntonic interventions with clients and relevant community groups can be very helpful.

- There should be an appreciation for the various levels in the individual's system at which intervention can be made.
- Liaising and collaborating with relevant specialist workers and/or voluntary organizations, services and community groups is essential.
- It is helpful to enable interventions to occur within or through the natural systems, structures and/or settings of the individual's family/community, if appropriate.

SERVICE PLANNING AND DELIVERY

In planning services, the following is considered necessary:

- Obtain clear demographic information on the ethnic distribution of the population in the catchment area served.
- Obtain as much information as possible (available national and local statistics, commissioning research, from community groups, community leaders,

user networks, etc.) about the patterns of substance misuse in the various communities (Daniel, 1993).

- Monitor the representation of the client profile in your service.
- Information about the perception of substance misuse problems in different communities, attitudes towards substance misuse and seeking help for problems among different communities is crucial for providing a culturally competent service. For example, some 'racial' and cultural groups may show a preference to use services which have staff from the same 'racial' and cultural group, while others may prefer exactly the opposite (Abdul-rahim *et al.*, 1994). Sensitivity to these differences is very important if increase of access to minority ethnic groups is to be achieved.
- Depending on the local picture, a service should decide on which groups to prioritise and target. The target groups will dictate which approach is best to increase access and deliver a culturally competent service. Examples of possible options may include outreach work by a same 'race' worker which will be perceived as a positive attitude to the target group (e.g. Black members of staff, positive Black images in posters in reception area).
- Research shows that minority ethnic people view drugs services with suspicion with respect to links with authorities such as the police and the Home Office compared to White drug users (Abdulrahim *et al.*, 1994). This view deters them from seeking help even if they are aware of services. Lengthy assessment procedures that require the disclosure of detailed personal information are routine in services. When individuals from Black and minority ethnic groups overcome their suspicions to seek help from services, the assessment process may act to confirm their suspicions and may prevent them from engaging in treatment. Services need to adopt interventions to overcome the 'suspicion barrier' to increase access and retain individuals from Black and minority ethnic backgrounds. Publicity and reassurance about confidentiality and modifying the routine assessment process for individuals from Black and minority ethnic groups will be steps towards achieving this.
- To deliver an effective culturally competent service, substance misuse services should designate an individual responsible for co-ordinating this work. Larger services should have a group of staff drawn from different professions and from different levels of the organizational structure to work continuously on access issues.
- In areas where there are a number of substance misuse services, a forum to facilitate a co-ordinated response in providing culturally competent services to minority groups in the locality can be a useful measure. Such a group would not only help services share information and learn from each other's experience, but can also lead to collaborative work.
- Participation of individuals taking a lead role within a service in national groups such as the Black Drug Workers Forum will help to keep abreast of innovative and successful developments. Also it will provide much-needed support for individuals striving to deliver a 'racially' and culturally competent service and increase access of minority groups.

It is a fact that Black and minority ethnic people are under-represented among clients in substance misuse. This is a national problem and a complex one with research indicating a number of possible contributory factors (Khan, 1997). A service has to continually work towards tackling this problem and it is something that has to be worked upon on a day-to-day basis in our clinical practice and strategic planning. Initiatives taken by an Inner City London Health Service Trust, The Camden and Islington Substance Misuse Service, can be given as examples:

- A half-time dedicated charge nurse post to work on increasing access to Black and minority ethnic patients.
- A senior management equal access group.
- Initiating the setting up of the Ethnic Minorities Substance Misuse Forum for the North London Area.
- Sponsoring a conference on Drugs and 'Race'.
- Supporting an event looking at 'a day in the life of North Islington Drug Use', particularly focusing on drug use in the Black community.
- Survey on training needs of staff of the Drugs Service on 'race' and culture issues.
- Equal access awayday for the service.
- Development of a document entitled 'Guidelines for Cross-Cultural Working in Substance Misuse'.
- Translating information leaflets about the service into different languages and purchasing information leaflets on drug use in different languages.

LEARNING OUTCOMES

1. Some awareness by the trainee of the diversity of factors influencing drug use in different minority ethnic groups and of within group differences (e.g. Rowe and Grills, 1993; Henman, 1990; GGII, 1991).
2. Trainees will have an appreciation of the issues influencing access to traditional drug services and the disproportionately small numbers of individuals from other minority ethnic groups utilizing such services (e.g. Rowe and Grills, 1993; Awaih *et al.*, 1990).
3. Trainees should be aware that the client's perception of traditional services may be different from their own (e.g. confidentiality issues: Awaih *et al.*, 1990; Daniel, 1993).
4. Trainees will have an understanding of the different ways of carrying out an assessment which is appropriate to their client's culture.
5. An appreciation of the trainee's own stereotypes about cultural/racial factors and how that might impact on assessment, formulation and intervention (Coomber, 1991; Rowe and Grills, 1993).
6. Trainees should develop the ability to avoid pathologizing on the basis of cultural/'racial' factors.

METHODS OF TEACHING

Useful methods include:

- Lectures and handouts.
- Video (if available).
- Vignettes – role play to practise interviewing techniques and case formulation.
- Visit(s) to drug/alcohol agencies offering specialist services to different racial/cultural groups.

Useful resources include:
Institute for the Study of Drug Dependence, Waterbridge House, 32–36 Loman Street, London SE1 OEE (Tel: 020 7928 1211/Fax: 020 7928 1771).

North Thames Regional Drug Misuse Database, Centre for Research on Drugs and Health Behaviour, 200 Seagrave Road, London SW6 1RQ (Tel: 020 8846 6563/Fax: 020 8846 6555).

Suggested exercises

Exercise 1: Paired exercise on stereotypes of the ethnicity of drug users

Instructions
Ask the group to form pairs. Trainees are instructed to take it in turns to describe their assumptions and stereotypes about the ethnicity of drug users. Each person has five minutes and the whole group will then give individual feedback.

Timings
10 minutes paired discussion
2 minutes per person feedback
20 minutes general discussion

Aims
To articulate assumptions and stereotypes that everyone has about drug users.
To examine what effect this can have on our clinical work.
To generate alternative ways of dealing with these assumptions.

Notes for trainers
- Trainees may find it difficult to articulate what their assumptions are, and trainers will have to be sensitive to this.
- Trainers should provide support for the discomfort that may be generated within the participants.

Exercise 2: Exercise on confidentiality

Instructions
Divide the group into threes, where participants role play a client, a psychologist and an observer. Ask two participants to role play an initial assessment interview in which a Black or minority ethnic client expresses concerns about confidentiality. The third person should observe what occurs during the process. Trainers should name different combinations of ethnic groups for both clients and psychologists such as African-Caribbean male client and White female psychologist, Bangladeshi male client and African psychologist, etc. Ask everyone to come back to the larger group and feed back how they felt in their roles. Ask everyone to de-role. Have a general discussion in the large group

Timings
10 minutes for role play:
25 minutes for feedback and group discussion

Aims
- To explore what it feels like to be a client from a different ethnic group coming to a substance misuse service for the first time with fears about the confidentiality of the service.
- To find ways to overcome the suspicions and fears that the client may have during the interview.

Notes for Trainers
- Trainers can help trainees attend to the process that occurs between the client and psychologist.
- Trainers need to examine the power differential that operates between professionals and clients, and particularly between White professionals and Black and minority ethnic clients.

Annotated references

Abdulrahim, D. (1998) Power, culture and the 'hard to reach': The marginalisation of minority ethnic populations from HIV prevention and harm minimisation. In R. Barbour and G. Huby (Eds) *Meddling with Mythology: The Social Construction of Post-AIDS Knowledge*. New York: Routledge

This chapter provides an excellent summary of the wider issues in providing services for minority ethnic groups. It is based on the author's extensive experience of researching into the needs of Cypriot and other minority ethnic groups in London.

Baker, O. (1997) *Drug Misuse in Britain*. London: Institute for the Study of Drug Dependence

This is a biannual edited publication by the Institute for the Study of Drug Dependence. It assembles the best available studies and surveys on the prevalence of substance misuse.

Cochrane, R. and Howell, M. (1995) Drinking patterns of black and white men in the West Midlands. *Social Psychiatry and Psychiatric Epidemiology, 30,* 139–146

This epidemiological study challenges some of the myths about patterns of drinking among various racial groups; this also shows significant within-group variations: for example, high levels of alcohol consumption among Sikh men.

Daniel, T. (1992) *Drug Agencies, Ethnic Minorities and Problem Drug Use*. Executive Summary. London: The Centre for Research on Drugs and Health Behaviour

One of the series of executive summaries on key issues in the field of substance misuse.

Perera, J., Power, R. and Gibson, N. (1993) *Assessing the Needs of Black Drug Users in North Westminster*. London: The Hungerford Drug Project and the Centre for Research on Drugs and Health Behaviour

This is one of the best qualitative studies on the area, looking at the service needs as well as perceptions of existing services of Black and other minority ethnic groups in West London. The report clearly outlines the issues and makes specific recommendations.

Useful further reading

* Stereotypes: DAWN,1985; GGII, 1991; Thompson-Fullilove, 1993; Lillie-Blanton *et al.*, 1993.
* Perception of substance use in different ethnic groups, norms and changing views over time/location: Henman, 1990; GGII, 1991; Hickling and Griffith, 1994.
* mental health, ethnicity/culture and drugs interaction: Hickling and Griffith, 1994; Adebimpe, 1993.
* Prevalence and type of substance use across ethnic groups and comparing use in different countries/subcontinents (e.g., US vs UK vs Asia vs Africa) and the difficulties in interpreting these results: Vega *et al.*, 1993; DAWN, 1985; Daniel, 1993; Lillie-Blanton *et al.*, 1993; Adebimpe, 1993; Gfroerer *et al.*, 1993; Cheung, 1993.
* Factors influencing frequency and type of substance use across different cultures (e.g. economic, social, racism [individual and institutional], societal norms and attitudes, employment): Adebimpe, 1993; GGII, 1991; Henman, 1990; Rowe and Grills, 1993; Dorn, 1987.
* Factors influencing availability of substances (e.g. socio-political, economic): Henman, 1990.

Other useful modules:
Health Psychology
Sexual Health
Adult Mental Health

Chapter18
NEUROPSYCHOLOGY

Lesley Murphy

Introduction

The following guidelines outline some basic considerations when undertaking neuropsychological assessments and interventions with Black and minority ethnic people, and are not meant to be exhaustive.

Few clinical neuropsychologists would claim to have expert knowledge in this area. The history of the academic debate about 'race and intelligence' (see Howitt and Owusu-Bempah (1994) for a recent discussion on this), where the science of neuropsychology has often been pressed into the service of ideology, has almost certainly hindered the development of thinking in this area for practising clinicians. It may also be that, given the expert nature of neuropsychology and its close alliance to medicine, power imbalances between clinician and client are even greater within this field of psychology than in others and, therefore, require particular attention.

Neuropsychologists assess cognitive skills and abilities, and their impairment, via the observation of behaviour. The behaviour observed may be in naturalistic settings, or in response to more structured situations, the most structured being the administration of standardized assessment instruments. The behaviours observed, and the cognitive skills inferred from them, are determined by many variables including, importantly, learning history, which will vary with an individual's cultural background. This should be considered when behaviour is observed in naturalistic settings and there is a difference of culture between the observer and the observed.

It is crucial when administering standardized tests and interpreting test results, to take into consideration:

* the construct validity of tests used.
* the standardization sample used in the construction of test norms. Norms set on the basis of the performance of a particular sample should not be used to interpret the performance of people not represented by this sample.
* an individual's familiarity with the conventions of the test situation and with materials used.

DEMOGRAPHIC AND EPIDEMIOLOGICAL DETAILS

Prevalence of neurological impairment may be related to:

- age
- sex
- sociocultural and political factors (e.g. head injury, more frequent in young males and among asylum seekers)
- geographical factors (e.g. Huntington's disease, more prevalent in East Anglia and South Wales than rest of UK)
- ethnicity (e.g. sickle-cell anaemia, more prevalent in African, Middle Eastern and Indian populations).

More detailed information about the prevalence of particular types of impairment in particular groups of people can be found in neuropsychiatric texts such as Lishman (1987), the *Dictionary of Neuropsychology* (Beaumont *et al.*, 1996) or epidemiology texts concerning the particular impairment.

THEORY

The concepts and constructs, as well as the materials, used in the construction of neuropsychological tests arise out of current academic knowledge of cognitive functioning, and this knowledge, along with the rest of academic psychology, is embedded within Western culture. Given the relative lack of cross-cultural research in this area, it is hard to say how universally applicable these instruments may be.

This then is the context for the debate as to whether there are significant differences in basic cognitive functions between members of different ethnic groups. Significant differences have not been consistently demonstrated in the score patterns of various cognitive abilities or in neuropsychological functioning (e.g. Faulstitch *et al.*, 1987, Kaufman *et al.*, 1988, Vernon, 1979, all cited in Lezak, 1995), which might suggest a degree of universality. However, there may be great differences in scores on tests due to differences in learning history and experience, and caution should be exercised in interpreting such differences.

PRACTICE

Interviewing

Basic to all neuropsychological assessment is the need to take as thorough a personal history as is possible, taking account of the client's background, learning and educational history, occupation, interests and general beliefs and attitudes. Family members, friends and significant others will often be consulted in this process, and may be particularly rich sources of information when there is a cultural difference between the psychologist and the client. Cultural differences in knowledge base are to be expected and should be considered. These include consideration of the interviewer's cultural background and culturally determined beliefs, as well as those of the client. When a client's mother tongue is not English, and the interviewer does not speak the client's language, care must be taken in the choice of test and the interpretation of results. Lezak (1995, pp. 310–311) outlines some of the considerations necessary prior to assessment.

Assessment

Neuropsychological investigation is based on observing the behaviour of an individual in particular situations. Standardized tests are used as an opportunity for observing the performance of certain cognitive tasks in a controlled setting. In both functional assessment and the use of standardized measures, care must be taken in the interpretation of performance, when there are differences between the culture of the observer and the observed.

The culture-bound nature of tests, and therefore possible bias, does not necessarily mean that their use should be discounted with people who are not members of the group for whom the test was constructed. Formal standardized assessment tools may be used qualitatively, in that they can provide an opportunity to observe particular cognitive skills without reference to test norms. This principle is used in the WAIS-R-NI where the WAIS-R is extended, providing the opportunity for a qualitative, hypothesis-testing approach to assessment.

When English is not the client's mother tongue and their familiarity with English is slight, assessments which are largely mediated by language should not be used; otherwise the results will reflect a client's command of English, rather than cognitive process.

It is possible to work closely with interpreters in administering carefully selected tests. This entails professional translation of relevant tests and translations back into English. Where literal translations are inappropriate, a close equivalent may be used. Interpreters should be thoroughly briefed about the administration of tests. Interpreters should also be consulted in the process of qualitative interpretation of results, to access their views on the client's level of emotional arousal and the client's expectations of and response to the testing situation and the tests used. It should be noted that translations are not a substitute for validation of culturally appropriate tests. Alternative, non-verbally mediated assessments are available, and may be more appropriate. For example, the following can be useful in relation to:

Intellectual ability
* Raven's Progressive matrices
    standard
    coloured
    advanced
* Leiter International Performance Scale – this assessment is carried out completely with gestures – the examiner does not speak at all.
* Non-verbal Test of Cognitive Skills

These instruments will avoid skewing of test results by language difference, but examiners should remain aware of possible differences between individuals in familiarity with the materials used (e.g. items of clothing in the Leiter scale) and with the conventions of the testing situation which may affect results.

WAIS-R has been translated into different languages. However, caution should be taken in administering these versions, as translation does not necessarily imply cultural validity and re-standardisation may not have been undertaken.

Memory

The assessment of non-verbal memory is less of a problem for non-English speakers but, again, examiners should be aware of the possible effect on performance of the use of culture-specific materials. If verbal memory problems are suspected, the best approach is to obtain professional translations of verbal memory assessments into the client's mother tongue and use an interpreter (when the examiner is not familiar with the language being used). The same caveat about the validity of translation as mentioned in relation to the WAIS-R is relevant here as translation does not address the possible culture-specificity of concepts and constructs used. The appropriateness of test norms should also be considered here.

Luria's Neuropsychological Battery (in translated form) has been used to assess people from a range of ethnic backgrounds and this work has demonstrated between-group differences in cognitive schemata used in thinking and problem-solving (see Lezak, 1995, p.717). These findings may prove useful in the establishment of appropriate norms for different groups.

Certain frequently used neuropsychological and intellectual tests were standardized on White English-speaking people and have clear cultural biases. In the WAIS-R, certain sub-tests are particularly culturally biased. The information subscale is a test of learned knowledge and is not appropriate for clients not educated in Britain. Similarly, the vocabulary subtest is sensitive to socio-economic and cultural factors. Clinical judgement can be used to decide whether it will be useful to administer parts of the WAIS-R when assessing clients from Black and minority ethnic backgrounds as an observation tool, but great caution should be exercised in interpreting test scores.

Report writing

Communication of test results and observations should make explicit the limitations of the assessment on the basis of cultural specificity and validity. Reports of assessments should include statements about the examiner's judgement of the validity of any tests used for the particular individual, and a discussion of all factors which might have influenced test performance and which would suggest caution in the interpretation of results.

Intervention

When planning neuropsychological rehabilitation programmes, the following should be taken into account:

- The client's beliefs about/constructions of health and illness. For example, neurological disability may be regarded as something which has to be accepted and rehabilitation may not be acceptable to the client or their family. (For further discussion on this issue, see the Health Psychology Module.)
- The client's, or client's relatives', ability to give informed consent to, or to refuse, intervention.
- Cultural issues when caring for a disabled person need to be considered. For example, for someone who has never been expected to prepare hot drinks or a meal, the inclusion of such activities in a rehabilitation programme may not be appropriate.
- The gender and age of staff working directly with clients may be an issue.
- Time of year, time of day or day of the week may affect when interventions should be carried out to take account of a client's religious beliefs and observances.

The client's family should be closely involved in this process, so that realistic and appropriate goals can be set. When there are differences in the construction of the problem and response to it between professionals and families, respectful negotiation will be required in order to maximize the changes of a positive outcome. (See also the Child, Adolescent and Family Module, the Adult Mental Health Module and the Primary Care Module for further discussion of these issues.)

SERVICE DELIVERY

Attempts to provide more culturally appropriate and inclusive neuropsychological assessment and intervention have clear resource implications, including the employment of professional, skilled interpreters and funding for the development of a range of culture-specific assessment instruments.

Other relevant issues will be covered in other modules. For example, the use of psychometrics to classify rather than to assess function, and to determine access to care, or type of care, is more appropriately addressed in other modules.

LEARNING OUTCOMES

It is acknowledged that following clinical psychology training, it is not expected that a newly qualified clinical psychologist should be competent in neuropsychology. Therefore, the following points should be regarded as desirable for those trainees who have undertaken a neuropsychology placement. These outcomes also apply to all neuropsychological work, regardless of the ethnicity or culture of the client.

1. Trainees should demonstrate their awareness of the importance of a thorough pre-assessment individualized history-taking, including questions to establish the learning history, education, occupation, interests, beliefs and expectations of the client.

2.   Trainees should be able to select the tests most appropriate for the client. This will include a good understanding of the validity criteria for formal tests; an ability to critically evaluate tests against these and an awareness of factors related to culture, language and learning history which may suggest caution in interpretation of scores against norms.
3.   Trainees should demonstrate in their report writing an awareness of factors, including those related to culture, language and learning history, which may influence test performance.
4.   Trainees should demonstrate their awareness of the importance of inclusion of a client's family in assessment and intervention.
5.   Trainees should be able to demonstrate awareness and understanding of the way in which neuropsychological theories and testing have and can reinforce discriminatory practices and racist ideologies.

METHODS OF TEACHING

A good starting point is to practise assessments (e.g. WAIS subtests) in pairs or small groups, followed by a plenary discussion of what each test measures, cultural sensitivity or bias and ecological validity.

Further teaching may be conducted using role play, presentation of key reading with discussion, setting up a debate for and against neuropsychological assessment with all people of all cultures, brainstorming ways and methods of assessment and intervention.

Suggested exercises

Exercise 1: Bias in assessment

Description
A specific vignette could be chosen or developed from clinical experience. The vignette should indicate the age, gender and ethnicity of the client, who could be suffering from memory difficulties. The referrer has specified neuropsychological testing by a clinical psychologist to ascertain the possible reasons for the memory difficulties and the nature and extent of the difficulties. The exercise is designed to enable trainees to consider ways to develop an appropriate and sensitive approach to neuropsychological testing.

Instructions
Small groups of four to five to discuss and identify the process of the neuropsychological assessment, including the stages of: discussion with the referrer, choosing appropriate tests, the planning of the assessment itself and the feedback given to the minority ethnic client. They are also to discuss and identify the sources of potential bias in the assessment process which could affect the validity of the assessment. The group is to prepare a

---

poster, perhaps with a flowchart of the process of assessment, indicating stages where bias is possible. The group must attempt to redesign the assessment process and content to minimize bias as much as possible.

The small groups can present their poster and suggestions to minimise bias to the larger group for further discussion.

The larger group can jointly attempt to identify ideas for good practice in neuropsychological testing with Black and minority ethnic people.

Timings
The exercise could take a total of 90–100 minutes. This would allow small group discussions to take approximately 60 minutes, with a large group discussion lasting approximately 35–40 minutes.

Aims
1. To enable trainees to think critically about the assessment process itself in working with Black and minority ethnic people.
2. To enable trainees to be creative in generating ways to manage and minimize bias in assessments with Black and minority ethnic people.
3. To enable trainees to share experience or knowledge of good practice in neuropsychological testing with Black and minority ethnic people.

Exercise 2: Assessing with interpreters

Description
Vignettes could be developed where the client is from a minority ethnic background, e.g. an asylum seeker who has experienced repeated blows to the head resulting in loss of consciousness. The client is referred to a clinical psychologist for a neuropsychological assessment of their difficulties in memory. The client does not speak any English at all.

The exercise is designed to enable trainees to develop conceptual and clinical skills in working with interpreters in neuropsychological assessments.

Instructions
Small groups of four are given the same or different vignettes. The small group plans together what preparation is needed to conduct a neuropsychological assessment with this client, including planning how to use an interpreter in the assessment process. The small group agree their individual roles as clinician, client, interpreter and observer. The group role plays:

- the beginning of the assessment where the client is provided with an explanation of the process of the assessment and the role of the interpreter;
- the administration of one particular sub-test with the help of the interpreter (e.g. digit span, similarities, current affairs).

The 'interpreter' may speak in English, but rephrase what the clinical psychologist is saying in layperson's terms. This requires the clinical psychologist to use more jargon than they may ordinarily use. Another variation could be that the client's ears are blocked by fingers or ear plugs are used, except when the interpreter is speaking.

The role play can be repeated with people changing roles but maintaining a focus on specific aspects of the assessment. The role of the observer is to provide feedback on:

- potential points of miscommunication or misunderstanding by either client, clinician or interpreter;
- potential points at which the validity of the assessment or later test-results could be questioned.

Following a de-role, the small group can discuss the process of the role play and ideas on how a neuropsychological assessment could be conducted more easily and in a way which minimizes the invalidation of the assessment when working with interpreters.

A large group discussion could focus on points raised in the final small group discussions (as above).

Timing
Allow at least 90 minutes for this exercise. The preparation for the role play, including preparation of how an interpreter could be used in the assessment, could take up to 20 minutes. The role plays and small group discussions must be given at least one hour. The large group discussion can take up to 40 minutes.

Aims
1. To enable trainees to consider the issues involved in planning and conducting a neuropsychological assessment with a client who does not speak English.
2. To enable trainees to explore the conceptual and methodological difficulties and the strategies in conducting neuropsychological assessments with the aid of an interpreter.
3. To enable trainees to begin developing skills in using interpreters in the assessment process.

> *Materials*
> Vignettes, interview rooms and some testing materials may be helpful (e.g.
> blocks, WAIS-R, forms, short stories).

Annotated reference

Kaufman, A.S., McClean, J.E. and Reynolds, C.R. (1988) Sex, race, residence region and education differences on the 11 WAIS-R subtests. *Journal of Clinical Psychology, 44*, 231–248

In this study Kaufman *et al.* investigate the differences in WAIS-R subtest scores according to five variables: sex, race, residential region, education and age. This is an American study and the 'race' variable refers to a comparison between Caucasians ('Whites') and Americans of African ancestry ('Blacks') – all other racial groups were excluded. 'Blacks' scored consistently lower on all subtests than 'Whites', with the greatest discrepancies being on the Block Design and Vocabulary subtests. The authors suggested that every short form of the WAIS-R consisting of the Vocabulary-Block design dyad was not to be recommended as this would unfairly penalize Black adults. However, overall level of education had significant main effects and may account for the difference across subtest scores.

A later related study subjected the same data to factor analysis (Kaufman, McClean and Reynolds, 1991. *Journal of Clinical Psychology, 47*, 548–557). Results showed that the factor patterns across all groups were very similar to each other indicating that the underlying abilities are identical for these groups. These results are limited to a comparison of American Caucasians and Americans of African ancestry. The socio-cultural and educational status of Black African-Americans may not be comparable to other Black groups and generalization to comparisons with other groups will be limited. Lezak (1995) points out that the effect of level of education on test scores is more potent and pervading.

Other useful modules
*   Older Adults
*   Learning Disabilities
*   Adult Mental Health
*   Child, Adolescent and Family
*   Health Psychology
*   Primary Care

Chapter 19

FORENSIC CLINICAL PSYCHOLOGY [1]

Gill Aitken

Introduction

This module is divided into three broad sections. The first section, 'The Role and Responsibilities of Clinical Psychologists in Forensic Settings' argues a case for why forensic clinical psychologists should be concerned with issues of 'race' and culture in working with the forensic client group. This is developed in the second section, 'Demography and Research Findings', by exploring the effects for Black and minority ethnic groups of the application of this medico-legal framework and wider psychiatric diagnostic practices against a background of the history of wider societal racialized practices. The term 'racialized' is used to denote that in the UK context all of us are socialized into a world in which the terms 'invisible' and 'race' are ever present in our social and institutional structures, i.e. in the fabric of our society, our own development and ways of thinking and relating. 'Race' then provides an ever present framework in which we relate to ourselves and others, whether within or across cultural interactions (Carter, 1995). In this sense racialization is not synonymous with racism – i.e. with its discriminatory effects (however unintended) (Ridley, 1995).

In particular, this second section illustrates how unless clinicians are aware of a number of limitations with the research process and of how racialized assumptions enter clinical decision-making processes, then Black people are particularly vulnerable to being diagnosed as 'bad', 'mad' and/or 'irrational' and to have needs problematized or obscured (see also Introductory Module). It is important here to acknowledge that people of Black and/or minority ethnic heritages have a history of developing a range of strategies of resistance in surviving and challenging multiple oppressions, and may also elect particular routes into psychiatric and non-psychiatric forensic services. However, the focus in this module is to engage with personal, professional and disciplinary reflexivity in relation to the regulation and control by dominant groups in White British society.

Issues for us as practitioners (irrespective of how similarly or differently we might 'racially' or culturally identify with our clients) are further highlighted in

---

1. Owing to external constraints on word limits, this is a shortened version of the module as originally prepared. The full version is available on request to the author.

the final section 'Assessment and Therapy'. In particular, the issues of trust, the need to be aware of the limitations of assessment tools, the importance of reflecting on how we work with (and communicate our assessment/evaluation of) our clients are illustrated in a brief case scenario for trainees to work through.

Throughout this module, the aim is to identify some of the key criticisms of existing service provision, and to provide references and interpretations which may be useful as initial resources in a move to contributing to the development of more appropriate and sensitive service provision for all our clients.

THE ROLE AND RESPONSIBILITIES OF CLINICAL PSYCHOLOGISTS IN FORENSIC SETTINGS

Clinical psychologists in NHS forensic settings are typically employed in high (e.g. special hospitals), medium (regional units) and/or low (high dependency) secure services across adult, child and adolescent and/or people with learning disabilities specialities. This spectrum of services was developed to provide in-patient and/or out-patient based assessment, care and management of three broad categories of people: (i) those who have come into contact with the criminal justice system, (ii) those identified as presenting a substantial risk to others, and/or (iii) those identified as having mental health/incapacity needs/personality disorder which is treatable (Reed, 1994, Warner, 1994).

Within Britain, there are four main sources of referrals for admission to the different levels of secure care: young offenders' institutions or prison (remand or sentenced prisoners), community settings, general hospitals and from within the configuration of secure services themselves. Across the secure settings, recent years have witnessed an increase in prison referrals and more recently (re-)admissions from community settings (McKenna, 1996; see also Health Advisory Committee for the Prison Service, 1997). Although service provision is associated with the 'mentally disordered offender', in practice this also covers people who are judged to have a propensity to offend, or for people with similar needs who may or may not have a formal mental health/personality disorder diagnosis under the Mental Health Act, 1983 (NW AFMHS, 1998). However, the public's association between criminality, mental illness and violence is strong, with males diagnosed with schizophrenia portrayed as the typical 'mentally disordered offender' (Buchanan and David, 1994; Gilligan, 1997). Not surprisingly, much of the literature and research in the forensic mental health field focuses on the identification of, or association between, particular offender types, mental illness or personality diagnoses and/or risk management (e.g. Crighton, 1999; Farrington, 1997; Kemshall, 1999).

Historically, little attention has been paid to the ways that racialized assumptions and practices enter into the process of routes into and out of the different levels of secure mental health settings. Although there has been long-standing criticism of existing service provision and processes, change seems to be tortuously slow. With the recent publication of the MacPherson Report (1999) following the death of Stephen Lawrence, institutional racism is defined as:

The collective failure of an organization to provide an appropriate and professional service to people because of their colour, culture or ethnic origin. It can be seen or detected in the processes, attitudes and behaviour which amount to discrimination, ignorance, thoughtlessness and racist stereotyping which disadvantage minority, ethnic people.

This has contributed to wider public debate about the ways in which institutions and professions associated with, in particular, the criminal justice system provide less than equitable and just services to people of Black, South Asian, Asian and/or minority ethnic heritages.

Within mental health forensic services, as with other mental health specialities, the target of critics has been the profession of psychiatry with its power to prescribe medication and with the legal powers to determine who should be detained under the Mental Health Act (1983). This power exceeds that available to anyone else in British society (Ndegwa, 1998) to influence the pathways into and out of secure mental health settings. However, forensic clinical psychologists are increasingly being called upon, or offer services, to provide psychological (risk) assessments and reports for referring agencies (e.g. courts, probation, social services). Further, as part of multi-disciplinary team working, clinical psychologists are playing a greater role in the decision making process when working with in-patients to make evaluations about admission and discharge routes, as well as therapeutic intervention possibilities. As highlighted throughout this Training Manual, rarely are questions about the cultural appropriateness of our methods and techniques for evaluating clients, and the role of possible emotional and other structural differences between client and therapist pivotal to clinical psychology's concerns (Embleton, Tudor and Tudor, 1994).

As indicated above, forensic clinical psychologists in secure mental health systems are an integral part of the interface between the medical and legal systems. In our roles, we are part of (at least) a triangular relationship comprising the client, the therapist/clinical psychologist and society (public, criminal justice system etc.). In managing these relational aspects we are likely also to have to manage conflicting interests (Welldon, 1994). For example, the interests of the client are likely to conflict with wider society's agendas, and as clinical psychologists we have responsibilities and duties to both, as well as our own profession. One reading of the MacPherson Report is that it is not professional to remain unaware of, or uninterested in, the effects of our assumptions, practices and policies on all members of society. As argued elsewhere (Aitken, 2000) the challenge to us is whether as clinical psychologists we can engage in a process of self and professional development to become at least aware of (the effects of) racialized assumptions and practices, and at most to commit to developing more racially and culturally appropriate and sensitive services. Here, some of the key criticisms of existing service provision are identified, as are a number of references, issues and strategies. These may be useful as initial resources in contributing to the development of more appropriate and sensitive service provision. The focus will be on in-patient forensic mental health care.

DEMOGRAPHY AND RESEARCH FINDINGS

The [in]visibility and problematization of 'race' and cultural issues

The ethnic monitoring of different populations (e.g. general population, prison populations, secure setting populations), referral rates, index offences or diagnoses is either strikingly absent or where present subject to criticism (Fernando *et al.*, 1998). Such criticism includes that researchers ignore issues of cultural validity or ignore the cultural bias in the instruments used and in the process of data collection. Often researchers make use of simplified ethnic categories or collapse categories into assumed homogeneous grouping which further mask the complexities of 'race', ethnicity and culture (Smaje, 1995). In absolute numbers, the figures for people of minority ethnic origins across the different populations, as above, are consistently lower than for those identified as White British. This may in part account for why a cultural or racial neutral stance is often taken in the interpretation or analysis of data for policy making. Consequently, policy making tends to be organized around levels of secure care, offending or diagnostic categories but which leaves the identification of the needs of people of diverse cultures in service provision obscured (see below). This has been noted in the consistent over-or under-representation of Black and minority ethnic people compared to the national demographics within particular offending/patient populations or forms of treatment, and which is cited as reflecting racialized assumptions and practices. This clearly is of concern to those of us working in forensic mental health settings. Further, women often remain invisible relative to male peers when gender is not the focus of research. Often because of small numbers 'no significant differences' are found, resulting in gender categories being collapsed into overriding categories relating to 'race', index offence or diagnostic category. This has particular implications for the position of Black and minority ethnic women, who are subject to further forms of marginalization and pathologizing on the basis of the interrelations between racialized and gendered assumptions in the interface between the legal and medical systems (Sayal, 1990; Torkington, 1991).

Some relevant details regarding demography and research findings follow:

- Over-representation of people of Black, African, Caribbean, South Asian, Asian and/or 'other' cultural heritages in prison populations (both remand and sentenced) relative to the demographics of general population: 15–24 per cent compared to 5.2 per cent respectively (Fernando, 1998; Home Office, 1996).
- Black people receive longer sentencing than White peers (Hood, 1992).
- Black people, and particularly second-generation males of African-Caribbean heritages, receive 3–17 times more diagnoses of schizophrenia relative to White peers (McGovern and Cope, 1987; see also Sayal, 1990 for discussion of the position of South Asian women). Minority ethnic people have been historically under-represented in the diagnostic category of personality disorder. However, recent research highlights that 'disturbed'

women as a 'group' are being increasingly diagnosed with personality disorder (particularly borderline personality disorder) within the penal and high secure hospital settings (e.g. Gorsuch, 1998; Gordon *et al.*, 1999), but with little analysis along ethnic/cultural dimensions.

- Black people are given lower rates of diagnoses of less severe forms of 'mental illness' or affective forms of the more severe diagnoses including categories of depression, anxiety or affective schizophrenia (Cochrane and Sashidharan, 1996).

- Over-representation of involuntary referrals (sectioning) from the community to psychiatric admission/secure settings (e.g. use of S136, MHA 1983) and general over-representation in psychiatric settings in relation to general population demography (Birrell and Partington, 1998; Browne, 1995; Cope and Ndegwa, 1990; Pipe *et al.*, 1991; Shaw *et al.*, 1999).

- Proportionately greater use of restrictive orders within secure settings relative to White peers, e.g. use of S41, Mental Health Act 1983 (Browne, 1990, 1995; Cope and Ndegwa, 1990; Pipe *et al.*, 1991).

- Transfer to, and longer duration at, higher levels of secure mental health care irrespective of diagnostic category, offender profile, presenting 'challenging' behaviour in relation to white peers (Fernando, 1998). Reports of increased rates of Black males referred to special/intensive care units within high secure settings (Gordonet *et al.*, 1998) and regional secure units (Lawson, 1998).

- Shorter stays but higher re-admission rates to lower levels of secure settings (Lawson, 1998; Wilson, 1998).

- Initial higher rates of forms of physical intervention/therapy (chemical – especially via depot injections, electro-convulsive therapy, seclusion) than White peers and less often referred to non-medicalized therapies, particularly psychotherapies (Chen *et al.*, 1991; Ndegwa, 1998; Special Hospitals Service Authority, 1993; Nadirshaw, 1999). Chemical treatments are typically taken orally or administered by injection such as depots which release medication into the body over a period of time. Reasons for the use of depots include ease of administration and ensuring treatment compliance. At present the little research on the possible differential effects of medication across ethnic groups/gender remains inconclusive. That there are cultural differences in the metabolism of neuroleptics and antidepressants including lithium which are not taken into account in psychiatric prescribing continues to be an ongoing and controversial debate.

- General findings (not analysed on 'racial' dimensions): across the levels of secure care between 19 per cent (of those with no index offence) and 82 per cent (of those with an index offence) of people in secure settings are placed in conditions of too high security (e.g. Shaw *et al.*, 1999, WISH, 1997).

THEORY

A range of concepts which inform psychological theory and practice are often referred to under the umbrella term of 'Eurocentrism' or 'Westernism' (see the

Introductory Module and Fernando, 1995). If we can accept the earlier reading of the MacPherson Report (1999) in relation to institutional racism, then part of our task as professional clinical psychologists is to learn about the history of the emergence of psychology as a discipline and profession, its uses and misuses; the history of Black and White-dominant relations and the interface between these. Learning about these histories provides us with resources to critically explore how these legacies inform our present day assumptions and practices about what are 'normative' and 'acceptable' ways of thinking, feeling, acting and relating (Aitken, 1996; Fernando, 1995b, 1998).

Given the context of notions of risk and dangerousness in the evaluation of the 'mentally disordered offender', Fernando's model of how the association between racialized assumptions and diagnosis emerge is useful. Myths become confused with (scientific) facts and categories with stereotypes (Fernando, 1998, p.71) in the construction of psychosis, and in perpetuating the association with 'dangerousness'.

The model proposed by Fernando (1998, p.73) illustrates how racialized assumptions can inform clinical practice with people identified as 'fitting' particular cultural stereotypes, as in the over-representation in particular diagnostic categories and pathways into secure care. As Lipsedge (1994) and Gordon *et al.* (1998) note the report of the Special Hospital Service Authority (1993) concluded that the deaths of three Black men in a special hospital reflected the effects of racial prejudice on the forms of treatment made available. Wilson's (1998) analysis also highlights how people who do not fit particular cultural stereotypes are at risk of not receiving the care that they need – citing the case of Christopher Clunis. Christopher Clunis is a man of African-Caribbean heritage, with a history of diagnosed psychiatric illness. In 1992 he attacked and killed a stranger, Jonathan Zito. Wilson (1998) reviews the inquiry reports which followed, and notes how he was 'regarded as a black man who went against type' rather than a 'person with a mental health problem'. This she argues shaped how he was not considered 'a risk to others' or with needs for 'sustained and consistent care and attention' (pp.189–190).

A deconstruction of research findings/trends
In the context of the above, there are many readings of the research trends and findings. In the culture of forensic mental health services there is a focus on risk assessment and management of re-offending behaviours, mental illness and association with violent and aggressive acts. These reinforce representations of the mentally disordered offender as 'dangerous' and 'complex cases'. If we consider that representations of Blackness and femaleness over the centuries have reflected physical, sexual, mental or moral danger, degeneration and irrationality (Aitken, 1996) and that there is a concomitant intervention focus on physical (institutional or drug compliance) management and containment rather than psycho-social or non-drug rehabilitative care or therapy in forensic contexts (Buchanan and David, 1994) and in services offered to Black people (Nadirshaw, 1999) then such trends can be deconstructed. That is, these representations and constructions can act as preconditions to position Black people as especially

vulnerable to be diagnosed as 'bad', 'mad' and irrational within particular sub-classifications of mental illness (Browne, 1990; Fernando, 1998) and to receive particular forms of treatment (Black Health Workers and Patients Group, 1983). This is not the same as saying we can attribute all Black people's presence in forensic mental health contexts to misdiagnosis, but that the situation is complex. For example, the findings of consultation exercises between the NHS representatives and minority ethnic communities (National Health Service Task Force, 1994b) highlighted the history of wider societal racialized practices and lack of societal resources available to the Black population which contribute both to distress, experienced/mental health needs as well as to the mistrust held by members of ethnic communities of White dominant institutions. Thus, when in distress Black people may access mental health services later, and in crisis, relative to the general population. Further, there was a perception that Black people are more likely to be taken into the criminal justice system, and once there misdiagnosed or receive diagnosis at the more severe end of the mental health system.

PRACTICE

Assessment and therapy

The forensic mental health client group is usually referred for assessment, therapy and/or rehabilitation as a condition of external (e.g. courts, social services) or internal (e.g. in-patient multidisciplinary teams) institutional authorities. These involuntary routes into assessment and therapy are likely to constrain the development of therapeutic relations not usually found in other therapy contexts (Welldon, 1994), and the issue of lack of trust can be anticipated as a key dynamic in any potential therapy/therapist–client encounter. From the preceding sections, we can start to understand how the issue of trust can be heightened in assessment and therapy encounters for the Black clients for whom we receive referrals. This is particularly so when considering that staff/professionals hold the ultimate power in determining or evaluating the progress of a client in the forensic mental health system in relation to location and forms of management and care, discharge, access to families and so forth.

When called upon to undertake risk assessments or assessments for therapeutic intervention there is an assumption that we use 'objective', standardized assessment screens and tools. In commenting upon the lack of research on psychometric properties of instruments used, Ndegwa (1998) cites the four considerations that Marsella and Kameoka (1989) propose to meet the notion of cultural equivalence: linguistic, conceptual, scale and norm-equivalence (see also Primary Care, Neuropsychology, and Introductory modules). However, rarely are the tools available 'culture free' or validated for being culture sensitive. Although some tools' guidelines may recommend qualification to any interpretations of findings (categorization, diagnosis) the risk is that such qualification remains peripheral to the overall 'objective' assessment findings. Yet categorization/diagnosis is inevitably based on 'clinical judgement' (e.g.

Fernando, 1995a; Good, 1994) and if we adopt a racially/culturally neutral (read 'objective') approach then we risk masking the ways in which racialized assumptions enter into our practices.

For example, generic models of risk assessment are used to identify 'Risk Factors' (always to include the issue of risk of harm to self or others). These factors centre on a client's history, levels of, for example, arousal, symptomatology, concurrent substance misuse, situational factors, clinical diagnosis, ideation, plan and intent. The outcomes of these judgements are made on the degree of insight and functional or social competency which, in turn, have implications for recommendations for form and type of care. As highlighted in an exploration of stereotypes of Black and minority ethnic people there is an association of excess of 'deficits' grounded in theories of biological and cultural essentialism. Stereotypes associated with people of African and Caribbean origins include excess of family instability, criminality, irrationality, physicality, aggressiveness and dangerousness, over-sexualization, users of illicit drugs and lack of intellectual capacity. In the context of people of South Asian or Asian heritages, stereotypical associations link with notions of excess of cultural repressiveness, overconformity, passivity, extremism, propensity to somatize, lack of psychological mindedness (e.g. Webb-Johnson, 1991). As Ndegwa (1998) cautions 'people making decisions ... which impact on Black people need to appreciate the limitations of research knowledge and methods of research as well as the fact that biased perceptions of Black people affect decisions that are presented as clinical opinion' (p.142).

In conclusion, throughout this module, I have attempted to illustrate how racialized and cultural assumptions are part of all of our lives. These are, however, played out with differential effects for the people we work with. In particular, I focused on some of the adverse implications for Black and minority ethnic people in the forensic mental health services. The issue is not to deny that this occurs, but to start to develop a reflective eye in a move to develop more culturally appropriate and sensitive methods and processes of assessment and therapy. To facilitate this a case scenario is provided later in this module.

LEARNING OUTCOMES

Trainees should be able to:

1. Identify a range of issues about why forensic clinical psychologists should be concerned with 'race' and culture in working with the forensic client group.
2. Demonstrate increased awareness and knowledge about how the unquestioning application of the medico-legal framework and wider psychiatric diagnostic practices mitigate against the provision of just and equitable services.
3. Demonstrate increased awareness of how power relations within forensic settings contexts are played out along dimensions of culture, professional, mental health and forensic structures.
4. Demonstrate increased recognition of the importance of our own personal,

professional and institutional cultural heritages which necessarily enter assessment and therapy encounters.

METHODS OF TEACHING

The following may be useful:

- The module as example of how to deconstruct research and clinical findings.
- Case study/role play/group discussion.
- Experiential learning – bringing in own experiences.

These can be expanded upon by visits to high dependency, medium secure units, special hospitals and contact with voluntary agencies. National networks related to forensic issues include the BPS DCP Forensic SIG; Women in Special Hospitals; Justice for Women; as well as regional networks

Suggested exercises

One case example is provided to stimulate discussion and exploration of issues that can arise in working in forensic mental health settings. As noted elsewhere there is no 'easy' cookbook technique (Aitken, 1998) to working with cultural and racial dynamics (see also Patel, 1998), and the importance of reflective practice and supervision cannot be overemphasized.

Exercise 1

Aims
1. To put learning and theory into practice and to engage in a process of awareness in combination with action and reflective practice.
2. To identify the complexities of working with power relations in the context of forensic mental health services.
3. To identify wider practice implications (outside of direct client contact) within an organization.

Timing
Allow about an hour.

15 minutes for small group discussion
15–20 minutes for paired role play and paired observation
10 minutes for small group feedback
20 minutes for group preparation of reformulation of presenting difficulty

Referral scenario

You are in a multi-disciplinary team (MDT) meeting and are asked to take on an in-patient who has been on the unit for seven months for a cognitive behavioural approach to 'anger management'. The client is described as a single, male African Caribbean in his forties. The staff report concerns about his expression of magical powers which form the content of verbal and written threats to harm/kill staff, and in his identifying as an alien. His last route in to the unit was from the community (it is documented that he alleged it was in response to racial abuse). He is diagnosed with 'paranoid schizophrenia' and receives neuroleptics in the form of depots. He has over 20 years' contact with mental health services, with multiple admissions to a secure unit and is currently on a Section 41.

Instructions

Small group discussion

- In your role as a clinical psychologist in an MDT how do you initially respond to the team's request for you to undertake 'anger management' with the client?
- What personal and professional assumptions and factors would you consider important to be alert to when first meeting the man, and why?
- How would these assumptions and factors influence the ways in which you approach working with the man and in the assessment and formulation of his 'presenting distress' and therapeutic approaches?

Role play

Role play for five minutes. Divide group into pairs to try out how you would introduce yourself to the client and what issues you would make explicit with him. An observer to be assigned to (i) the therapist and (ii) the client. Role players given two minutes to get into role. Prior to role play, therapist to state where the client is to be seen (e.g. on ward, off ward, degree of observation by other staff members), who is to be present, and security precautions (if any) to be taken (in most secure settings staff are automatically issued with an alarm and keys for doors in and out of wards).

The observers' role is to reflect on how socio-cultural issues influenced the encounter from the point of view of the person they are observing and the perceived implications for the therapeutic alliance.

Small group discusson

Group of four to discuss what assumptions/experiences they drew on to role play, make evaluations, and to reflect on the feelings invoked/evoked for them. To explore what could be different and how this might differentially impact on the therapeutic alliance. Group to de-role by, for example, stating their names.

Exercise 2: Large group discussion: choose from among the following

Referral
When receiving referrals, often the expectation is that a (psycho-educative) cognitive-behavioural approach to addressing issues of the 'here and now' problems with 'anger' or 'delusional' beliefs will be undertaken. Not only might this risk unproblematically accepting referrals (which themselves could be influenced by cultural biases), but it also risks masking the role of socio-cultural influences in a person's development. This also raises the issue of the role of clinical psychologist in educating the MDT about the role and autonomy of forensic clinical psychologists in assessment for type and form of therapy interventions, and the role of socio-cultural factors in influencing types of referrals/clinical decision-making processes.

Trust and development of therapeutic alliance within forensic settings
Consider the role of involuntary routes into system/referral for therapy work; therapist's awareness of own personal and professional identifications/client's identifications; awareness of therapist's position as being part of different systems in relation to client (acknowledging power relations), issues of client's interests and limited confidentiality. To what extent are the foregoing made explicit with the client?

Racial identification
The automatic assumption that a person identifies with a particular racial/cultural identity is problematic and we need to consider the importance of (changing) self identifications (and the meanings of such identifications). While staff may identify the client as being of a particular cultural heritage, e.g. African-Caribbean, a client may be ambivalent about such an identification and may overtly identify, for example, with a dominant ethnic group. Further early experiences of (familial) deprivation are said to be common in the forensic client population (Welldon, 1994). We need to consider different approaches to working with a client. For example, if working with understandings at the personal and familial level how do we keep in mind psychosocial and systemic influences throughout life which influence a racial world view whereby the person has learned to devalue or avoid her/his own 'race' (e.g. Carter, 1995). As an acceptable therapeutic alliance is developed, therapists may find increasing examples of subtle and overt forms of racialized incidents disclosed (as out 'there', i.e. outside the therapy context), general inequalities in White–Black relations, and the importance of power relations played out within and outside family of origin. How do we create the conditions for such disclosures and not silence the client? Do we link the 'out there' to 'in here' (the actual/symbolic identification of the therapist with wider systems), and are we able to tolerate this and not be overwhelmed, destroyed nor to be

defensively 'attacking' of the client. We must be aware of over-identification with the client in which therapeutic shifts and changes may be minimal.

Magical powers/alienness
Black clients can feel a heightened sense of vulnerability and powerlessness: for example, if a member of a numerically minority ethnic group; if being on a Section under the MHA; if diagnosed with mental illness or a victim of other stereotypes of Blackness. Do the clients feel pressure to confront/deny their own needs, but experience this as increasing their levels of anxiety. How do they cope? Do strategies heighten the client's (and therapist's) sense of anxiety about 'dangerousness', 'alienness' and hopelessness about discharge back into the community? Can we understand and contextualize how magical powers may be developed and elaborated on over the years to increase a sense of power in a personal and socio-cultural-political context?

Reformulation of distress
What are the implications of (diagrammatic) reformulations of presenting distress being shared with the client to explicitly incorporate 'race', mental health labels and family relations as pain inducing experiences? Do we link these to clients' articulations of powerful feelings such as rage, anger, humiliation, shame, envy, betrayal and need in relation to (Black) family of origin, wider (White) society and experience of the dynamics of the (White/secure) institution in reproducing these relations? When do we decide to explicitly raise issues of 'race' versus entering the therapy encounter with the view and the assumption that they are ever present (both from therapists and client's perspective) (Carter, 1995).

Levels of working in the system
To what extent do we work with the client in isolation from wider relations within our institutional setting? We might consider the importance of working with care teams to explore how patterns of staff–client relationships and clinical decisions could be informed by socio-cultural issues. We might reflect on the position of other minority ethnic clients across the unit in terms of possible relative isolation, marginalization, problematization and non-representation.

Annotated references

Aitken, G. (1996) The present absence/pathologised presence of Black women in mental health services. In E. Burman, G. Aitken, P. Alldred, R. Allwood, T. Billington, B. Goldberg, C. Heenan, A. Gordo Lopez, D. Marks and S. Warner. *Psychology, Discourse, Practice: From Regulation to Resistance.* London: Taylor and Francis

The chapter cited particularly focuses on the way that psychology affects inequalities as structured around 'race' and gender in the context of clinical psychology services within National Health Service settings.

Carter, R. (1995) *The influence of 'race' and racial identity in psychotherapy*. New York: Wiley

This book, written in a North American context, highlights the importance of cultural issues in self and professional development and the implications for therapy encounters and argues for the development of a racially inclusive model of psychotherapy.

Fernando, S., Ndegwa, D. and Wilson, M. (1998) *Forensic Psychiatry, Race and Culture*. London: Routledge

This is an important book for readers interested in working in the area of forensic-related mental health services. It is divided into four sections covering Background, Clinical Issues, Public Policy and Future Prospects. In a useful final section the authors suggest and evaluate different ways in which service provision could be more just.

Fernando, S. (Ed.) (1995) *Mental Health in a Multi-Ethnic Society: A Multi-Disciplinary Handbook*. London: Routledge

An edited collection of 13 chapters from a multi-disciplinary perspective, focusing on the development of community care in mental health service provision. The first section describes the socio-political-historical context from which service provision has emerged and is developing and includes chapters on legal frameworks and the experience of sectioning for Black and minority ethnic populations.

Torkington, P. (1991) *Black Health – A Political Issue: The Health and Race Project*. Liverpool: CARJ-LIHE.

This three-section book reports on an action research project exploring issues of 'race' and class in the area of sickness and health. In the second section, the sixth article, which focuses on mental illness, provides a very clear case study of the process of sectioning, the interface between the medico-legal system and the ways in which racialized assumptions and practices influence the type and form of treatment made available.

Other useful modules

Psychosocial rehabilitation (Long-term needs)
Adult Mental Health
Learning Disabilities
Research

Chapter 20
RESEARCH

Brigid MacCarthy and Richard Hallam

Introduction

In designing this module we assumed that only a limited amount of time would be devoted to this topic – perhaps two or three half days at most – and so we felt that discussion of some key issues was probably the best approach. Clinical psychology has a predilection for empiricism, giving rise to the expectation that there must exist 'methods' which will allow questions concerning the cultural context of 'disorder' and 'abnormal experience' to be 'researched'. A simple résumé of research methods will not do, however, because the uses to which empirical information are put depend so heavily on the theoretical paradigm that frames the research question, the methods used and the interpretation of results. The positivist framework that assumes the independent existence of 'disorders' which, although perhaps shaped by cultural factors, can be found universally is familiar to psychologists and its methods need no introduction. Research of this type is considered below, more as an attempt to identify its strengths and weaknesses when applied to understanding cultural difference than to hold it up as an example of good practice. Within the social sciences generally, research is guided by many different conceptual frameworks such as those modelled on language and discourse, social relations, social structure and phenomenology. It is beyond the scope of clinical psychology training courses to come to grips with all of these paradigms and their associated methodologies.

To resolve this dilemma (as a compromise), we have selected a limited number of articles which highlight methodological problems and choices and some from psychiatric epidemiology, some from medical anthropology. This selection is arbitrary, but the texts chosen are relevant. Their choice may also be an analogue of the therapeutic 'difference that makes a difference': they are probably familiar to readers, but may not have been considered in this context and so may stimulate a new perspective.

GENERAL REFERENCES

The following references provide a general introduction to frameworks for research which differ from the positivist/empiricist paradigm familiar to psychologists

- Alasuutari, P. (1995) *Researching Culture*. London: Sage. (This text includes considerations on the conduct of research.)
- Smith, J.A., Harré, R. and Langenhove, L.V. (1996) *Rethinking Methods in Psychology*. London: Sage.
- Richardson, J.T.E. (Ed.) (1996) *Handbook of Quantative Research Methods for Psychology and the Social Sciences*. Leicester: BPS Books.

SELECTED ARTICLES

The problems associated with translating ideas from alternative paradigms into research findings are not, of course, unfamiliar. These are perhaps best debated as concrete applications rather than as rarefied theoretical abstractions. Therefore, it is suggested that teaching focus on the reading of articles which describe a piece of research. To render this reading meaningful, some pertinent questions have been raised about the material which should help to produce a critical reading of it and facilitate group discussion. The first three articles concern various forms of emotional distress; the next four relate to major mental disorders and the last three to pathways into care and healing.

Psychological distress

1. Brown, G.W., Harris, T.G., Hepworth, C. (1995) Loss, humiliation and entrapment among women developing depression: a patient and non-patient comparison. *Psychological Medicine, 25, 7–21*

The work of George Brown and colleagues represents a good example of qualitative analysis, based on the interpretation of responses to interview questions, being used within a positivist philosophy of science. The meaning of events and life difficulties is inferred from contextual information and is subsumed within concepts (e.g. loss, danger) assumed to have universal validity across human and, to some extent, mammalian species. The ratings of these concepts are based on an empathic understanding of the meaning of certain situations, with 'objectivity' guaranteed by inter-rater agreement. The interpretation of the data ignores self-reported feelings, even though an attempt is being made to produce a causal analysis of syndromes largely characterized by feelings (e.g. depression). This is presumably because the interpretation of 'subjective' feelings is assumed to be prone to greater bias than 'objective' context. The events subsumed under concepts such as loss are taken as potential etiological factors producing psychiatric states, themselves regarded as universally valid entities.

Learning outcome
Trainees should be able to demonstrate an awareness of the issues/parameters to be considered in answering the questions which follow.

How does Brown's methodology and theory relate to cultural difference? Consider the following:

- Are concepts of depression, loss and humiliation valid cross-culturally? Does the understanding of cultural context require that raters be members of the culture concerned? (Note that Brown *et al.* make no comment on this even though they are working in a multiethnic Inner London borough.)
- Can a 'severe event' (according to Brown's definition, one requiring long-term overall unpleasantness) be judged on the basis of the respondent's description of their life situation, ignoring its emotional impact?
- Similarly, can events with psychological significance (such as humiliation) be rated with sufficient validity, especially when there is any degree of 'difference' between the rater and respondent? At what point and for what reasons might validity be questioned?
- To what extent are concepts like loss, humiliation and defeat culturally specific and related to the Western concept of the person?
- Can an adequate conceptualization of cultural difference be derived from ratings of psychological attributes? For example, would Brown's theory have anything to say about cross-cultural differences in 'defeat' events, or the fact that two-thirds of provoking events for depression concern a relationship with a sexual partner?

2. Kleinman, A. and Kleinman, J. (1991) Suffering and its professional transformation: Toward an ethnography of interpersonal experience. *Culture, Medicine and Psychiatry*, 15, 3, 275–301

This article nicely illustrates some of the dilemmas of understanding 'difference'. 'Experience near' categories are needed to understand human suffering as it is experienced; 'experience distant' categories are also needed in a second stage of analysis to provide an 'existential appreciation of shared human conditions'. The authors are trying to balance the sin of 'cultural solipsism' (we can only understand our own culture) with the sin of a 'universal science of human suffering' which dehumanizes and decontextualizes. They regard any professional language as potentially dehumanizing and argue for an understanding that is informed by history, politics and literature. They seem to imply that there are human existential universals that can always be sympathetically understood without recourse to theory.

Learning outcome
Trainees should be able to demonstrate an awareness of the issues/parameters to be considered in answering the following questions:

- Can a middle ground between universalism and relativism be found?
- How much of an individual's culture do we need to know in order to grasp the 'panhuman in the experience of distress'?
- Are there any legitimate arguments for a 'universal science of human suffering'? Would such a science necessarily be dehumanizing?

3. Good, B. J. (1977) The heart of what's the matter: The semantics of illness in Iran. *Culture, Medicine and Psychiatry*, 1, 25–58

This article gives a thorough background to some fieldwork in Iran in which the folk category of 'heart distress' was investigated. It describes the social setting, therapeutic options, local medical tradition and concepts, commonly reported antecedents and associated meanings for the term. It criticizes assumptions made in earlier studies of ethnomedicine based on an empiricist theory of language and offers a social communication model instead in which powerful polysemous symbols (such as heart distress) are used rhetorically to achieve social effects, either unconsciously or deliberately.

Learning outcome
Trainees should be able to demonstrate an awareness of the issues/parameters to be considered in answering the following questions:

The research methods (interviews and survey of 750 people) are not described in any detail and the case material is anecdotal. Can the empirical findings be relied upon to give a valid picture of heart distress?

Would it be appropriate to conduct a similar analysis of a Euroamerican folk category such as depression? What would this add to the way 'depression' is routinely assessed by clinical psychologists?

In understanding someone from a different race or culture are we putting an exotic gloss on their experiences while ignoring the culturally specific nature of our own assessment categories?

What research methods could be adopted to test Good's notion that reporting distress communicates an intention to influence the social setting and relieve stress?

Major mental disorder

Attempts to compare manifestations of major mental disorders across cultures tend to follow either a narrowly universalist (or 'etic') or a strongly relativist (or 'emic') approach. Findings from either research tradition have generated valuable insights, but it is important to be clear about the strengths and limitations of each position in designing research and evaluating results.

The universalist tradition assumes that the experience and nosology of major mental disorders are unproblematically universal, transcultural phenomena, reflecting underlying, presumably biologically driven, disease entities. The standard research strategy which flows automatically from these assumptions, is to develop maximally objective measures to identify and classify the disease entity under examination in a highly reliable way across all cultures. The relativist position assumes that an episode of illness is a product of the interaction of a malfunction in the organism, pain behaviour, and the recognition and curative responses prevalent in the social context in which the episode occurred. In other words, major mental disorders are strongly shaped by cultural pressures.

Research conducted from the universalist perspective is well adapted to comparing the incidence and prevalence of clearly defined disorders. Findings can help to identify key socio-cultural aetiological factors which may explain variance in rates of specific disorders. However, it can only measure whether more or less of a pre-determined hypothetical disease entity exists. The validity of the category in a particular cultural context cannot be tested, nor can 'universalist' research easily investigate any of the processes which converge to shape an episode of illness.

Research conducted from the relativist perspective can explore a range of processes which contribute to the construction of an episode of mental illness within a specific cultural context. Its methods are geared to ensuring the validity of the measures and constructs employed, but do not lend themselves easily to cross-cultural comparisons. These approaches have, therefore, produced little systematic research, but have raised critical awareness of the limitations of the universalist approach. The sets of articles summarized below are designed to highlight the contrasts in approach and conclusions from these different traditions.

Schizophrenia
1. Sartorius, N., Jablensky, A., Korten, A., Ernberg, G., Anker, E.M., Cooper, J.E. and Day, R. (1986) Early manisfestations and first contact incidence of schozophrenia in different cultures: *Psychological Medicine, 16*, 909–928

The World Health Organization (WHO) have been responsible for a series of studies looking at transcultural variations in the incidence and outcome (Sartorius *et al.*, 1986) of schizophrenia using a methodology firmly rooted in the universalist tradition. In the study of incidence, attempts were made to identify every person living in closely defined catchment areas of mental health services in 12 centres in 10 countries around the world presenting for the first time with a potentially schizophrenic illness. Their mental state and behaviour were assessed in detail, using highly standardized measuring instruments. These instruments operationalized the detection and quantification of phenomena considered by psychiatrists trained in the Western psychiatric tradition to be diagnostic of schizophrenia. The instruments were carefully translated and standardized in the language of each participating centre, and raters were trained in their use to a high degree of reliability. The two-year pattern of course and treatment and social outcome was explored.

Considerable debate has surrounded the interpretation of the findings of these studies. Incidence rates were shown to vary between 0.7 per 10,000 population in Aarhus, Denmark, to 1.4 per 10,000 in Nottingham, UK. Some commentators read this as demonstrating that nuclear schizophrenia occurs at effectively the same rate throughout the world – giving strong support to an essentially biological model for its aetiology – while others argue that the results show there are statistically significant differences in its prevalence. A somewhat separate argument focuses on the much more marked discrepancies between centres in the clinic-diagnosed rates of schizophrenia. Here the argument is that the interest in so-called 'nuclear' schizophrenia is misplaced, since clinically more significant issues are revealed by the big cross-cultural differences in clinical practice shown by the broader definition figures. Prognosis was demonstrably better in less industrialized societies.

2.   Kleinman, A. (1987) Anthropology and psychiatry: The role of culture in cross-cultural research on illness. *British Journal of Psychiatry, 151*, 447–454

This article takes a critical look at the methodology of the WHO study. Kleinman highlights the way that validity has been ignored or sacrificed in the interests of achieving high reliability. He argues that, as a result, the WHO work commits a 'category fallacy' through failing to verify the meaning of careful measurements in a particular social system.

3.   Edgerton, R.B. (1966) Conceptions of Psychosis in Four East African Societies. *American Anthropologist, 68*, 408–425

By contrast, this study explored, from a strongly relativist and anthropological perspective, how four neighbouring societies understood and responded to severe mental disorder. No standardized measuring instruments were used. The aim was to map out a culturally contextualized account of how each society categorized and explained marked deviations in behaviour. There was no reliance on assumptions about the universality of the division between normal and pathological behaviour. Interestingly, the constellation of behaviours categorized as severely pathological was similar among the four societies, and closely resembled the broad cluster of symptoms and signs recognized by Western psychiatry as diagnostic of schizophrenia. However, the study's methodology allowed variations in emphasis to be noted, and to map those and differing aetiological explanations onto core cultural features, such as preferred explanations for misfortune.

4.   Waxler, N.E. (1974) Cultural and Mental Illness: A social labelling perspective. *Journal of Nervous and Mental Disease, 159*, 379–395

Writing from a social labelling perspective, and comparing research findings from cultures distributed between the developed and developing world, the author demonstrates that the construction and maintenance of symptomatology is socially driven. She argues for the significance of factors such as aetiological explanations – whether pathological change is located within the person and the degree of control over treatment procedures maintained by the patient and family – in determining outcome.

Learning outcome
Trainees should be able to demonstrate an awareness of the issues/parameters to be considered in answering the following questions:

- Can the kinds of questions addressed by research within a universalist framework usefully inform clinical psychology practice?
- How can we be sure that results based on universalist research methods are valid for people from Black and minority ethnic backgrounds?
- Can a relativist approach be used to make comparisons between different communities/societies?
- What scope is there for research programmes to combine these approaches? Are they necessarily mutually contradictory in their aims?

Healing and pathways into care

The management and therapeutic response to episodes of ill-health, physical or mental, is also highly culturally determined. Yet, there is surprisingly little research literature in the field which includes ethnicity or 'race' as an independent variable. Conventionally, psychotherapy outcome research is geared to exploring differences between the efficacy of decontextualized treatment approaches. If demographic differences in responsiveness are explored, these tend to be limited to sex and age. That this should continue to be the case, despite a wealth of literature on cross-cultural differences in healing practices from medical anthropology and sociology, is all the more surprising. Two pairs of articles are presented below to highlight the contrast in methods and areas of concern between work which lacks a cross-cultural perspective and work from an anthropological tradition, the first relating to pathways into care and the second to therapeutic effectiveness.

1. Gater, R., Sousa, B., Barrientas, G. *et al.* (1991) The pathways to psychiatric care: a cross-cultural study. *Psychological Medicine, 21,* 761–774

The classic work of Goldberg and Huxley from an epidemiological tradition, quantified the filtering process which determines which episodes of psychological disturbance will be identified and managed as a formal episode of mental illness. Their research demonstrated how individuals are passed up a treatment hierarchy to receive care from increasingly specialized health service providers. Their work revolutionized thinking about the objectivity of the recognition of minor disturbance but the social and cultural factors which influenced this process were not analysed.

Building on this approach, the WHO conducted a multi-centre study, exploring the factors associated with delays in referral to mental health services. Using a rigorously quantitative approach, the study identified a tendency to consult native healers and a somatic presentation as leading to longer delays in contacting services. The study did not attempt to relate these pathway variations to social or cultural factors. However, the aim of the study was to improve the quality of available mental health care.

2.   Zola, I.K. (1973) Pathways to the doctor – from person to patient. *Social Science and Medicine, 7*, 677–689

Although the research method used in this study is a semi-structured interview leading to some quantification of results, the main thrust of the article is the interpretation of cross-cultural difference. The contention is that the patient's views of health and sickness, and his/her expectations of the encounter with the doctor, form a meaningful whole within the patient's cultural context, and that these variables are the key to understanding when and how the patient chooses to consult. Thus, this study could be seen as putting flesh on the bones of the first filter identified by Goldberg and Huxley. However, for Zola, the key variables are social in origin and require analysis at a level more abstract than the decontextualized behaviour of a set of individuals.

Process and outcome

1.   Stiles, W.B., Shapiro, D.A. and Elliott, R. (1986) Are all psychotherapies equivalent? *American Psychologist, 41*, 165–180

This review of process and outcome research in psychotherapy aims to resolve a paradox thrown up by aggregated findings: no major differences can be found in the effectiveness of psychological therapies despite apparent technical diversity in therapeutic methods. The debate hinges on how real the apparent equivalence is, and the authors discuss three levels of potential diversity: outcomes may be less equivalent than findings suggest, if measured more sensitively; therapies may share a common core of therapeutic processes (i.e. what people do in therapy may be more similar than superficial differences suggest); the mechanism for change in therapy may be largely universal, despite real differences in therapeutic technique. The review concludes that the paradox can only be resolved by increasing specificity in both process and outcome measures. Assessment of either should be conducted at the level of single, brief exchanges or 'events' within sessions.

Explicit discussion of the impact of cultural variables on process or outcome is limited to a brief acknowledgement that cultural values may impinge on ratings of effectiveness, as cultures will vary in what is considered a desirable effect, and in concepts of normality. Indeed, the literature in this area is strikingly devoid of discussion of the influence of 'race', class and culture.

2.   Parkin, D. (1979) Straightening the paths from the wilderness: the case of divinatory speech. *Journal of the Anthropological Society of Oxford, 4*, 147–161

This article analyses contrasting therapeutic processes within two small-scale Kenyan societies. Examples of the work of three types of diviners from those societies are presented verbatim and each is subjected to a detailed discourse analysis. The output of the analyses is to understand the thematic logic underlying each of the divinations. Most of the logic is held in common, despite considerable differences in the social circumstances and style of the diviners. Parkin argues that 'orderless deep-structure semantics' pose the emotional and intellectual questions which the people within a society seek to solve, and that the different forms of diagnosis and treatment offered by the divinatory process are surface semantics. Both semantic levels reflect key cultural themes, as well as elucidating the mechanism for therapeutic change within these small social groups.

Learning outcome

Trainees should be able to demonstrate an awareness of the issues/parameters to be considered in answering the following questions:

- Does Goldberg's filter model provide an adequate framework for analysing any system of help seeking, independent of context? If not, what are the minimum additional features we need to consider?
- Is it sufficient to introduce culture as an extra variable in Paul's assessment matrix of treatment x therapist x client x problem x setting or, instead, is outcome research too ready to assume that underlying mechanisms for change are entirely universal?
- If we apply Parkin's techniques to analysing Western treatments such as cognitive behaviour therapy or psychoanalysis, what 'key cultural themes' might emerge?

SAMPLING

Researching 'race' and culture raises a number of specific methodological problems in defining a sample, in addition to all the usual difficulties in selecting an appropriate design capable of testing a hypothesis. More qualitative methods do not entirely avoid these problems either, although they become more pressing the more large-scale and impersonal the research strategy.

What follows is a brief list of issues which should be taken into account together with some references which explore the implications of the issue in an applied context.

Definition of ethnicity

See Introductory Module for a discussion on terminology. For research purposes, a choice must be made between the various definitional dimensions (e.g. self- versus other-ascription; birthplace; political versus genetic definitions) which should be driven by the demands of the hypothesis under test. Once made, the chosen dimension must be rigorously applied.

Case identification

Ethnic groups subject to comparison may be differentially visible, making case finding less reliable in one group than another. For example, this has been thought to have contributed to inflating estimates of pathology in groups associated with distinctive physical appearances in bounded contexts such as hospital in-patient settings.

Census data

Large-scale surveys concerned with estimating population rates rely heavily on census information to calculate incidence and prevalence. The UK census has a number of problems when reporting data related to ethnicity. Glover (1991) carries an extensive review of factors affecting the validity of findings based on census data.

Identification of an appropriate comparison group

In community surveys, a common technique is to compare near neighbours of differing ethnicity. However, this strategy ignores the fact that many sub-communities have their own unique history, and that individuals whose ethnicity differs from that which predominates locally are likely to be unrepresentative of their ethnic group. See London (1986) for a detailed discussion of this and other case identification points applied to large-scale comparative studies.

False assumption of homogeneity within broadly defined ethnic groups

Studies employing broad ethnic categories such as 'Asian' risk making unjustified generalizations which may apply to some subgroups but not others. See Wilson and MacCarthy (1994) for a discussion of findings in the light of this point, and Wade Smith (1993) for the implications of this for conducting survey research among Black Americans.

Factors affecting participants' willingness to co-operate

Communities with large numbers of recent migrants often have strained relationships with procedures perceived as bureaucratic, such as form-filling and structured interviews, and migrants may be reluctant to, or fearful of, participating in any study which could conceivably impinge on their relationship with the Home Office. Levels of literacy or primary preference for a non-written language can also discriminate non-randomly between potential study participants.

Translation

Research conducted within an emic tradition fosters rich descriptions of phenomena within closely specified cultural contexts. Research which seeks to make comparisons between, rather than within, cultures will require the design of measuring instruments which can be used with equal validity in different cultural contexts. Either a new instrument may be developed and be subjected to psychometric assessment in each ethnic/cultural group under study, or an instrument with proven reliability and validity in one ethnic/cultural group may be 'translated' and psychometrically tested in another. In either case, translation is a complex technical task, which is described in considerable detail in the following article.

Flaherty, J.A., Gaviria, F.M., Pathak, D. *et al.* (1998) Developing instruments for cross-cultural research. *Journal of Nervous and Mental Disease, 176,* 257–263

The authors define five dimensions of cross-cultural equivalence: content; semantic; technical; criterion; conceptual. Strategies for achieving each type of equivalence are outlined. It is acknowledged that aiming to achieve all five types of equivalence may be unrealistically ideal, but argue that it is inadequate, at the other extreme, simply to translate the terminology of a well-established instrument without further attempts at validation. Finally, the authors advocate developing conceptually equivalent instruments which do not share item content or format, pointing out that such efforts test the limits of cross-cultural, etic research work.

Other useful modules
Introductory Module
Adult Mental Health
Neuropsychology

Chapter 21

PROFESSIONAL AND ORGANIZATIONAL ISSUES

Zenobia Nadirshaw

Introduction

Psychologists are poorly informed about issues of 'race', culture and ethnicity and have become socialized into a system which supports the status quo – rarely challenging prevailing beliefs of implicit ideology within the profession. The aim of this module is, therefore, to add weight to the preceding modules.

THE PROFESSION AND ITS CONTEXT

Clinical psychology as a profession

Points to consider:
* The history of the profession, particularly that of its relationship to the medical profession in the earlier days. The development and growth of clinical psychology as an independent profession but practised within institutional systems which are powerful and 'control' others (Newnes, 1996).
* The BPS and its related sub-systems, including the establishment of the Standing Committee for the Promotion of Equal Opportunities (SCPEO) following on from the Presidential Task Force which addressed issues about providing services in a multicultural context.
* The BPS Division of Clinical Psychology's Special Interest Group in 'Race' and Culture was established in 1991 to inform the DCP on issues and practices that unfairly discriminate against Black and minority ethnic people in relation to:
    (a) the selection and recruitment of Black and minority ethnic trainees (Boyle *et al.*, 1993; Nadirshaw, 1994);
    (b) the ethnocentric course content and curriculum (Nadirshaw, 1998a);
    (c) the Charter and Register of Chartered Psychologists, established in 1990;
    (d) the perceived lack of career progression within the NHS for Black and minority ethnic clinical psychologists.

Work in the Health Service

The majority of clinical psychologists work within an NHS setting. Health care is provided via primary care, secondary care and tertiary care. Professionals within the NHS are in positions of power, both in terms of the organization of service provision and the potential to construct definitions of mental illness and health which affect the lives of vulnerable people. While power continues to be vested in psychiatrists and in the predominant use of the medical model in mental health settings, clinical psychologists also share this power. Thus, it is our responsibility to be aware of this to improve services and make them relevant to *all* sections of the population.

The implications for Black and minority ethnic communities in Britain are significant. The discrimination and disadvantage that occurs within service provision to these groups is evident from the material in this Training Manual. Attitudinal and behavioural practices and prejudices in the form of organized power directly and indirectly discriminate and form the basis of our professional structures and systems, which in turn maintain the status quo.

PERSONAL AND PROFESSIONAL PRACTICE

1. Psychologists must understand and be aware of the social, political and professional issues which underpin current thinking within the NHS (Newnes, 1996).
2. Psychologists should be aware that professional ethos and ideology may conflict with their personal values and belief systems (Richardson, 1996).
3. The value base of clinical psychology is not neutral, and is arguably reflective of the values held in the dominant culture in Britain (Nadirshaw, 1999).
4. Work within the NHS setting gives rise to ethical issues and moral responsibilities at an individual and team level (for example, equal opportunity issues of access to services). An appreciation of the ethical issues within the NHS system and the legal aspects of working within the NHS system needs to be expanded. That is, the NHS and the mental health care system is for *all* sections of society, including Black and minority ethnic people. Issues such as patients' rights, consent to treatment, the Mental Health and Education Acts, clinical responsibility and confidentiality all need to be scrutinized for their application to people from Black and minority ethnic groups.
5. Psychologists must be aware of their professional power. Professional power resides in:
    *   access of relevant knowledge, experience and expertise which it is claimed is only available to members of the professional group;
    *   the authority to take decisions over lives of others;
    *   being able, on terms available to the professions, to dispense with or withhold information from service users;
    *   being able to structure face-to-face interactions (interviews, meetings, reviews) in ways which are advantageous to the professional person (content of agenda, procedures, time and location of meeting);

- successfully perpetuating a mystique and notion of exclusivity surrounding professional knowledge and expertise.

CLINICAL PSYCHOLOGY COMPETENCIES

Skills in assessment, formulation, team work, teaching, consultation, research and evaluation need to be adapted to the actual needs of the client population so as to make clinical psychology more appropriate and accessible to an ethically diverse population. Further core competencies such as the ability to deconstruct our knowledge base and practice should be considered essential. Good professional practice would identify indicators which would be directly related to issues of equality, fairness and effectiveness under whatever model of intervention used by psychologists is most appropriate for Black and minority ethnic people (consultancy, skills sharing) at an individual, family, group or community level (Mahtani and Marks, 1994; Webster, 1996).

ORGANIZATIONAL CHANGE AND SERVICE DEVELOPMENT

Increasingly, the value base and philosophical approach of the profession has to incorporate principles of equity of access, equal opportunity in service delivery and staffing, and anti-discriminatory practice. There has to be a major organizational change and paradigm shift within The British Psychological Society, the Division of Clinical Psychology and individual Heads of Services to address issues at national and European levels for *all* sections of British society. Trainees and recently qualified psychologists can also play a very active part in changing the status quo. An 'energizing' of the BPS needs to take place with a clear paradigm shift to address issues of 'race' and culture (Nadirshaw, 1998a), as indicated in Figure 21.1

As there is no single prescription for achieving these paradigm shifts, there has to be a major organizational change within the BPS, the Council and all its sub-systems (see Figure 21.2).

There needs to be:

- **Board level commitment and accountability** in the form of a council member taking the lead on these issues, becoming a 'product champion', driving the issues forward and ensuring that they do not fall off the Council's agenda. Assistance from the Society's Standing Committee for the Promotion of Equal Opportunities and the Division of Clinical Psychology's Special Interest Group in 'Race' and Culture in Clinical Psychology would be of benefit to this person.
- **Executive team leadership**. Visible leadership in the Society's sub-systems as well as in the main central office would encourage staff to incorporate these issues as an integral part of their work. A key senior manager could be given the responsibility to undertake detailed work necessary to develop a coherent and effective strategy (including an implementation plan).

From	To
Being treated separately.	Being mainstreamed with overall agenda.
Treating Black and minority communities as a homogenous group.	Acknowledging the extensive diversity that exists.
Moving from consultation with community groups.	Moving into the world of action in working with community groups.
Providing Eurocentric models of mental health care.	Providing culturally and 'racially' competent services.
Treating employment practice and service delivery issues separately.	Integrating staffing issues and appropriate psychological care.
Treating Black and minority ethnic groups as a problem.	Recognizing issues of fairness and equity as part of the overall solution to the Society's strategic plan and organizational objectives.

Figure 21.1 *A paradigm shift for the BPS*

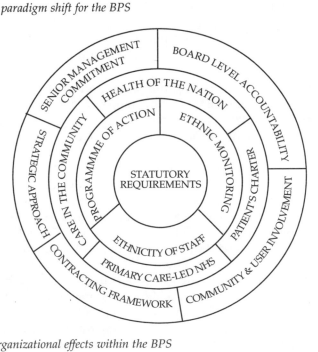

Figure 21.2 *Organizational effects within the BPS*

- **Public participation.** Psychological policy, practice and research has to be informed by views of users and recipient of services and a coherent strategy developed as informed by the views of all sections of British society, which is governed by the principles of equality, anti-discrimination and anti-racist practice. We have a duty to be open and accountable, to enable all clients to understand the role and function of clinical psychology and to be informed in decision-making.
- **Commitment to action following consultation** needs to be made where consultation with Black and minority ethnic people has been sought. It is important to shift the firmly entrenched status quo, to reveal the language of exclusion and segregation behind the language of inclusion and élitism and to remove the reinforcers that maintain the status quo.

In addition, the role of the Division of Clinical Psychology and of the associated training and validation Committee must provide evidence and guidance on preparing trainees to work in a multiethnic and multiracial context on how trainees are prepared to meet the psychological needs of Black and minority ethnic communities and how courses are organized to manage and work-through 'difference' and diversity in a constructive manner.

The Committee for Training in Clinical Psychology could:

- Identify and incorporate statutory/mandatory requirements to ensure the inclusion of a module on 'values' within the curriculum which could detail principles, criteria, competencies and a clear interpretation of responsible practice in relation to working with Black and minority ethnic people (Nadirshaw, 1999). This could also address related issues in supervisor training and ensure that Continuing Professional Development activities incorporate topics of 'difference', working with diversity, equality and anti-racist principles.
- Take responsibility for ensuring that as part of the Course Accreditation process, all courses demonstrate their competence to meaningfully address issues of racism and cultural difference at all levels of training.
- Identify criteria by which courses can be accredited as competent in their teaching and practice in this area.
- Revise the current core competencies for clinical practice to ensure that they include competencies related to the application of clinical psychology to Black and minority ethnic people (Nadirshaw, 1999).
- Ensure that teaching on racism and cultural difference is adequately represented and integrated at all levels of the training. This needs to be monitored, supported and facilitated. Monitoring could take the form of proper scrutiny of a framework which builds into it:
  (a) evidence of mainstreaming issues of equality and opportunity and the use of anti-racist principles within the formal teaching curriculum;
  (b) identification of a senior member of the academic training establishment with the responsibility for ensuring that curriculum decisions are made and implemented;

(c) evidence of individual and group work with clients from Black and minority ethnic backgrounds;

(d) satisfactory supervision from supervisors competent in addressing issues of racism and cultural difference;

(e) steps taken by courses to increase the number of trainees and staff from Black and minority ethnic groups (Bender and Richardson 1990, Boyle *et al.* 1993);

(f) Consider the Learning Outcomes outlined later in this section for all trainees.

Individual Heads of Department within the NHS could regularly monitor their own services: (1) reviewing the ethnic composition of existing personnel and recruitment policies, (2) reviewing the training and supervision needs of the department in relation to the ethnic make-up of the population it serves, (3) comparing a cohort of their referred clients with the expected referral profile based on epidemiological data and the social demography of their catchment area, (4) getting a better understanding of how Black and minority ethnic people are under-served by the use of inappropriate psychological therapy and interventions despite progress made within various fields (e.g. in behavioural/cognitive therapies with different client populations (Kasvikis, 1995)), (5) identifying the steps that need to be taken to get to know the Black and minority ethnic communities within their area, (6) making their services more accessible and user-friendly by rethinking ways in which services are offered and where, (7) establishing and maintaining links and credibility with the community groups and the Black Voluntary Sector with relation to the shared expectations of services offered.

Qualified and Trainee Clinical Psychologists as part of their contribution to addressing the needs of a diverse, multiethnic society, could develop accurate assessment, meaningful and appropriate interventions which are culturally contextualized, dealing with differences in language and meaning and exploring the role of the 'change agent', in their work with the minority ethnic voluntary sector (Webster, 1996; Mahtani and Marks, 1994).

LEARNING OUTCOMES

1. To be aware of the bias in service provision and service delivery in clinical psychology and its origin in the Eurocentric value base of the profession.

2. To understand the history of clinical psychology and to revisit the value base against which the work of clinical psychology can be understood (patients' rights, consent to treatment/effects of psychotropic medication, balancing the personal and political, addressing inequalities based on power and domination).

3. To have a better understanding of the barriers to access to clinical psychology services as experienced by Black and minority ethnic people as a result of:
   • lack of information about available services

- suspicion and fear related to the use of ethnocentric psychological models and practices which may have little meaning or impact on the lives of Black or minority ethnic people.

4. To understand the role and responsibility of clinical psychology services in developing appropriate and culturally competent models of service to Black and minority ethnic clients by relocating the problem from the purely individual to the socio-economic and socio-political nature of psychological problems.

5. To understand the clinical psychologist's role as 'change agent' in the provision and delivery of services (e.g. networking with the Black voluntary sector, primary care teams, Patient's Councils, use of legislation and Government Acts like the Patient's Charter, Disability Discrimination Act, Race Relations Act).

6. To be aware of ways in which a culturally sensitive, anti-racist perspective can be incorporated in all aspects of service delivery.

7. To develop a more pluralistic approach which reflects psychological reality more adequately for all sections of British society and to refocus from the scientific framework of psychology to the personal. The aim is to achieve a measure of objectivity while at the same time acknowledging and working through the powerful impact and effects of attitudes beliefs and value systems (embedded in labelling) which can result from a White, middle-class Eurocentric position.

8. To understand the limitations of the current theoretical frameworks for practice and academic research which continue to be developed from within the narrow confines of a universalist approach.

METHODS OF TEACHING

Facilitate guided discussion of relevant conceptual issues.

Other useful modules
Introductory Module
Service Delivery sections of other modules

REFERENCES

Abdulrahim, D. (1992) *Working with Diversity: HIV Prevention and Black and Ethnic Minority Communities*. London: North East and North West Thames Regional Health Authorities

Abdulrahim, D. (1998) Power, culture and the 'hard to reach': The marginalisation of minority ethnic populations from HIV prevention and harm minimisation. In R. Barbour and G. Huby (Eds.) *Meddling with Mythology: The Social Construction of Post-AIDS Knowledge*. New York: Routledge

Abdulrahim, D., White, D., Phillips, K., Boyd, G., Nicholson, J. and Elliot, J. (1994) *Ethnicity and drug use: Towards the design of community interventions*. Vol. I. London: AIDS Research Unit, University of East London

Abrol, S. (1990) Curriculum and culture. *Special Children*. February, 8–10

Adebimpe, V.R. (1993) Race and Crack Cocaine. *JAMA*, 270, 1, 45

Adler, L. (ed.) (1989) *Cross-cultural Research in Human Development: Lifespan Perspectives*. New York: Praeger

Advisory Centre for Education (ACE) (1989) *Asian Children with Special Needs*. London: London Advisory Centre for Education (Education Advice Service)

Advisory Council on the Misuse of Drugs (1998) *Drugs and the Environment*. London: HMSO

Ahmad, W.I.W., Baker, M.R. and Kernohan, E.E.M. (1990) Race, Ethnicity and General Practice. *British Journal of General Practice*, June, 223–224

Ahmed, S., Cheetham, J. and Small, J. (Eds.) (1986) *Social Work with Black Children and their Families*. London: B.T. Batsford

Ahmed, S.M. and Ali, M.R. (1993) *National Survey on Drug Abuse in Pakistan*. Islamabad: Ministry of Health

Ahmed, T. and Webb-Johnson, A. (1995). Voluntary groups. In S. Fernando (Ed.) *Mental Health in a Multi-ethnic Society. A multi-disciplinary Handbook.* London: Routledge

Ahmun, V. (1997) Taking things forward: Underpinning issues faced by Black professionals. *Black Drugs Workers Forum News*, 3, 3–4

Aitken, G. (1996) The present absence/pathologised presence of Black women in mental health services. In A. Burman, G. Aitken, P. Alldred, R. Allwood, T. Billington, B. Goldberg, C. Heenan, A. Gordo Lopez, D. Marks, and S. Warner. *Psychology, Discourse, Practice: From Regulations to Resistance*. London: Taylor and Francis

Aitken, G. (1998) Working with, and through, professional and 'race' differences: Issues for clinical psychologists. Special Issue Race and Culture. *Clinical Psychology Forum*, 118, 11–17

Aitken, G. (2000) Clinical psychology in a cold climate: Towards culturally appropriate services. In J. Batsleer and B. Humphries (Eds.) *Welfare, Exclusion and Political Agency*. London: Routledge, 79–101,

Akbar, N. (1996) An interview with Naim Akbar. *Journal of Black Therapy*, Spring, 1, 2, 3–50

Akinsola, H.A and Fryer, T. (1986). A comparison of patterns of disability in severely mentally handicapped children of different ethnic origins. *Psychological Medicine*, 16, 127–133

Alcohol Concern (1995) *Alcohol and the Asian, African and Caribbean Communities: Research and Practice*. London: Alcohol Concern

Alibhai-Brown, Y. (1990) Still Papering Over the Cracks. The *Guardian*, 10 September

Alibhai-Brown, Y. and Montague, A. (1992) *The Colour of Love. Mixed Race Relationships*. London: Virago

American Psychological Association Office of Ethnic Minority Affairs (1993) Guidelines for providers of psychological services to ethnic, linguistic and culturally diverse populations. *American Psychologist, 48,* 1, 45–48

Anderson, H. and Goolishian, H. (1992) The client is the expert: a not-knowing approach to therapy. In S. McNamee and K.J. Gergen (Eds.) *Therapy as Social Construction*. Thousand Oaks: Sage

Anderson, W.T. (1990) *Reality Isn't What It Used To Be*. New York: Harper and Row

Arean, P.A. and Gallagher-Thompson, D. (1996) Issues and recommendations for the recruitment and retention of older ethnic minority adults into clinical research. *Journal of Consulting and Clinical Psychology, 64,* 5, 875–880

Armstrong, F., Lemanek, K. Pegelow, C.H., Gonzalez, J.C. and Martinez, A. (1993) Impact of lifestyle disruption on parent and child coping, knowledge, parental discipline in children with sickle cell anaemia. *Children's Health Care, 22,* 3, 189–203

Athey, J. and Ahearn Jr, F. (1991) The mental health of refugee children: An overview. In: F. L. Ahearn and J.L.Athey (Eds.) *Refugee Children: Theory, Research and Services*. Baltimore: Johns Hopkins University Press

Atkinson, D., Morton, G. and Sue, D. (1989) A minority identity model. In D.Atkinson *et al*. (Eds.) *Counselling American Minorities: A Cross-Cultural Perspective*. Dubuque, Iowa: W.C. Brown, 35–52

Awaih, J., Butt, S. and Dorn, N. (1990) 'The last place I would go': Black people and drug services in Britain. *Druglink*, Sept./Oct., 14–15

Awaih, J., Butt, S. and Dorn, N. (1992) *Race, Gender and Drugs Services*. London: ISDD

Azmi, S., Emerson, E., Caine, A. and Hatton, C. (1996) *Improving Services for Asian People with Learning Disabilities and Their Families*. Manchester: Hester Adrian Research Centre/The Mental Health Foundation

Azmi S., Hatton, C., Emerson, E., Caine, A., (1997) Listening to Adolescents and Adults with Intellectual Disabilities from South Asian communities. *Journal of Applied Research in Intellectual Disabilities. 10,* 3, 250–263

Bahl, V. (1993) Access to health care for black and ethnic minority elderly people: general principles. In A. Hopkins and V. Bahl (Eds.) *Access to Healthcare for People from Black and Ethnic Minorities*. London: Royal College of Physicians

Bailey-Holgate, G. (1996) Educating young adults about sickle cell and thalassaemia. *Health Visitor, 69,* 499–500

Baker, O. (1997) *Drug Misuse in Britain*. London: Institute for the Study of Drug Dependence

Balarajan, R. (1996) Ethnicity and variations in mortality from coronary heart disease. *Health Trends, 28,* 45–51

Balarajan, R. (1997) Patterns of mortality among Sri Lankans in England and Wales. *Health Trends, 29,* 3–5

Balarajan, R. and Busulu, L. (1990) Mortality among Immigrants in England and Wales, 1979–83. In M. Britton (1990) *Mortality and Geography: A Review in the Mid-1980s*. Series DS. No.9. London: OPCS

Balarajan, R. and Yuen, P. (1986) British smoking and drinking habits: Variation by country of birth. *Community Medicine, 8,* 237–239

Balarajan, R., Yuen, P. and Raleigh, V.S. (1989) Ethnic differences in general practitioner consultations. *British Medical Journal, 29,* 9, 959–960

Baldwin, S. (1985) Sheep in wolf's clothing: Impact of normalisation teaching on human services. *International Journal of Rehabilitation Research, 8,* 131–142

Balint, M. (1964) *The Doctor, His Patient and The Illness.* (2nd ed.) New York: Churchill Livingstone

Banks, N. (1992) Identity work with black children: Approaches for clinical use. *Clinical Psychology Forum, 46,* 2–6

Banks, N. (1992) Some consideration of 'racial' identification and self-esteem when working with mixed ethnicity children and their mothers as Social Services clients. *Social Services Research, 3,* 32. Department of Social Policy and Social Work, University of Birmingham

Banks, N. (1996) Young single white mothers with black children in therapy. *Clinical Child Psychology and Psychiatry, 1,* 1, 19–28

Barn, R. (1993) *Black Children in the Public Care System..* London: BT Batsford/BAAF

Barn, R. (1994) Race and ethnicity in social work: Some issues for anti-discriminatory research. In B. Humphries and C. Truman (Eds.) *Re-thinking Social Research.* Aldershot: Avebury

Baxter, C. (1990). Parallels between the social role perception of people with learning difficulties and black and ethnic minority people in Britain. In A. Brechin and J. Walmsley (Eds.) *Making Connections.* London: Hodder and Stoughton in association with Open University Press

Baxter, C. (1994) Sex Education in the multiracial society. In A. Craft (Ed.) *Practice Issues in Sexuality and Learning Disabilities.* Routledge: London

Baxter, C. (1998) Learning Difficulties. In S. Rawaf and V. Bahl (Eds.) *Assessing the Health Needs of People from Minority Ethnic Groups.* London: Royal College of Physicians/Faculty of Public Health Medicine in conjunction with the Department of Health

Baxter, C., Poonia, K., Ward, L., and Nadirshaw, Z. (1990) *Double Discrimination. Issues and Services for People with Learning Difficulties from Black and Minority Ethnic Minority Communities.* London: King's Fund/Commission for Racial Equality. December

Beaumont, J.G., Kenealy, P.M. and Rogers, M.J.C. (1996) *The Blackwell Dictionary of Neuropsychology.* Oxford: Blackwell

Begum, N. (1995) *Beyond Samosas and Reggae: A Guide to Developing Services for Black Disabled People.* London: King's Fund

Beh-Pajooh, A. (1991) Social interactions among severely handicapped children, non-handicapped children and their mothers in an integrated playgroup. *Early Child Development and Care, 74,* 83–94

Belgrave, F. and Lewis, D. (1994) The role of social support in compliance and other health behaviours for African Americans with chronic illnesses. *Journal of Health and Social Policy, 5,* 3–4, 55–68

Beliappa. J. (1991) *Illness or Distress? Alternative Models of Mental Health.* London: Confederation of Indian Organisations (UK)

Bender, M. and Richardson, A. (1990) The ethnic composition of clinical psychology in Britain. *The Psychologist, 2,* 6, 250–252

Bennett, D.H. (1991) The historical development of rehabilitation services. In F. N. Watts and D.H. Bennett (Eds.) *Theory and Practice of Psychiatric Rehabilitation.* Chichester: John Wiley

Bentall, R.P. (1990) (Ed.) *Reconstructing Schizophrenia.* London, New York: Routledge

Bernal, M. and Knight, G. (Eds.) (1993) *Ethnic Identity: Formation and Transmission amongst Hispanics and Other Minorities.* New York: State University of New York Press

Bernstein, M.H. (Ed.) (1991) *Cultural approaches to parenting.* Newark: Lawrence Erlbaum

Berrios, G. (1991) Delusions as 'wrong' beliefs: A conceptual history. *British Journal of Psychiatry, 159,* 6–13

Bhatt, C. (1985) *HIV and Black Communities: A Report of the African HIV Working Group.* London: The HIV Project and the New River Health Authority Health Promotion Department

Bhopal, R. (1997) Is research into ethnicity and health racist, unsound or important science? *British Medical Journal, 314,* 1751–1756

Bhugra, D. and Cordle, C. (1986) Sexual Dysfunction in Asian couples. *British Medical Journal, 292,* 111–112

Bhugra, D. *et al.* (1997) Incidence and outcome of schizophrenia in Whites, African-Caribbeans and Asians in London. *Psychological Medicine, 27,* 791–798

Birchwood, M. *et al.* (1992) The influence of ethnicity and family structure on relapse in first-episode schizophrenia. A comparison of Asian, Afro-Caribbean and White patients. *British Journal of Psychiatry, 161,* 783–790

Birrell, D. and Partington, D. (1998) Patient Needs Assessment: Adult Forensic Services. Unpublished Report held at Mental Health Services of Salford Trust, Prestwich

Black Health Workers and Patients Group (1983) Psychiatry and the corporate state, *Race and Class, 25,* 249–264

Black People First (1994) Conference Report, Black People First, Instrument House, 207–215 King's Cross Road, London WC IX 9DB

Bostock, J. (1991) Developing a radical approach: the contributions and dangers of community psychology. *Clinical Psychology Forum, 33,* 2–6

Bostock, J. (1998) Developing coherence in community and clinical psychology: the integration of idealism and pragmatism. *Journal of Community and Applied Social Psychology, 8,* 363–371

Bott, D. and Hodes, M. (1989) Structural therapy for a West African family. *Journal of Family Therapy, 11,* 169–179

Bourne, J., Bridges, J. and Searle, L. (1994) *Outcast England: How Schools Exclude Black Children.* London: Institute of Race Relations

Boyce, W. (1990) Developing a Resource Centre for Black Afro-Caribbean Elders, Baseline, 2–19

Boyd-Franklin, N. (1989) *Black Families in Therapy: A Multisystems Approach.* (2nd ed.) New York: Guildford University Press

Boyle, M. (1990) *Schizophrenia – A Scientific Delusion?* Routledge: London

Boyle, M. (1999) Diagnosis. In C. Newnes, G. Holmes and C. Dunn (Eds.) *This is Madness. A Critical Look at Psychiatry and the Future of Mental Health Services.* Ross-on-Wye: PCCS

Boyle, M., Baker, M. and Charman, T. (1993) Selection for clinical psychology courses: a comparison of applicants from ethnic minority and majority groups to the University of East London. *Clinical Psychology Forum, 56.* June, 9–13

Braham, B., Rattansi, A. and Skellington, R. (Eds.) (1992) *Racism and Anti-racism: Inequalities, Opportunities and Policies.* London: Open University and Sage

Brechin, A. and Swain, J. (1988) *Changing Relationships. Shared Action Planning with People with a Mental Handicap.* London, Harper and Row

Breggin, P. (1993) *Toxic Psychiatry,* London: Fontana

Brickman *et al.* (1982) Model of helping and coping. *American Psychologist, 37,* 368–384

British Journal of Guidance and Counselling (1993) Jan., 2, 1, Symposium on Transcultural Counselling

Bronfenbrenner, U. (1993) Ecological Systems Theory. In. R.K.Wozniak and K.Fischer (Eds.), *Development in Context.* Newark, New Jersey: Lawrence Erlbaum

Brookins, C. (1996) Promoting ethnic identity development in African American Youth: The role of rites of passage. *The Journal of Black Psychology, 22,* 3, 388–417

Brown, M. T. and Brown, J. L. (1995) Counselor supervision cross-cultural perspectives. In J. G. Ponterotto, J. M. Casas, L. A. Suzuk, C. M. Alexander (Eds.) *Handbook of*

Multicultural Counseling. Newbury Park: Sage, 263–286

Browne, D. (1990) *Black People, Mental Health and the Courts*. London: National Association for the Care and Resettlement of Offenders (NACRO)

Browne, D. (1995) Sectioning: the Black experience. In S. Fernando (ed.) *Mental Health in a Multi-Ethnic Society: A Multi-disciplinary Handbook*, London: Routledge

Brummer, N. and Simmonds, J. (1992) 'Race' and culture: The management of 'difference' in the learning group. *Social Work Education, 11*, 1, 54–64

Brunning, H. and Burd, M. (1993) Clinical Psychologists in Primary Care. *Clinical Psychology Forum, 58*, 27–31

Buchanan, A. and David, A. (1994) Compliance and the reduction of dangerousness. *Journal of Mental Health, 3*, 427–429

Bucke, T. (1997) Ethnicity and contacts with the Police: Latest findings from the British crime survey. *Home Office Research Findings, 59*

Burnham, J. and Harris, Q. (1996) Emerging Ethnicity: A Tale of Three Cultures. In K. Dwivedi and V. Varma (Eds.) *Meeting the Needs of Ethnic Minority Children. A Handbook for Professionals*. London: Jessica Kingsley

Cambell, D., Draper, R. and Huffington, C. (Eds.) (1991) *A Systemic Approach to Consultation*. London: Karnac

Castleton, J. and Francis, R. (1996) *African-Caribbean Drug Use, Risk Behaviour and Attitudes to Drugs*. The Warehouse, Cottage Street, Brierley Hill, Dudley, West Midlands DY5 1RE

Catalano, R.F. *et al.* (1993) Using research to guide culturally appropriate drug abuse prevention. *Journal of Consulting and Clinical Psychology, 61*, 5, 804–811

Centres for Disease Control and Prevention (1994) Summary of notifiable diseases, United States. *MMWR, 43*, 1–80

Chadwick, P., Birchwood, M. and Trower, P. (1996) *Cognitive Therapy for Delusions, Voices and Paranoia*. London: Wiley

Chaudhury, S. and Au, A. (1994) The usage of the Mental Health Service by the elderly from ethnic minorities. *PSIGE Newsletter*, June, 50, 40–43

Cheetham, J., James, W., Loney, M., Mayor, B. and Prescott, W. (Eds.) (1981) *Social and Community Work in a Multi-Racial Society*. London: Harper and Row

Chen, E. Harrison, G. and Sandon, P. (1991) Management of the first episode of psychotic illness in Afro-Caribbean patients. *British Journal of Psychiatry, 158*, 517–522

Cheung, Y.W. (1993) Approaches to Ethnicity: Clearing roadblocks in the study of ethnicity and substance use. *International Journal of Addictions, 28,*12, 1209–1226

Chevannes, M. and Tait, T. (1997) *A Study to Study the Accommodation Support and Care Needs of Individuals With Learning Disability from the Asian Communities in Leicestershire*. Leicester: De Montfort University and Mary Seacole Research Centre

Christopher, E. (1980) *Sexuality and Birth Control in Social and Community Work*. London: Temple Smith

Cline, T. and Frederickson, N. (1996) *Curriculum Related Assessment, Cummins and Bilingual Children*. Clevedon, Avon: Multilingual Matters

Clulow, C. (1993) Marriage across frontiers: national, ethnic and religious differences in partnership. *Sexual and Marital Therapy, 8*, 1, 81–87

Coard, B. (1971) *How the West Indian Child is made Educationally Subnormal in the British School System*. London: New Beacon

Cochrane, R. and Bal, S. (1989) Mental hospital admission rates of immigrants to England: a comparison of 1971 and 1981. *Social Psychiatry and Psychiatric Epidemiology, 24*, 2–11

Cochrane, R. and Bal, S. (1990) The drinking habits of Sikh, Hindu, Muslim and white men in the West Midlands: a community survey. *British Journal of Addiction, 85*, 759–769

Cochrane, R. and Howell, M. (1995) Drinking patterns of black and white men in the West

Midlands. *Social Psychiatry and Psychiatric Epidemiology, 30,* 139–146

Cochrane, R. and Sashidharan, S. (1996) *Mental health and ethnic minorities: Review of the literature and implications for services, in NHS Centre for Reviews and Dissemination,* Report No. 5. York: University of York, 105–126

Cohen, P. (1992) It's racism what dunnit: Hidden narratives in theories of racism. In J. Donald and A. Rathansi (Eds.) *'Race', culture and difference.* London: Sage and Open University

Coleman, D. and Salt, J. (1996) *Ethnicity in the 1991 Census: Demographic Characteristics of the Ethnic Minority Populations. Vol.1.* London: OPCS

Coleman, R. (1999) *Recovery – An Alien Concept.* Handsel: Gloucester

Commander, M.J., Sashi Dharan, S.P., Odell, S.M. and Surtees, P.D. (1997) Access to mental health care in an inner-city health district. II: Association with demographic factors. *British Journal of Psychiatry, 170,* 317–320

Commission for Racial Equality (1987a) *Employment of Graduates from Ethnic Minorities: A Research Report.* London: CRE

Commission for Racial Equality (1987b) *Formal Investigation: Chartered Accountancy Training Contracts.* London: CRE

Commission for Racial Equality (1989) *Racial Discrimination in Liverpool City Council:* Report of a Formal Investigation into the Housing Department. London: CRE

Commission for Racial Equality (1992) *Ethnic Minorities in Great Britain: Settlement Patterns. 1991.* Census Statistical Paper 1. London: CRE

Commission for Racial Equality (1993) *Country of Birth: Settlement Patterns. 1991.* Statistical Paper 5. London: CRE

Commission for Racial Equality (1997) *CRE Factsheet: Employment and Unemployment.* London: CRE

Commission for Racial Equality (1999a) *CRE Factsheet: Racial Attacks and Harassment.* London: CRE

Commission for Racial Equality (1999b) *CRE Factsheet: Criminal Justice in England and Wales.* London: CRE

Compton, A.Y. (1989) Multicultural perspectives in sex education. *Sexual and Marital Therapy* 4,1: 75–85

Coomber, R. (1991) Beyond the 'Black drug worker'. *Druglink,* 17

Cooper, A. (1997) Thinking the unthinkable: 'White liberal' defences against understanding anti-racist training. *Journal of Social Work Practice, 8,* 2, 127–137

Cope, R. and Ndegwa, D. (1990) Ethnic differences in admission to a regional secure unit. *Journal of Forensic Psychiatry, 3,* 365–378

Coyne, J.C. (1982) 'A critique of cognition as casual entities with particular reference to depression. *Cognitive Therapy Research, 6*

Crighton, D. (1999) Risk assessment in forensic mentalhealth. *British Journal of Forensic Practice, 1,*118–26

Cross, M. and Smith, D. (Eds.) (1987) *Black Youth Futures: Ethnic Minorities and the Youth Training Scheme.* London: National Youth Bureau

Cross, W.E.J. (1971) The Negro-to-Black conversion experience. *Black World, 20,* 13–27

Cross, W.E. (1991) *Shades of Black: Diversity in African American Identity.* Philadelphia, PA: Temple University Press

Cross, W.E.J. (1995) The psychology of nigrescence. Revising the cross model. In J.G. Ponterotto, J.M. Casas, L.A. Suzuk, C.M. Alexander (Eds.) *Handbook of Multicultural Counseling.* Newbury Park: Sage, 93–122

Cruikshank, J. and Jackson, S. (1985) Similarity of blood pressure in blacks, whites and Asians in England: the Birmingham study. *Journal of Hypertension, 3,* 365–367

Curry, A. (1964) Myth, transference and the black psychotherapist. *Psychoanalytic Review, 51,* 7–14

CVS (1998*). Ethnicity and Difficulties. Moving towards Equity in Service Provision.* London: CVS Consultants and Asian People's Disability Alliance in conjunction with the Department of Health

Dagnino, N. (1992) Responding to the psychosocial needs of refugee children: a multifaceted approach. In M. McCullin (Ed.) *The Psychological Wellbeing of Refugee Children.* Geneva: International Catholic Child Bureau

Dalal, F.N. (1993) 'Race' and Racism: An Attempt to organise Difference. *Group Analysis,* 26, 277–293

Daniel, T. (1992) *Drug Agencies, Ethnic Minorities and Problem Drug Use.* Executive Summary. London: The Centre for Research on Drugs and Health Behaviour

Daniel, T. (1993) Ethnic minorities use of drug services. *Druglink,* Jan/Feb. 16–17

d'Ardenne, P. (1986) Sexual dysfunction in a transcultural setting: assessment, treatment and research. *Sexual and Marital Therapy,* 1, 1, 23–34

d'Ardenne, P. (1996) Sexual health for men in culturally diverse communities – some psychological considerations. *Sexual and Marital Therapy,* 11, 3, 289–296

d'Ardenne, P. and Mahtani, A. (1999) Transcultural Counselling in Action. (2nd ed.) London: Sage

Dasen, P. (1984) The cross-cultural study of intelligence: Piaget and the Raoule. *International Journal of Psychology,* 19, 4–5, 407–434

Davids, F.M. (1992) The cutting edge of racism: An object relations view. Paper presented at Applied Section of the Psychoanalytic Society, London, 28 October

Davids, F.M. (1997) Frantz Fanon. The struggle for inner freedom. *Psychoanalytic Psychotherapy in South Africa.* 5, 1, 54–75

Davis, H. and Russell, P. (1989) *Physical and Mental Handicap in the Asian Community. Can My Child Be Helped?* London: National Children's Bureau

DAWN (1985) *Black women and dependency: a report on drug and alcohol use.* London: DAWN

De Cock, K.M. and Low, N. (1997) HIV and AIDS, other sexually transmitted diseases, and tuberculosis in ethnic minorities in UK: Is surveillance serving its purpose? *British Medical Journal,* 314, 1747–51

de Silva, P. (1993) Buddhism and Counselling. *British Journal of Guidance and Counselling,.* 21, 1, 30–33

de Silva, P. and Rodrigo, E. (1995) Sex therapy in Sri Lanka: Development, problems and prospects. *International Review of Psychiatry,* 7, 241–246

Delaney, C. (1995) Rites of passage in adolescence. *Adolescence,* 30, 120, 891–897

Department of Health (1995) *The Health of the Nation: A Strategy for People with Learning Disabilities.* Wetherby: Department of Health

Department of Health (1998) *Signposts for Success in Commissioning and Providing Health Services for people with Learning Disabilities.* Author: M. Lyndsey. Wetherby: Department of Health

DeZulueta, F. (1990) Bilingualism and family therapy. *Journal of Family Therapy,* 12, 225–265

Dobbins, J.E. and Skillings, J.H., (1991) The utility of race labelling in understanding cultural identity: A conceptual tool for the social science practitioner. *Journal of Counselling and Development,* 70, 37–44

Donald, J. and Rattansi, A. (Eds.) (1992) *Race, Culture and Difference.* London: Sage and Open University

Donnison, J. and Burd, M. (1994) Partnership in Clinical Practice. *Clinical Psychology Forum,* 65, March

Dorn, N. (1987) *Social deprivation and drug problems in the European Communities.* Brussels: EEC

Dowd, J. and Bengston, V.L. (1978) Ageing in minority population. An examination of the double jeopardy hypothesis. *Journal of Gerontology,* 33, 3, 427–436

Dwivedi, K. and Varma, V. (1996) *Meeting the Needs of Ethnic Minority children: A handbook for professionals.* London: Jessica Kingsley

Ealing Community Health Council (1990) Provision of health services to the immigrant elderly in Ealing (unpublished)

Ebrahim, S., Smith, C. and Giggs, M. (1987) Elderly immigrants – a disadvantaged group? *Age and Ageing, 16,* 249–255

Edwards, G. (1989) Finding the Broad Street Pump. *Primary Prevention in Mental Health Changes, 7,* 2, April

Eisdorfer, C. (1981) Foreword. In T. Amos, and S.Harrell (Eds.) *Other Ways of Growing Old: Anthropological Perspectives.* Stanford, CA: Stanford University Press

Elam, G., Fenton, K., Johnson, A., Nazroo, J. and Ritchie, J. (1999) *Exploring Ethnicity and Health.* London: SCPR

Ellahi, R. (1992). Research into the needs of Asian families caring for someone with a mental handicap. *Mental Handicap, 20,* 4 134–136, December

Ellerbrock, T.V., Bush, T.J., Chamberland, M.E. and Oxtoby, M.J. (1991) Epidemiology of women with AIDS in the US, 1991 through 1990. A comparison with heterosexual men with AIDS. *JAMA, 265,* 22, 2971–5

Embleton Tudor, L. and Tudor, K. (1994) The personal and the political: power, authority and influence in psychotherapy. In P. Clarkson and M. Pokorny (Eds.) *The Handbook of Psychotherapy.* London: Routledge

Emerson, E. (1990) Consciousness raising, science and normalisation. *Clinical Psychology Forum, 30,* 36–39

Emerson, E., Azmi, S., Hatton, C., Caine, A. (1997) Is there an increased prevalence of severe learning disability among British Asians? *Ethnicity and Health 2,* 4: 317–321

Emerson, E. and Hatton, C. (1999) Future trends in the ethnic composition of British society and among British Citizens with Learning Disability. *Tizard Learning Disability Review, 4,* 4. Pavilion Publishing Ltd. Brighton

Eron, J.B. and Lund, T.W. (1996) *Narrative Solutions in Brief Therapy.* New York: Guilford

Essed, P. (1991) *Understanding Everyday Racism: An Interdisciplinary Theory.* Thousand Oaks: Sage

Eysenck (1971) *Race, Intelligence and Education.* London: Temple-Smith

Falicov, C. (1995) Training to think culturally: A multi-dimensional comparative framework. *Family Process, 34,* 373–388

Faloon, I.R.H. (1988) Expressed Emotion: current status. *Psychological Medicine, 18,* 269–74

Fanon, F. (1965 [French 1961]) *The Wretched of the Earth.* London: Macgibbon and Kee. Reprinted by Penguin in 1967

Fanon, F. (1986 [French 1952]) *Black Skins, White Masks.* London: Pluto Press

Farrington, D. (1997) Advancing knowledge about the early prevention of adult antisocial behaviour. Paper given at the High Security Psychiatric Services Commissioning Board (Department of Health) Network meeting on 'Primary prevention of adult antisocial behaviour', London, 5–6 June

Farroqi, A. (1993) How can family practice improve access to health care? In A. Hopkins and V. Bahl, (Eds.) *Access to Health Care for People from Black and Ethnic Minorities.* London: Royal College of Physicians

Fatimilehin, I. and Coleman, P. (1998) Appropriate services for African-Caribbean families: Views from one community. *Clinical Psychology Forum, 111,* 6–11

Fatimilehin, I. and Coleman, P. (1999) 'You've got to have a Chinese chef to cook Chinese food' Issues of power and control in mental health services. *Journal of Community and Applied Social Psychology 9,* 101–117

Fatimilehin, I. and Nadirshaw, Z. (1994). A cross-cultural study of parental attitude and beliefs about learning disability. *Mental Handicap Research, 7* 3, 202–227

Faulkner, J. and Kich, G.K. (1983) Assessment and engagement stages in therapy with the inter-racial family. *Family Therapy Collections, 6*, 78–90

Faulstich, M.E., McAnulty, D.A., Carey, M.P. and Gresham, F.M. (1987) Topography of human intelligence across race: Factorial comparison of black–white–WAIS-R profiles for criminal offenders. *International Journal of Neuroscience, 35*, 181–187

Fenton, K., Davidson, O., Mudan-Chinouya, M. and Miller, D. (1999) The Mayisha Study: engaging African communities in sexual behaviour research. 10th Conference on the Social Aspects of AIDS, London

Fenton, K. and Johnson, A.M. (1997) Race, ethnicity and sexual health: Can sexual health programmes be directed without stereotyping? *British Medical Journal, 314*, 1698–1699

Fenton, S. and Sadiq, A. (1993) The sorrows of my heart: sixteen Asian women speak about depression. London: CRE.

Fernando, S. (1984) Depression in Ethnic Minorities. In A.W. Burke (Ed.) *Racism and Mental Illness. Transcultural Psychiatry*: Spring. Sage Publications on behalf of McGill University, London

Fernando, S, (1988) *Race and Culture in Psychiatry.* London: Croom Helm

Fernando, S. (1991) *Mental Health, Race and Culture.* London: Macmillan Education, in conjunction with MIND

Fernando, S. (1995a) Social realities and mental health. In S. Fernando (Ed.) *Mental Health in a Multi-ethnic Society. A Multi-disciplinary Handbook.* London: Routledge

Fernando, S. (Ed.) (1995b) *Mental Health in a Multi-ethnic Society: A Multi-disciplinary Handbook.* London: Routledge

Fernando, S. (1998) Part 1: Background. In S. Fernando, D. Ndegwa and M. Wilson. *Forensic Psychiatry, Race and Culture.* London: Routledge

Fernando, S., Ndegua, D. and Wilson, M. (1998) *Forensic Psychiatry, Race and Culture.* London: Routledge

Ferns, P. (1992) Promoting Race Equality through Normalisation. In H. Brown and H. Smith (Eds.) *Normalisation: A Reader for the Nineties.* London: Routledge

Ferns P. and Madden M. (1995). Training to promote race equality. In S. Fernando (Ed.) *Mental Health in a Multi-ethnic Society. A Multi-disciplinary Handbook.* London: Routledge

Fitzgerald, M. (1993) *Ethnic Minorities and the Criminal Justice System.* Royal Commission on Criminal Justice Research Study London: HMSO

Fitzgerald, M. and Hale, C. (1996) Ethnic minorities: victimisation and racial harrasment. Findings from the 1998 and 1992 British Crime Surveys. *Home Office Research Studies, 150.* London: HMSO

Flaskerad, J.H. and Hu, L.T. (1994) Participation in and outcome of treatment for major depression among low-income Asian Americans. *Psychiatric Research, 5*, 3, 289–300

Flood-Page, C. and Mackie, A. (1998) Sentencing practice: An examination of decisions in Magistrates Courts and the Crown Courts in the mid-1990s. *Home Office Research Study 180.* London: HMSO

Frankenberg, R. (1993) *White Women, Race Matters: The Social Construction of Whiteness.* Minneapolis: University of Minnesota Press

Freud, S. (1915) The Unconscious, Vol.14 of The Standard Edition of the Complete Psychological Works of Sigmund Freud. Ed. and Trans. James Strachan, London: Hogarth

Freud, S. (1923) *On Metapsychology. The Theory of Psychoanalysis.* London: Penguin

Frosh, S. (1997) *For and Against Psychoanalysis.* London: Routledge

Fryer, D. (1998) Editor's Preface. *Journal of Community Applied Social Psychology, 8*, 75–88

Fryer, P. (1984) *Staying Power. The History of Black People in Britain.* London: Pluto

Gaber, I. and Aldridge, J. (Eds.) (1994) *In the best interest of the Child: Culture Identity and Transracial Adoption.* London: Free Association

Gardiner, L. (1971) Therapeutic relationships under varying conditions of race. *Psychotherapy, 18,* 78–87

Geller, J. (1990) Clinical guidelines for the use of involuntary outpatient treatment. *Hospital and Community Psychiatry, 41,* 749–755

Gfroerer, J., Flewelling, R. and Folsom, R. (1993) Race and Crack Cocaine. *JAMA, 270,* 1, 46

GGII (1991) High-Fliers: Asian drug abuse. *GGII,* Jan, 13–16

Ghuman. P. (1999) *Asian Adolescents in the West.* Leicester: BPS Books

Gibbs, S. (1994) Post war social reconstruction in Mozambique: Reframing children's experience of trauma and healing. *Disasters, 18,* 268–276

Gibson, H.B. (1992) The Emotional and Sexual Lives of Older People. London: Chapman and Hall

Gillam, S.J., Jarman, B., White, P. and Law, R. (1989) Ethnic Differences in Consultation Rates in Urban General Practice. *British Medical Journal, 299,* 953–957

Gillborn, D. and Gipps, C. (1996) Recent Research on the Achievements of *Ethnic Minority Pupils* OFSTED Report. London: HMSO

Gilligan, J. (1997) Founder's Lecture: Sixth International Conference of the International Association for Forensic Psychotherapy. London: 25 April

Glover, G.R. (1991) The use of inpatient psychiatric care by immigrants in a London borough. *International Journal of Social Psychiatry, 37,* 121–134

Good, B. (1994) *Medicine, Rationality and Experience: An Anthropological Perspective.* Cambridge: Cambridge University Press

Gordon, H. Hammond, S. and Veeramani, R. (1998) Special care units in special hospitals. *Journal of Forensic Psychiatry, 9,* 3, 571–587

Gordon, J.U. (1994) *Managing Multiculturalism in Substance Abuse Services.* London: Sage

Gorsuch, N. (1998) Unmet need among disturbed female offenders. *Journal of Forensic Psychiatry, 9* 3, 556–570

Gournay, K. (1995) Reviewing the review, *Nursing Times, 91,* 18

Groth-Marmat, G. (1990). *Handbook of Psychological Assessments.* London: Wiley

Griffiths, P., Gossop, M., Powis, B. and Strang, J. (1993) Reaching hidden populations of drug users by privileged access interviewers: Methodological and practical issues. *Addiction, 90,* 607–614

Griffiths , P., Gossop, M., Wickenden, S., Dunworth, J., Harris, K. and Lloyd, C. (1997) A transcultural pattern of drug use: qat (khat) in the UK. *British Journal of Psychiatry, 170,* 281–284

Grossman, F.M., Herman, D.O. and Matarazzo, J.D. (1985) Statistically inferred vs. empirically observed VIQ-PIQ differences in the WAIS-R. *Journal of Clinical Psychology, 41,* 268–272

Haines, A. *et al.* (1987) Blood pressure, smoking, obesity and alcohol consumption in black and white patients in general practice. *Journal of Human Hypertension, 1,* 39–46

Hardiman, R (1982) White Identity Development: A process oriented model for describing the racial consciousness of white Americans. Unpublished PhD Dissertation. University of Massachusetts, Amherst. *Abstracts International, 43,* 104A

Hardy, K. and Laszloffy, T. (1995) The cultural genogram key to training culturally competent family therapists. *Journal of Marital and Family Therapy, 3,* 227–237

Hare, B. (1985) Stability and change in self-perception and achievement among black adolescents: A longitudinal study. *Journal of Black Psychology, 112,* 29–42

Harkness, S. (1992) Human development in psychological anthropology. In T. Schwartz, G. White and C. Lutz (Eds.) *New Directions in Psychological Anthropology.* Cambridge: Cambridge University Press

Harrison, G., Owens, D., Holton, A., Neilson, D., Boot, D. (1988) A prospective study of severe mental illness among Afro-Caribbean patients. *Psychological Medicine, 18,* 643–657

Harwood, R. Miller, J. and Irizarry, N. (Eds.) (1995) *Culture and Attachment: Perceptions of the Child in Context* New York: Guilford

Haskey, J. (1990) The Ethnic Minority Populations of Great Britain. Estimates by ethnic group and country of birth. *Population Trends, 60,* 35–38

Haworth, R. (1998) Mental health professionals' accounts of clients who are from ethnic minorities. Clinical Psychology Forum, Special issue: *Race and Culture, 118,* 6–10

Hays, P. A. (1995) Multicultural applications of cognitive behavioural therapy. *Professional Psychology: Research and Practice, 25,* 3, 309–315

Health Advisory Committee for the Prison Service [England and Wales] (1997) *The Provision of Mental Health Care in Prisons.* London: HAC

Helms, J.E. (1984) Toward a theoretical explanation of the effects of race on counselling. A Black and White Model. *The Counselling Psychologist, 12,* 4, 153–165

Helms, J.E. (Ed.) (1990) *Black and White Racial Identity: Theory, Research and Practice.* Westport, CT: Greenwood Press

Helms, J.E. (1994) Racist identity and 'racial' constructs. In E.J. Trickett, R. Watts and D.Birman (Eds.) *Human Diversity.* San Francisco: Jossey-Bass

Helms, J.E. (1995) An update of Helms' White and People of Colour Racial Identity Models. In J.G. Ponterrotto, J.M. Casas, L.A. Suzuk, C.M. Alexander (Eds.) *Handbook of Multicultural Counselling.* Newbury Park: Sage, 181–217

Helms, J.E. and Piper, R.E. (1994) Implications of racial identity theory for vocational psychology. *Journal of Vocational Behaviour, 44,* 124–38

Henderson, P. (1995) *Drugs Prevention* London: Home Office

Henman, A.R. (1990) Coca and Cocaine: Their role in 'traditional' cultures in South America. *Journal of Drug Issues, 20* 4, 577–588

Henriques, J., Hollway, W., Urwin, C., Venn, C. and Walkerdine, V. (1984) *Changing the Subject: Psychology, Social Rregulation and Subjectivity.* London: Methuen

Hernstein, R. J. and Murray, C. (1994) The Bell curve: intelligence and class structure in American Life. New York: Free Press

Hickling, F.W. and Griffith, E.E. (1994) Clinical perspectives on the Rastafari movement. *Hospital and Community Psychiatry, 45,* 1, 42–48

Higgs, R. and Dammers, J. (1992) Ethical Issues in Counselling and Health in Primary Care. *British Journal of Guidance and Counselling, 20,* 1

Hillier, S., Huq, A., Loshak, R., Marks, F. and Rahman, S. (1994) An evaluation of child psychiatric services for Bangladeshi parents. *Journal of Mental Health, 3,* 332–337

Hillier, S., and Rahman, S (1996) Childhood development and behavioural and emotional problems as perceived by Bangladeshi parents in East London. In D. Kelleher and S. Hillier (Eds.) *Researching Cultural Differences in Health.* London: Routledge

Hiro, D. (1992) *Black British, White British: A History of Race Relations in Britain.* London: Paladin

Ho, D.Y. (1981) Traditional patterns of socialisation in Chinese society. *Acta Psychologica Taiwanica, 23,* 2, 81–95

Ho, M. (1987) *Family Therapy with Ethnic Minorities.* Thousand Oaks: Sage

Ho, M. (1992) *Minority Children and Adolescents in Therapy.* Thousand Oaks: Sage

Holland, S. (1988) Defining and Experimenting with Prevention. In D. Ramon (Ed.) *Psychology in Transition.* London: Pluto

Holland, S. (1990) Psychotherapy, oppression and social action: Gender, race and class in black women's depression. In R, Perlberg and A. Miller. (Eds.) *Gender and Power in Families.* London: Routledge

Holland, S. (1991) From Private Symptoms to Public Action. *Feminism and Psychology, 1,* 1, 58–62

Holland, S. (1996) From social abuse to social action: A neighbourhood psychotherapy and social action project for women. In J. Ussher and P. Nicholson (Eds.) *Gender Issues in Psychology*. London: Routledge

Holliday, B. and Curbeam, B. (1996) The Parental Belief Interview. In R.L. Jones (Ed.) *Handbook of Tests and Measurements for Black Populations, Vol 1*, Hampton Virginia: Cobb and Henry

Home Office (1996). *Race and the Criminal Justice System*. London. HMSO

Home Office (1997) *British Crime Survey*. London: HMSO

Home Office (1998). *Race and the Criminal Justice System*. London: HMSO

Hood, R. (1992) *Race and Sentencing: A Study in the Crown Court*. Oxford: Clarendon Press

Hopkins, A. and Bahl, V. (Eds.) (1993) *Access to Health Care*. London: Royal College of Physicians

Howitt, D. (1991) *Concerning Psychology: Psychology Applied to Social Issues*. Buckingham: Open University Press

Howitt, D. and Owusu-Bempah, J. (1994) *The Racism of Psychology: Time to Change*. London: Harvester Wheatsheaf

Hudson, B. (1989) Discrimination and disparity: The influence of race on sentencing. *New Community, 16*, 1

Huffington, C. and Brunning, H. (Eds.) (1994) *Internal Consultancy in the Public Sector*. London: Karnac

Hunt, H. (1989) An assertiveness and self-confidence group for women: A primary prevention project in primary care. *Clinical Psychology Forum, 22*, 19–23, August

Ineichen, B. (1980) Mental illness among New Commonwealth migrants to Britain. In A. Boyce (Ed.) *Mobility and Migration*. London: Taylor Francis

Ineichen, B., Harrison, G., Morgan, H.G. (1984) Psychiatric Hospital Admissions in Bristol: 1. Geographical and Ethnic Factors. *British Journal of Psychiatry, 145*, 600–604

Jackson, B. (1975) Black Identity Development. *Journal of Education Diversity, 2*, 19–25

Jackson, H. and Westmoreland, G. (1992) Therapeutic issues for black children in foster care. In L. Vargas and J. Koss-Chioino (Eds.) *Working with culture: Psychotherapeutic Interventions with Ethnic Minority Children and Adolescents*. San Francisco: Jossey-Bass

Jackson, J. (1971) Compensatory care for the black aged. In Minority Aged in America. Occasional paper #10, Institute of Gerontology. University of Michigan – Wayne State University. Ann Arbor, 15–23

Jackson, J. (1996) An experimental procedure and scales for assessing attachment relationships in African-American infants – Alternatives to Ainsworth methods. In R.L. Jones (ed.) *Handbook of Tests and Measurements for Black Populations* Hampton, Virginia: Cobb and Henry

Jahoda, G. and Lewis, I. (Eds.) (1988) *Cross Cultural Studies in Child Development*. London: Croom Helm.

Jareg, E. (1992) Basic therapeutic actions: Helping children, young people and communities to cope through empowerment and participation. In M. McCullin (ed.) *The Psychological Wellbeing of Refugee Children*. Geneva: International Catholic Child Bureau

Jenkins, R. (1986) Social anthropological models of inter-ethnic relations. In J. Red and D. Mason (Eds.) *Theories of Race and Ethnic Relations*. Cambridge: Cambridge University Press, 170–186

Jennings, S. (1996) *Creating Solutions: Developing alternatives in Black Mental Health*. London: King's Fund

Jensen, A.R. (1969) How much can we boost IQ and scholastic achievement? *Harvard Educational Review, 39*, 1, 1–123

Johnson, A.M., Wadsworth, J., Wellings., K. and Field, J. (1994) *Sexual Attitudes and Lifestyles*. Oxford: Blackwell

Johnson, M. and Caroll, M. (1995) *Dealing with Diversity: Good Practice in Drug Prevention Work with Racially and Culturally Diverse Communities*. London: HMSO

Johnstone, L. (1993) Family Management in 'schizophrenia': Its assumptions and contradictions. *Journal of Mental Health, 2,* 255–269

Johnstone, L. (1995) What clinical psychology trainees will discover about psychiatric rehabilitation. *Clinical Psychology Forum, 82,* 27–29

Jones, E. (1993) *Family Systems Therapy*. Chichester: Wiley

Jones, T. (1996) *Britain's Ethnic Minorities*. London: Policy Studies Institute

Kakar, S. (1978) (1981) *The Inner World: A Psychoanalytic Study of Childhood and Society in India*. New Delhi: Oxford Indian Paperbacks

Kakar, S. (1981) *The Inner World: A Psychoanalytic Study of Childhood and Society in India*. (2nd ed.). Oxford: Oxford University Press

Kakar, S. (1982) *Shamans, Mystics and Doctors*. London: Unwin Paperbacks

Kakar, S. (1984) *Shamans, Mystics and Doctors: A Psychological Inquiry into India and its Healing Tradition*. London: Unwin Paperbacks

Kapasi, R. (1996*). Reaching people: Guidelines for the Development and Evaluation of Sexual Health Materials in a Multiracial Society*. Birmingham: Aquarius

Kardiner, A. and Ovesey, L. (1951) *The Mark of Oppression*. New York: World

Kareem, J. (1992) The Nafsiyat Intercultural Therapy Centre: Ideas and experience in intercultural therapy. In J. Kareem and R. Littlewood (Eds.) *Intercultural Therapy, Themes, Interpretations and Practice*. Oxford: Blackwell

Kareem, J. and Littlewood, R. (Eds.) (1992) *Intercultural Therapy: Themes, Interpretations and Practice,* Oxford: Blackwell

Karenga, M. (1992) *Introduction to Black Studies*. Inglewood, California: Kawaida Publications

Kasvikis, Y. (1995) *25 years on Scientific Progress in Behavioural and Cognitive Therapies*. Vol. 1, Athens, Greece: Ellinika Grammatta Publishers, Akadimias 88, Athens, Greece

Kat, B. (1994) The contribution of psychological knowledge to primary health care taking a step back to go forward. *Clinical Psychology Forum, 65,* 23–26, March

Katz, J.H. (1978) *White Awareness: Handbook for Anti-Racism Training*. Oklahoma City: University of Oklahoma Press

Katz, J.H. and Ivey, A. (1977) White awareness: The frontier of racism awareness training. *The Personnel and Guidance Journal, 55*: 489–499

Kaufman, A.S., McLean, J.E. and Reynolds, C.R. (1988) Sex, race, residence, region and education differences on the 11 WAIS-R subtests. *Journal of Clinical Psychology, 44,* 231–248

Kavanagh, D. (1992) Recent developments in expressed emotions and schizophrenia. *British Journal of Psychiatry, 160,* 601–620

Keese, E. (1995) Psychology meets haematology: A role for psychologists in the management of sickle cell disease? *Clinical Psychology Forum, 83,* 29–32

Kemshall, H. (1999) Risk Assessment and Risk Management: Practice and Policy Implications. *British Journal of Forensic Practice, 1,* 1 27–36

Kerwin, C. and Ponterotto, J. (1995) Biracial identity development. Theory and Research. In J. Ponterotto, J. Casas, L. Suzuki and C. Alexander (Eds.) *Handbook of Multicultural Counselling*. Newbury Park: Sage

Khan *et al.* (1995) *An Investigation into Drugs Issues in the Asian Community in Dudley*. Catalyst Community Services Agency, 1, Causeway, Blackheath, B65 8AA

Khan, K. (1997) Race and Drugs Project – Race, Drugs, Europe: Specialist Drugs Services and Managing Change to Meet the Needs of Black and Other Visible Minority Drug Users. Vol. 1, London: Department of Sociology, City University

Kim, U. and Berry, J.W. (Eds.) (1993) *Indigenous Psychologies, Research and Experience in Cultur-*

al Context. Vol. 17, Cross-Cultural Research and Methodology Series. Thousand Oaks: Sage

King, M., Coker, F., Leavey, G., Hoare, A., Johnson-Sabine, F. (1994) Incidence of psychotic illness in London: Comparison of ethnic groups. *British Medical Journal, 309,* 1115–1119

Kingsbury, S. (1994) The psychological and social characteristics of Asian adolescent overdose. *Journal of Adolescence, 17,* 131–135

Kitzinger, S. and Kitsinger, C. (1999) *Talking with children about things that matter.* London: Rivers Oram/Pandora List

Kleinman, A. (1987) Anthropology and Psychiatry. The role of culture in cross-cultural research on Illness. *British Journal of Psychiatry, 151,* 447–454

Koch, H.C.H. (1986) Anxiety and depression: a community mental health perspective. In H.C.H. Koch (Ed.) *Community Clinical Psychology,* London: Croom Helm

Kovel, J. (1988) (1984 2nd edition, 1970 1st edition) *White Racism: A Psychohistory.* London: Free Association

Koyano, W. (1989) Japanese attitudes towards the elderly: a review of research findings. *Journal of Cross-Cultural Gerontology, 4, 4,* 335–345

Krause, I.B. (1994) Numbers and meaning: A dialogue in cross-cultural psychiatry. *Journal of the Royal Society of Medicine. 87,* 278–282

Krause, I.B. (1989) Sinking heart: a Punjabi communication of distress. *Social Science in Medicine. 29, 4,* 563–75

Krause, I. and Miller, A. (1995) Culture and Family Therapy. In S. Fernando (ed.) *Mental Health in a Multi-ethnic Society: A Multi-disciplinary Handbook.* London: Routledge

Kreps, G. and Kunimoto, E. (1994) *Effective Communication in Multicultural Health Care Settings.* Thousand Oaks: Sage

Kuipers, L. and Bebbington P. (1988) Expressed emotion research in Schizophrenia: Theoretical and clinical implications. *Psychological Medicine, 18,* 893–909

Lago, C. and Thompson, J. (1996) *Race, culture and counselling.* Buckingham: Open University Press

Lamb, M., Sternberg, K., Hwang, C. and Broberg, A. (Eds.) (1992) *Child Care in Context: Cross-Cultural Perspectives.* Newark: Lawrence Erlbaum

Landman, R. (1994) 'Let's talk about Sex'. Accessing sex education services for black people with learning difficulties. Workshop held at Avoncroft College, Bromsgrove, 18 and 19 January 1994. Birmingham: E Birmingham Health Promotion Service

Lau, A. (1984) Transcultural issues in Family Therapy. *Journal of Family Therapy, 6,* 91–112

Lau, A. (Ed.) (2000) *South Asian Children and Adolescents in Britain.* London: Whurr

Laungani, P. (1992) Cultural variations in the understanding and treatment of psychiatric disorders: India and England. *Counselling Psychology Quarterly, 5, 3,* 231–244

Lawson, (1998) A study of an intensive care unit in a regional secure setting. Unpublished report held at Edenfield Centre, Prestwich, Manchester

Leary, K. (1997) Race self-disclosure and 'forbidden talk': Race and ethnicity in contemporary clinical practice. *Psychoanalytic Quarterly, 66,* 163–189

Lee, C.C., Oh, M.Y. and Mountcastle, A.R. (1992) Indigenous model of helping in non-western countries: Implications for multicultural counselling. *Journal of Multicultural Counselling and Development, 20,* January, 3–10

Leff, J.P. and Vaughn, C. (1981) The role of maintenance therapy and relatives – expressed emotion in the relapse of schizophrenia: A two year follow up. *British Journal of Psychiatry, 139,* 102–104

Leitner, M. *et al.* (1993) *Drug Usage and Drugs Prevention: The Views and Habits of the General Public.* London: HMSO

Levine, R. (1995) Infant environments in psychoanalysis: A Cross-Cultural View. In J. Stigler, R. Schweder and G. Herdt (Eds.) *Cultural Psychology: Essays on Comparative*

Human Development. Oxford: Oxford University Press

LeVine, R., Dixon, S., Levine, S., Richman ,A., Leiderman, P., Keefer, C. and Brazelton, T. (1996) *Childcare and Context, Lessons from Africa*. Cambridge: Cambridge University Press

Lewis, G., Croft-Jeffreys, C. and David, A. (1990) Are British psychiatrists racists? *British Journal of Psychiatry, 157*, 410–415

Lewis, J.A., Sperry, L. and Carlson, J. (1993) *Health Counseling*. Pacific Grove, LA: Brooks/Cole

Lezak, M. (1995) *Neuropsychological Assessment*. (3rd ed.) New York: Oxford

Liberman, R.P., Mueser, K.T., Wallace, C.J., Jacobs, H.E., Eckman, T. and Mussel, H.K. (1986) Training skills in the psychiatrically disabled: Learning competence and coping. *Schizophrenia Bulletin, 12*, 631–47

Lillie-Blanton, M., Anthony, J.C. and Schuster, C.R. (1993) Probing the meaning of racial/ethnic group comparisons in Crack Cocaine smoking. *JAMA, 269*, 8, 993–997

Lipsedge, M. (1993) Mental health: Access to care. In A. Hopkins and V. Bahl (Eds.) *Access to Health Care for People from Black and Ethnic Minorities*. London: Royal College of Physicians

Lipsedge, M. (1994) Dangerous stereotypes. *Journal of Forensic Psychiatry, 5*, 14–19

Lishman, W.A. (1987) *Organic Psychiatry*. (2nd ed) Oxford: Blackwell

Littlewood, R. (1986) Ethnic minorities and the Mental Health Act. Patterns of explanation. *Bulletin of the Royal College of Psychiatrists, 10*, 306–8

Littlewood, R. (1993) Ideology, camouflage or contingency? Racism in British psychiatry. *Transcultural Psychiatric Research Review, 30*, 243–290

Littlewood, R. (1994) How universal is something we can call therapy? In J. Kareem, and R. Littlewood. (Eds.) *Intercultural Therapy – Theories, Interpretation and Practice*. Oxford: Blackwell

Littlewood, R. and Lipsedge, M. (1982) *Aliens and Alienists: Ethnic Minorities and Psychiatry*. Harmondsworth: Penguin

Littlewood, R. and Lipsedge, M. (1988) Psychiatric illness among British Afro-Caribbeans. *British Medical Journal, 296*, 950–951

Littlewood, R. and Lipsedge, M. (1989) *Aliens and Alienists: Ethnic Minorities and Psychiatry*. (2nd ed.) London: Unwin Hyman

Littlewood, R. and Lipsedge, M. (1997) *Aliens and Alienists. Ethnic Minorities and Psychiatry*. (3rd ed.) London: Unwin Hyman

Logue, B.J. (1990) Modernisation and the status of the frail elderly. *Journal of Cross-Cultural Gerontology, 5*, 349–374

Lokare, V. (Ed.) (1992) *Counselling Psychology Quarterly, 5*, 3, Special Issue on Transcultural Counselling

London, M. (1986) Mental illness among immigrant minorities in the United Kingdom. *British Journal of Psychiatry, 149*, 265–273

Lonner, W. and Ibrahim, F. (1996) Appraisal and assessment in cross-cultural counselling. In P. Pedersen, J. Dragims, W. Lonner and J. Trimble (Eds.) *Counselling Across Cultures*. (4th ed.) Thousand Oaks: Sage

Lousada, J. (1994) Some thoughts on the adoption of anti-racist practice. *Journal of Social Work Practice, 8*, 2, 151–159

Lovell, A. (1990) (ed.) *Health in any Language*. Department of Health. London: NETRHA

Low, N., Daker-White, G., Barlow, D. and Pozniak, A.L. (1997) Gonorrhoea in inner London: Results of a cross-sectional study. *British Medical Journal, 314*, 1717–1723

MacCalman, J.A. (1990) *The Forgotten People: Carers in Three Ethnic Communities in Southwark*. London: King's Fund Centre

MacPherson, W. (1999) The Stephen Lawrence Inquiry: Report of an Inquiry by Sir

William MacPherson of Cluny, advised by Tom Cook, The Right Reverend Dr John Sentamu, Dr Richard Stone. London: HMSO

Mahoney, M.J. (1993) Introduction to special section: Theoretical developments in the cognitive psychotherapies. *Journal of Consulting and Clinical Psychology*, 61, 2, 187–193

Mahtani, A., Davidson, O., Kell, P. and Miller, D. (in preparation) Psychological and medical priorities of ethnic minority attenders at a London sexual health clinic: a pilot needs assessment

Mahtani, A. and Huq, A. (1993) The use of a Western model across cultures. *British Journal of Guidance and Counselling*, 21, 1

Mahtani, A. and Marks, L. (1994) Developing a primary care psychology service that is racially and culturally appropriate. *Clinical Psychology Forum*, 65, 27–31

Maitra, B. (1995) Giving due consideration to the family's racial and cultural background. In P. Reder and C. Lucey (Eds.) *Assessment of Parenting, Psychiatric and Psychological Contributions*. London: Routledge

Maitra, B. and Miller, A. (1996) Children, families and therapists: Clinical considerations and ethnic minority cultures. In K. Dwivedi and V. Varma (Eds.) *Meeting the Needs of Ethnic Minority Children. A Handbook for Professionals*. London: Jessica Kingsley

Malhotra, H. and Wig, N. (1975) Dhat syndrome: a culture-bound sex neurosis of the orient. *Archives of Sexual Behaviour*, 4, 519–528

Mama, A. (1992) Black women and the British state. In P. Braham, A. Rattansi and R. Skellington (Eds.) *Racism and Antiracism*. London: Sage

Mama, A. (1995) *Beyond the Masks: Race Gender and Subjectivity*. London: Routledge

Manthorpe, J. and Hettiaratchy, P. (1993) Ethnic minority elders in the UK. *International Review of Psychiatry*, 5, 171–178

Markides, K.S. and Miranda, M.R. (Eds.) (1997) *Minorities, Aging and Health*. Thousand Oaks: Sage

Mars, M. (1989) Child sexual abuse and race issues. In *After Abuse*. Papers on caring and planning for a child who has been sexually abused. London: British Agencies for Adoption and Fostering

Marsella, A. and Kameoka, V. (1988) Ethno-cultural issues in the assessment of psychopathology. In S. Wetzler (Ed.) *Measuring mental illness: Psychometric Assessment for Clinicians*. Washington, DC: APA

Martindale, B. (1989) Becoming dependent again: The fears of some elderly persons and their younger therapists. *Psychoanalytic Psychotherapy*, 4, 1, 67–75

Matarazzo, J.D. and Herman, D.O. (1985) Clinical uses of the WAIS-R: base rates of differences between VIQ and PIQ in the WAIS-R standardisation sample. In B Wolman,. (Ed.) *Handbook of Intelligence: Theories, Measurements and Applications*. New York: Wiley

Mather, M. and Marjot, D. (1992) Alcohol-related admissions to a psychiatric hospital: A comparison of Asians and Europeans. *British Journal of Addiction*, 87, 327–329

Maximé, J. (1986) Some psychological models of Black self-concept. In S. Ahmed, J. Cheetham and J. Small (Eds.) *Social Work with Black Children and Their Families*. London: B.T. Batsford

McAdoo, H. and McAdoo, J. (1985) *Black Children*. Beverley Hills: Sage

McAdoo, H. (1996) *Black Families*. Third edition. Beverley Hills: Sage

McCormick, A., Fleming, D., Charlton, J. (1995) *Morbidity Statistics from General Practice: Fourth National Study*. London: HMSO

McGoldrick, M. (1994) Culture, race, class and gender. *Human Systems*, 5, 131–153

McGoldrick, M., Pearce, J. and Giordano, J. (1982) *Ethnicity and Family Therapy*. New York: Guilford Press

McGovern, D. and Cope, R. (1987) The compulsory detention of males of different ethnic groups with special reference to offender patients. *British Journal of Psychiatry*, 150,

505–512

McGovern, D. and Cope, R.V. (1987) First psychiatric admission rates of first and second generation African Caribbeans. *Social Psychiatry, 22,* 139–149

McIntyre, P. (1998) White Privilege: Unpacking the invisible knapsack. In M. McGoldrick (Ed.) *Revisioning Family Therapy: Race, Culture and Gender in Clinical Practice.* New York: Guilford

McIver, S. (1994). *Obtaining the Views of Black Users of Health Services.* London: Kings Fund

McKeigue, P. and Karmi, G. (1993) Alcohol consumption and alcohol-related problems in African-Caribbean and South Asians in the UK. *Alcohol and Alcoholism, 28,* 1–10

McKenna, J. (1996) In-patient characteristics in a regional secure unit. *Psychiatric Bulletin, 20,* 264–268

McMunn, A., Mwanje, R. and Pozniak, A.L. (1997) Issues facing Africans in London with HIV infection. *Genitourinary Medicine, 73,* 157–158

McRoy, R., Zurcher, L., Lauderdale, M.. and Anderson, R. (1984) The identity of transracial adoptees. *Social Casework, 65,* 1, 34–39

Mehta, G. (1993) The Ethnic Elderly. *Journal of Community Nursing, 6,* 16–20

Mental Health Foundation (1996). *Building Expectations.* London

Messent, P. (1992) Working with Bangladeshi families in the East End of London. *Journal of Family Therapy, 14,* 287–304

Midence, K., Fuggle, P. and Davies, S. (1993) Psychosocial aspects of sickle cell disease (SCD) in childhood and adolescence: A review. *British Journal of Clinical Psychology, 32,* 271–280

Milner, D. (1990) *Children and Race: Ten years on.* Sussex, London: Ward Lock

Mirza, H. (1992) *Young, Female and Black.* London: Routledge

Mirza, H., Pearson, G. *et al.* (1991) *Drugs, People and Services in Lewisham. Drug Information Project.* Monograph, Goldsmiths College, London: University of London

Mitchell, P. (1992) *The Psychology of Childhood.* London: The Falmer Press

Modood, T. (1997) Employment. In T. Modood, R. Berthoud, J. Lakey, J. Nazroo, P. Smith, S. Virdee and S. Beishon (Eds.) *Ethnic Minorities in Britain: Diversity and Disadvantage.* London: Policy Studies Institute

Modood, T., Berthoud, R. Lakey, J., Nazroo, J., Smith, P., Virdee, S. and Beishon, S. (Eds.) (1997) *Ethnic Minorities in Britain: Diversity and Disadvantage: The Fourth National Survey of Ethnic Minorities.* London: Policy Studies Institute

Mohamed, C. and Smith, R. (1997) Race in the therapy relationship. In M. Lawrence, and M.Maguire *Psychotherapy with Feminist Perspectives.* London: Macmillan

Montalvo, B. and Guttierrez, M. (1988) The emphasis on cultural identity: A developmental-ecological constraint. In C. Falicov (Ed.) *Family Transitions: Continuity and Change Over the Life Cycle.* New York: Guilford

Moodley, P. (1993) Setting up services for ethnic minorities. In D. Bhugra and J. Leff, J. (Eds.) *Principles of Social Psychiatry.* Oxford: Blackwell

Moodley, P. and Perkins, R. (1991) Routes to psychiatric in-patient care in an inner London borough. *Social Psychiatry and Psychiatric Epidemiology, 26,* 47–51

Morelli, G. and Tronick, E. (1991) Efe multiple caretaking and attachment. In J. Gerwitz and W. Kurtines (Eds.), *Intersections with Attachment.* New Jersey: Lawrence Erlbaum

Muhammed, S. (1991) *Improving Health Services for Black Populations. Share, 1,* London: Kings Fund

Murray, S.A. and Graham, L.J.C. (1995) Practice based health needs assessment: Use of four methods in a small neighbourhood. *British Medical Journal, 310,* 1443–1448

Nadirshaw, Z. (1991a) *Gearing up for Good Practice. Implications in the assessment and care management of black and ethnic people and the difficulties of their carers.* Occasional Paper No.2. London Boroughs Disability Resource Team. May

Nadirshaw, Z. (1991b) Assessment of learning difficulties in ethnic minority clients. *Ethnic Minorities Health. Current Awareness Bulletin*, 2, i–iii January. Medical Library, Bradford Royal Infirmary, Bradford BD9 6RJ

Nadirshaw, Z. (1993) The implications for equal opportunities training in clinical psychology: A realist's view. *Clinical Psychology Forum*, 54, 3–6

Nadirshaw, Z. (1997) Cultural Issues. In J. O'Hara, and A. Sperlinger (Eds.). *Adults with Learning Disabilities: A Practical Approach for Health Professionals*. London: Wiley

Nadirshaw, Z. (1998) Clinical psychology. In K. Bhui and D. Olajide (Eds.) *Cross Cultural Mental Health Care. Contemporary Issues in Service Provision*. London: Routledge

Nadirshaw, Z. (1998) Community care: Whose benefit? *Learning Disability Practice. Vol. 1.1*. London: R C N

Nadirshaw, Z. (1999) Clinical psychology. In K. Bhui and D. Objide (Eds.) *Mental Health Service Provision for a Multi-Ethnic Society*. London: W.B. Saunders

Nadirshaw, Z. (in press) *Learning Disabilities*. In D. Bhugra and R. Cochrane (Eds.) *Psychiatry in Multicultural Britain*. London: Royal College of Psychiatrists/Gaskell Publications

Nadirshaw, Z. and Goddard, S. (1999) *Rethinking Clinical Psychology: A Race Against Time for Minority Ethnic Communities in Mental Health Settings*. London: Department of Health

Naoi, M. (1976) Review of *The Honourable Elders. Social Gerontology*, 4, 58–60

National Association of Health Authorities (1988) *Actions not Words: A Strategy to Improve Health Services for Black and Minority Ehnic Groups*. Birmingham: NAHAT

National Health Service Task Force (1994a) *Time for Action Now – Regional Race Programme: Greater Manchester Seminar*. Manchester: Department of Health

National Health Service Task Force (1994b) *Black Mental Health – A Dialogue for Change*. London: Mental Health Task Force

Nazroo, J.Y. (1997) *Ethnicity and Mental Health: Findings from the National Community Survey*. Londn: Policy Studies Institute

Ndegwa, D. (1998) Part 2: Clinical Issues. In S. Fernando, D. Ndegwa and M. Wilson *Forensic Psychiatry, Race and Culture*. London: Routledge

Neal, A. and Wilson, M. (1989) The role of skin colour and features in the black community: Implications for black women and therapy. *Clinical Psychology Review*, 9, 323–333

Newnes, C. and MacLachlan, A. (1996) The anti-psychiatry placement. *Clinical Psychology Forum*, 93, 24–27

Newnes, C. (1996) The Development of Clinical Psychology and its Values. Paper presented at the BPS/DCP Annual Conference, Brighton (unpublished)

NHS Centre for Reviews and Dissemination Social Policy Research Unit (1996) *Ethnicity and Health: Reviews of Literature and Guidance for Purchasers in the Areas of Cardiovascular Disease, Mental Health and Haemoglobinopthies*. CRD Report 5. York: York Publishing

Niemeyer, R.A. (1993) An Appraisal of Constructivist Psychotherapies. *Journal of Consulting and Clinical Psychology*, 61, 2, 221–234

Nobles, W. (1971) Black people in White insanity: An issue for black community mental health. *Journal of Afro-American Issues*, 4, 21–7

Nobles, W. and Goddard, L. (1996) The African based child rearing opinion survey: A research instrument for measuring Black cultural values. In R. Jones (Ed.) *Handbook of Tests and Measurements for Black Populations*. Hampton, Virginia: Cobb and Henry Publishers

Norman, A. (1985) *Triple Jeopardy: Growing Old in a Second Homeland*. Policy Studies in Ageing No.3, Centre for Policy on Ageing

Norman, A. (1988) *Mental Dsorder and Elderly Members of Ehnic Minority Groups. Mental Health Problems in Old Age, A Reader*. Buckingham: Open University

Stoyle, J. (1993) *Caring for Older People: a Multicultural Approach. Oxford:* Stanley Thorne

Strang, J. and Gossop, M. (1994) *Heroin Addiction and Drug Policy: The British System.* Oxford: Oxford University Press

Sue, D.W. and Sue, D. (1990) *Counselling the Culturally Different. Theory and Practice.* (2nd ed.) New York: Wiley

Swindon and District Community Health Council (1993) Survey into the perceptions of local ethnic minorities on their access to health services (unpublished)

Szivos, S.E. and Griffiths, E. (1990) Consciousness raising and social identity theory: A challenge to normalization. *Clinical Psychology Forum, A, 28,* 11–15

Tackling Drugs to Build a Better Britain (1998) *The Government's Ten-Year Strategy for Tackling Drugs Misuse.* London: HMSO

Tamasese, K. and Waldegrave, C. (1993) Cultural and Gender accountability in the 'Just Therapy' Approach. *Journal of Feminist Family Therapy, 5,* 229–45

Tan, R. (1993) Racism and similarity: Paranoid-schizoid structures. *British Journal of Psychotherapy, 10,* 1, 33–43

Task Force to Review Services for Drug Misusers (1996*) Report of an Independent Review of Drug Treatment Services in England.* London: Department of Health

Taylor, P.J. and Gunn, J. (1999) Homicides by people with mental illness: myth and reality. *British Journal of Psychiatry, 174,* 9–14

Teague, A. (1993) Ethnic group: First results from the 1991 Census, *Population Trends,* 72, Summer, 12–17

Teteh, N., Langlis, Y., Wanigaratne, S., Job, N. *et al.* (1994) *Guidelines for Cross-Cultural Work.* North London Race and Culture Substance Misuse Forum, Camden and Islington Substance Misuse Service, National Temperance Hospital, London NW1 2LT

The Health of the Nation (1992) *A Strategy for Health in England.* Government White Paper. London: HMSO

The Sainsbury Centre for Mental Health (1998) *Keys to Engagement.* London: Sainsbury Centre

Thomas, L. (1992) Racism and psychotherapy: Working with racism in the consulting room – an analytical view. In J. Kareem and R. Littlewood (Eds.) *Intercultural Therapy, Themes, Interpretations and Practice.* Oxford: Blackwell

Thomas, L. (1995) Psychotherapy in the context of race and culture: A therapeutic approach. In S. Fernando (ed.), *Mental Health in a Multi-ethnic Society. A Multi-disciplinary Handbook.* London: Routledge

Thomas, P. (1997) *The Dialectics of Schizophrenia.* London and NewYork: Free Association Books

Thompson, C. (1991) Changing the balance: power and people who use services. *Community Care Project.* London. N.C.V.0

Thompson, R. (1993) (Ed.) *Religion, Ethnicity and Sex Education: Exploring the issues.* National Children's Bureau, 8 Wakely Street, London ECIV 7QE

Thompson-Fullilove M. (1993) Perceptions and Misperceptions of race and drug use. *JAMA, 269,* 8, 1034

Thornicroft, G. (1990) Cannabis and psychosis: Is there epidemiological evidence for an association? *British Journal of Psychiatry, 157,* 25–33

Tippell, S., Aston, F., Hunter, A. and Painter, J. (1990) *Cocaine Use: The US Experience and the Implications for Drug Services in Britain.* Community Drug Project, 30 Manor Place, London SE17 3BB

Tizard, B. and Phoenix, A. (1993) *Black, White or Mixed Race? Race and Racism in the Lives of Young People of Mixed Parentage.* London: Routledge

Tomlinson, S. (1989) Asian pupils and special issues. *British Journal of Special Education, 16,* 3, 119–122

Torkington, P. (1991) *Black Health – A Political Issue*. The Health and Race Project, Liverpool: CARJ-LIHE

Tout, K. (Ed.) (1993) *Elderly Care – A World Perspective*. London: Chapman and Hall

Transcultural Counselling (1993) Symposium papers. *British Journal of Guidance and Counselling, 21*, 2, January

Tribe, R. and Raval, H. (Eds.) (in press) *Working with Interpreters in Mental Health*. London: Routledge

Tribe, R. (1991) *Bicultural Workers – Bridging the Gap or Damming the Flow?* Paper presented at the 11th international conference of centres, institutions and individuals concerned with the care of victims of violence, health, political repression and human rights. Santiago, Chile. Available from the Medical Foundation for the Care of Victims of Torture, London

Van der Veer, G. (1992) *Counselling and Therapy with Refugees: Psychological Problems of Victims of War, Torture and Repression*. New York: Wiley

Vargas, L. and Koss-Chioino, J. (Eds.) (1992) *Working with Culture, Psychotherapeutic Interventions with Ethnic Minority Children and Adolescents*. San Francisco: Jossey-Bass

Vega, W.A., Gil, A.G. and Zimmerman, R.S. (1993) Patterns of drug use among Cuban-American, African-American and White Non-Hispanic boys. *American Journal of Public Health, 83*, 2, 257–259

Vernon, P.E. (1979) *Intelligence: Heredity and Environment*. San Francisco: W.H.Freeman

Voakes, R. and Fowler, Q. (Eds.) (1989) *Sentencing, Race and Social Enquiry Reports*. West Yorkshire Probation Service

Wade Smith, A. (1993) Survey research on African Americans. In J.H. Stanfield, H. and R.M. Dennis (Eds.) *Race and Ethnicity in Research Methods*. Thousand Oaks: Sage

Waldegrave, C. (1990a) Social justice and family therapy. *Dulwich Centre Newsletter*, No. 1. Adelaide, Australia

Waldegrave, C. (1990b) Just therapy. *Dulwich Centre Newsletter*, No.1, 5–46. Adelaide, Australia

Waldegrave, C. (1993) Other wisdoms, other worlds: Colonialisation and family therapy. *Dulwich Centre Newsletter*, No.1, 15–19. Adelaide, Australia

Walker, M. (1988) The court disposal of young males, by race, in London in 1983. *British Journal of Criminology, 28*, 4

Walker, M., Jefferson, T. and Senaviratne, M. (Eds.) (1989) *Ethnic Minorities, Young People and the Criminal Justice System*. Economic and Social Science Research Council

Ward, L. (1990). An umbrella for the sun? *Community Care, 6*, 843, 21–23

Warner, R. (1994) *Recovery from Schizophrenia Psychiatry and Political Economy*. London: Routledge

Watson, E. (1984) Health of infants and use of health services by mothers of different ethnic groups in East London. *Community Medicine, 6*, 127–135

Watts, F.N. and Bennett, D.H. (Eds.) (1991) *Theory and Practice of Psychiatric Rehabilitation* Chichester: Wiley

Webb-Johnson, A. (1991) A cry for change: an Asian perspective on developing quality mental health care. London: Confederation of Indian Organisations (UK)

Webb-Johnson, A. and Nadirshaw, Z. (1993) Good practice in transcultural counselling: An Asian Perspective. *British Journal of Guidance and Counselling, 21*, 1

Webster, A. (1996) Stress and Culture. Working in partnership with community groups. *Clinical Psychology Forum, 105*, July

Weingarten, K. (1998) The small and the ordinary: The daily practice of post-modern narrative therapy. *Family Process, 37*, Spring, 3–15

Welldon, E. (1994) Forensic psychotherapy. In P. Clarkson and M. Pokorny (Eds.) *The Handbook of Psychotherapy*. London: Routledge

Wetherell, M. and Potter, J. (1992) *Mapping the Language of Racism. Hemel Hempstead:* Harvester Wheatsheaf

Wheeler, E. (1994) Doing black mental health research, observations and experiences. In H. Afshar and M. Maynard (Eds.) *The Dynamics of 'Race' and Gender, Some Feminist Interventions.* London: Taylor and Francis

Whyche, L. and Novick, M. (1992) Standards for educational and psychological testing: The issue of testing bias from the perspective of school psychology and psychometrics. In A. Burlew, W. Benks, H. McAdoo and D. Azibo (Eds.) *African-American Psychology: Theory, Research and Practice.* Newbury Park: Sage

Wieselberg, H. (1992) Family therapy and ultra-orthodox jewish families: A structural approach. *Journal of Family Therapy, 14,* 3, 305–330

Williams, B. (1987) Looking for Linda. *Child Welfare, 66,* 3, May–June 14–18

(1989) Mental handicap and oppression. In A. Brechin, J. Walmsley (Eds.) *Making Connections. Reflecting on the Lives and Experiences of People with Learning Difficulties.* London: Hodder and Stoughton in association with Open University Press

Willis, C.F. (1983) *The Use, Effectiveness and Impact of Police Stop and Search Powers.* Home Office Research Unit

Wilson, A. (1987) *Mixed Race Children: A Study of Identity.* London: Allen and Unwin

Wilson, M. (1989) Child development in the context of the black extended family. *American Psychologist, 44,* 380–383

Wilson, M. (1992) Perceived parental activity of mothers, fathers and grandmothers in three-generational black families. In A. Burlew, W. Banks, H. McAdoo and D. Azibo (Eds.), *African-American Psychology: Theory, Research and Practice.* Newbury Park: Sage

Wilson, M. (1992) Service where it's due. *Social Work Today, 18*

Wilson, M. (1993a) *Black Women Survive Incest.* London: Virago

Wilson, M. (1993b) *Mental Health and Britain's Black Communities.* London: King's Fund Centre

Wilson, M. (1998) Part 3: Public policy. In S. Fernando, D. Ndegwa and M. Wilson (1998) *Forensic Psychiatry, Race and Culture.* London: Routledge

Wilson, M. and Francis, J. (1997) *Raised Voices: Afro-Caribbean and African Users' Views and Experiences of Mental Health Services in England and Wales.* London: MIND (National Association of Mental Health)

Wilson, M. and MacCarthy, B. (1994) GP consultation as a factor in the low rate of Mental Health Service use by Asians. *Psychological Medicine, 24,* 113–119

WISH (1997) *Listening to Women – A Force for Change: Annual Report 1996–1997.* London: WISH

Wolfensberger, W. (1972) *The Principles of Normalization in Human Services.* Toronto: National Institute on Mental Retardation

Wolfensberger, W. (1983) Social role valorisation: A proposed new term for the principle of normalisation. *Mental Retardation, 21,* 6

Wolfensberger, W. and Glenn, L. (1983) *Programme Analysis of Service Systems (PASS): A Method for Quantitative Analysis of Human Services.* Handbook. Toronto: National Institute on Mental Retardation

Woodcock, J. (1995) Healing rituals with families in exile. *Journal of Family Therapy, 17,* 397–409

Woollett, A. and White, D. (1992) *Families: A Context for Development.* London: The Falmer Press

World Health Organisation (1978) *Primary Health Care: Report of the International Conference at Alma-Ata.* Geneva: WHO

Wrench, J. (1990) New vocationalism, old racism and the Careers Service. *New Community, 16,* 3, 425–40

Zandi, T. *et al.* (1990) Children's attitudes towards elderly individuals: A comparison of two ethnic groups. *International Journal of Ageing and Human Development, 30*, 3, 161–174

Zilbergeld, B. (1978) *Men and Sex*. London: New English Library

INDEX

Note: Page numbers in **bold** type refer to **figures**. Page numbers in *italic* type refer to *tables*. Page numbers followed by 'n' refer to notes